Commander in Chief

Commander in Chief

PARTISANSHIP, NATIONALISM,
AND THE RECONSTRUCTION OF
CONGRESSIONAL WAR POWERS

Casey B. K. Dominguez

University Press of Kansas

Published by the University Press of Kansas (Lawrence, Kansas 66045), which
was organized by the Kansas Board of Regents and is operated and funded by
Emporia State University, Fort Hays State University, Kansas State University,
Pittsburg State University, the University of Kansas, and Wichita State
University.

This book will be made open access within three years of publication thanks
to Path to Open, a program developed in partnership between JSTOR, the
American Council of Learned Societies (ACLS), University of Michigan
Press, and the University of North Carolina Press to bring about equitable
access and impact for the entire scholarly community, including authors,
researchers, libraries, and university presses around the world. Learn more at
https://about.jstor.org/path-to-open/.

Library of Congress Cataloging-in-Publication Data is available.

Names: Dominguez, Casey B. K., author.
Title: Commander in chief : partisanship, nationalism, and the reconstruction
of congressional war powers / Casey B. K. Dominguez.
Description: Lawrence : University Press of Kansas, 2024. | Includes
    bibliographical references and index.
Identifiers: LCCN 2023037117 (print) | LCCN 2023037118 (ebook)
  ISBN 9780700636518 (cloth)
  ISBN 9780700636525 (ebook)
Subjects: LCSH: War and emergency powers—United States. | War and
emergency legislation—United States. | Executive power—United States. |
Presidents—United States. | United States—Politics and government. |
BISAC: POLITICAL SCIENCE / American Government / Legislative Branch |
POLITICAL SCIENCE / Political Process / Political Parties
Classification: LCC KF5900 .D66 2024 (print) | LCC KF5900 (ebook) |
DDC 342.73/0412—dc23/eng/20240117
LC record available at https://lccn.loc.gov/2023037117.
LC ebook record available at https://lccn.loc.gov/2023037118.

British Library Cataloguing-in-Publication Data is available.

For Gerardo, Erin, and Claire

Contents

Preface

As it is for most academics, the bulk of the work I do, and the most important work I do, is teaching undergraduates. The idea for this book came from conversations I had with students in my presidency class. Students in that class are always surprised to learn how much the political and constitutional center of gravity has shifted toward the presidency over time. They are amazed to learn that presidents did not always give speeches, or campaign for themselves, or claim the right to start wars. Those revelations prompt them to ask important normative questions about how the presidency should look, as well as empirical questions about how and why it has changed so much over time.

This project was inspired by questions that my students asked about how and why the president's war powers grew over time. I have always assigned my presidency students to read Louis Fisher's *Presidential War Power*, which documents both Congress's insistence on initiating wars in the early republic and its acquiescence to presidentially led wars in the modern era. My students asked great questions about why those enormous changes took place, and all of us were unsatisfied with the answers that I could give based on the existing scholarly literature. My own curiosity led me to want to know more about how Congress managed to exert authority over war powers in the early republic and to ask how that congressional control eroded over time.

Motivated by this question, I began a complicated, decade-long project of gathering and analyzing all of the congressional references to the commander in chief clause in published debates, from the Founding to World War I. I thought that perhaps I could code the speeches for whether they favored congressional or presidential dominance of war powers, and then run regressions on those data that would help me test some basic hypotheses about how legislators understood the constitutional balance of war powers.

As it turned out, the story that emerged as I read congressional speeches about the commander in chief clause was quite nuanced, and the context of each speech was too important to lose that detail in simplistic coding schemes. I had originally intended to write a journal article, but what emerged was a book, and a long one at that. It took me deeper into US history, into work on American political development, into questions about the impact of rhetoric and ideas on politics, and into the processes of constitutional interpretation than I originally anticipated.

As I read congressional speeches, it quickly became clear that members of Congress talked differently about the commander in chief clause in different contexts—that there were entirely different conversations about the president's capacity, and Congress's, to govern conquered territory, to discipline wayward officers, and to initiate hostile force. But there were also commonalities across those conversations, and across party lines, in the ways that members of Congress talked about war powers. I also realized that there some big changes in congressional rhetoric over time, especially after the Spanish-American War and in the lead-up to World War I.

In the chapters that follow, I describe the patterns that I observed when reading members of Congress's arguments about the commander in chief clause. Members of Congress in the early republic narrowly defined the war powers of the president as commander in chief, but they also tended to support broader war powers for presidents in their own party. They defined the commander in chief clause while repeating just a few simple stories that seemed to define the responsibilities of both Congress and the president. Then, enveloped by the nationalist rhetoric of the Spanish-American War, around the turn of the twentieth century, those stories began to change and members of Congress began to argue that the commander in chief deserved their deference on questions related to war.

The story that I tell in this book speaks perhaps more to scholars who want to understand how Congress interprets the Constitution than it does to undergraduates who want to understand why presidential war powers grew over time. But hopefully both scholars and students with an interest in the development of war powers in the US constitutional system will learn something from this work that inspires them to ask different and perhaps better questions in the future.

Acknowledgments

This book was under construction for a long time. I would like to acknowledge the patience of my editor at University Press of Kansas, David Congdon, and to thank him for having faith in my original vision for the project and for allowing me the time to revise the manuscript. I would also like to extend my heartfelt thanks to the anonymous reviewers who spent so much of their own time offering thoughtful, constructive criticism and helped push me to make this manuscript better and its scholarly contributions clearer. I would like to thank Louis Fisher for helpful comments about the initial book proposal. At various times, I also received encouragement and helpful input from a number of other political scientists, especially Terri Bimes, Justin Buchler, Brendan Doherty, Julia Azari, Amy Steigerwalt, and Nancy Kassop. All remaining mistakes are, of course, my own.

The project was supported by Faculty Research Grants from the University of San Diego, which allowed me to hire a number of undergraduates to help me gather data. Thank you to those students: Brendan Burton, Natasha Daulat, Ricardo Dixon, Mari Olson, Georgina Paz Santos, William Plimpton, Lavanya Sridharan, Kimberly Thoren, Parker Winship, Cynthia Villacis, Benjamin White, and Catherine Wineinger. Most of you have probably forgotten that you even worked on this project, but I have not, and I am grateful for your help.

I would especially like to thank my colleagues in the Department of Political Science and International Relations at the University of San Diego for their support. I could not have a better group of people to work with, and I am grateful for the opportunity to be a member of this community. Thank you to Dean Noelle Norton and to Del Dickson, Evan Crawford, Emily Edmonds-Poli, Kacie Miura, Lee Ann Otto, Michael Pfau, David Shirk, Avi Spiegel, Kira Tait, Andy Tirrell, Mike Williams, Randy Willoughby, and to my most reasonable friends, Tim McCarty and Cory Gooding. I would specifically like to thank Vidya Nadkarni for her mentorship and for teaching me that it is OK to put parenting first when children are little and to trust that scholarship would come along in due time.

My most heartfelt thanks always to my Knudsen family for their love and support. I especially thank Phil and Angela Knudsen, for always being my biggest cheerleaders; Elizabeth, Brandon, Shea, and Keeley Moggio for putting the fun into every summer; and Nick Knudsen for inspiring us all by working for democracy.

And finally, thanks to Gerardo, Erin, and Claire Dominguez. Nobody knows more than you do how many hours went into this project. It exists because you were willing to share me with it and to forgive me for the time it took away from being with you. I am very grateful to you for those sacrifices, and I hope you are proud of the result.

Introduction

Under the Constitution of 1787, the United States has fought four declared wars, dozens of other wars and military interventions, and one major civil war. The country has gone from a postcolonial backwater having no military to speak of to a global superpower with one of the most powerful militaries in the history of the world. Alongside all those conflicts and all that change, the constitutional system for managing war powers has evolved as well.

The US Constitution divides the federal government's authority over war and peace between the Congress and the president, but it does not appear to do so equally. It vests executive power in the president and names him the commander in chief. But it also grants to Congress a long list of specific powers over international affairs, including regulating foreign commerce, declaring war, defining international law, making rules about prisoners of war, raising armies and navies, appropriating money, making rules for governing the armed forces, and determining the terms of militias' service in repelling invasions, executing law, and suppressing insurrections. This textual distribution of powers has remained the same for more than two centuries. But our interpretations of the authority those words grant to Congress and to the president have changed dramatically over time.

In the early republic, the branches of government agreed that Congress had exclusive authority to initiate hostilities against foreign powers, in both declared and undeclared wars, and that presidents had a limited defensive power to "repel sudden attacks."[1] At the time of the Founding, understanding of defensive war was limited to when the nation was actually attacked, and Congress maintained authority over wars undertaken to defend national interests.[2] In those days, both presidents and members of Congress believed that the commander in chief's authority to employ and govern the use of force derived from congressional action and that Congress could regulate the use of force once initiated. Today, however, presidents argue that the Constitution itself grants them broad authority to determine whether military force is necessary, to give orders initiating the use of force, and to make decisions about how that force will be used.[3] Presidents now argue that their authority to initiate hostilities comes from the Constitution, not the laws passed by Congress, and that Congress has no business interfering with it. Surprisingly, today, Congress mostly defers to these claims. If an essential constitutional power, initiating the use of military force, has shifted from one branch of government to another over time, it is important to study how that happened.[4]

In this book, I focus on just one clause of the Constitution: the commander in chief clause. I trace how members of Congress talked about that clause, how they interpreted it, and what discretionary authority they ascribed to it between the nation's founding and World War I. The congressional record illuminates how different members of Congress, in different partisan relations to the president, facing different governing challenges, answered the following questions: What independent authority does the commander in chief clause bestow upon the person who is elected president? Where are the boundaries to that authority? What are the minimum "commander in chief" powers that Congress cannot take away from the president?[5] What is the maximum the "commander in chief" can do in the face of congressional silence? Or over Congress's objections? By examining every congressional reference to the clause from the Founding to World War I, I describe with new specificity how members' interpretations of the Constitution evolved in the period pre-dating the modern constitutional order.

Analysis of congressional references to the commander in chief clause contributes to the scholarly literature in several ways. First, it suggests a new way to divide the timeline of the modern presidency, especially as it relates to presidential war powers. My research shows that from the Founding until 1898, members of Congress repeatedly articulated one dominant interpretation of the commander in chief clause and the authority it conferred. This interpretation held that the clause granted the president only the type of authority held by any other military officer, which included some amount of discretion on the battlefield and no discretion in making policy about the initiation or scope of war and peace. But suddenly, around 1898, and continuing until World War I, a new and broader interpretation became dominant, which held that the president represented the nation and that therefore Congress owed him deference in policy-making decisions about the initiation and scope of war and peace. This finding informs scholarly debates about when war powers began to shift from Congress to the president, and suggests that the modern constitutional order for war powers has earlier roots than other scholars usually describe.

Secondly, the analysis in this book adds rich detail to our understanding of what it looks like when Congress interprets the Constitution. In particular, it shows that when members of Congress defined the boundaries between their war powers and the president's, they referred frequently to a limited set of simple stories that prescribed a particular interpretation of the commander in chief clause based on a select list of historical precedents, tied together with a particular logic. Those stories, or constitutional scripts, seemed to provide members of Congress with a shared, accessible language with which to understand novel dilemmas about interbranch relations. These scripts themselves are important, because the language members used to describe the boundaries of each branch's war powers correlated with the both the range of debates that took place in the legislature and the types of actions that Congress collectively took. While these stories feature prominently in congressional constitutional interpretations, it is important to be cautious about suggesting that the stories themselves affected the behavior of the individual members or the collective body at any given moment in time. If these constitutional stories shaped Congress's decision making, they were certainly only one of many factors that did so. As described in the following chapters, prior to World War I, even when members' constitutional rhetoric relied heavily on stories, their interpretations and actions were also clearly shaped by other factors like their own partisan relationship to the president, Congress's institutional resources, interpretations of other, nonconstitutional concepts like what constitutes "offense," and existing racial and international orders.

TIMING THE EMERGENCE OF THE MODERN CONSTITUTIONAL ORDER

Most people who study war powers in the US constitutional system agree that today, presidents dominate foreign affairs and decisions about the use of military force.[6] Presidents certainly claim a right to do so. Since the Truman administration, presidents have claimed broad authority to initiate hostilities and to ignore congressional attempts to limit that authority or ground it in law.[7] These presidential claims have not generally brought presidents into sustained conflict with Congress, which has, in recent years, adopted a deferential posture toward the president's war powers authority.[8] At the same time, Congress still involves itself in decisions about war policy.[9] There have been moments when Congress asserted its legislative authority over the initiation of force, most famously when it passed the War Powers Resolution in 1973.[10]

Congressional politics still affects presidential choices, and congressional pressure can alter the trajectory of conflicts and the use of force.[11] Congress and the president can each use their institutional strengths to reach constitutionally acceptable and authoritative decisions.[12] But practitioners in our political system in the twenty-first century do not systematically question the president's authority to lead decision making about or even initiate the use of force abroad in a broad range of circumstances.[13]

This institutional balance, sustained by bureaucratic capacity, law, treaties, and accepted rhetorical and political justifications, has been termed a modern "constitutional order." Stephen Griffin defines a constitutional order as a relatively stable pattern of institutional actions, constructed by multiple institutions, regarding constitutional powers. It is supported by widely held interpretations of the constitutional text, the structure and capacity of state institutions, and the political and policy objectives of officials.[14] Griffin's definition is based in Orren and Skowronek's ideas about political orders, defined by Rogers Smith as "a constellation of rules, institutions, practices, and ideas that hang together over time as other things change."[15] The modern constitutional order for war powers is supported by shared beliefs that the Constitution gives the president practical authority to conduct foreign and military affairs, including committing US forces to at least limited engagements, and that it gives Congress at least some shared authority over spending and authorizing major wars. It is supported by the national security state and a large standing military, all reporting to the president. It is also supported by bipartisan foreign policy commitments to assertively promoting US security, including the nation's economic interests and ideological commitments abroad, as defined largely (though not exclusively) in the executive-led national security bureaucracy. The courts have helped to create and sustain this constitutional order by deferring to the political branches and by rejecting Congress's attempts to use the courts to restrain presidential actions.[16]

In Griffin's description, as in the work of Louis Fisher and many others, this arrangement displaced an alternative, original constitutional order. Scholars show that, in the original constitutional order for war powers, Congress asserted and defended its rights to declare wars and authorize undeclared wars.[17] Courts largely ruled in favor of that dominance.[18] Presidents did not claim the right to initiate hostilities on their own constitutional authority, and presidential unilateralism was the carefully defended exception and not the rule. US security commitments focused on westward continental expansion rather than global leadership.[19] The capacity of the national security bureaucracy and the military was far more limited than it is today, and as William Adler argues, the secretary of war and field commanders had a great deal of independence from political control at the nation's periphery.[20]

Scholars make several different arguments about when this shift in constitutional orders took place. According to some, the shift to the modern constitutional order began in the late 1800s, with a gradual growth in authority as presidents began to unilaterally deploy force in order to "protect Americans abroad."[21] Another argument holds that the courts helped drive the shift in authority because although nineteenth-century court decisions largely affirmed the dominance of congressional authority over war powers, over time, outlying cases, especially *United States vs. Curtiss-Wright Export Corporation* (1936), helped to create a constitutional order that supported presidential unilateralism.[22]

Despite those earlier developments, most scholars date the beginning of the modern constitutional order for war powers as beginning in the mid-twentieth century. Many scholars point to a dramatic shift to the modern order when President Truman unilaterally initiated the Korean War, setting a precedent that potentially legitimated later actions.[23] Others argue that what was most important to establishing the new constitutional order was its institutionalization in the executive branch, which also began with the Cold War.[24] Still others argue that as the Cold War brought global superpower status to the United States, that status required a unitary foreign and military policy process led by the president, and so the modern constitutional order followed from that security need.[25]

There are also explanations for the shift to the modern constitutional order for war powers that center Congress. Some scholars specifically attribute the growth of presidential war powers in the modern era to congressional deference to the president after World War II.[26] Others attribute postwar changes to the internal structure of Congress during the Cold War, when defense related committees began to be filled with hawks.[27] John Hart Ely argues that Congress acquiesced to presidential leadership during the Vietnam War in part to avoid responsibility for what happened there.[28] For her part, Mariah Zeisberg posits that Congress helped to construct the national security order that legitimized a broader definition of national defense.[29]

In addition, some scholars argue that the modern constitutional order for war powers was paradoxically further institutionalized with the passage of the

War Powers Resolution in 1973, which unintentionally empowered the presidency by seeming to recognize a presidential right to deploy troops into hostile situations for up to sixty days. The legislative history of the War Powers Resolution shows that congressional collective action problems and party politics affected its passage and helped to create the contradictions in its text that led to that expansion of presidential power.[30] Congress's posture of deference, emphasis on local domestic politics, and agreement with Cold War logic also helped to build and sustain this modern order.[31]

In general, though, most scholars agree that the president began to dominate war powers around the middle of the twentieth century.

On the other hand, some who study American political development caution against such clearly defined periodizations.[32] They argue that what appear to be periods of stability are usually composed of multiple orders, or patterned interactions of different origins, centered in institutions but also in constant political interaction. And indeed, within each of the periods roughly defined by the "original" and "modern" constitutional orders, there are actions that do not fit with the synthesis of the time period—such as when Polk unilaterally started the Mexican war, or when Eisenhower expressed deference to Congress about the possibilities of going to war over Taiwan.[33] In both time periods, Congress was sometimes proactive about dictating policy to the president and sometimes reacted, often deferentially, to presidential overreach. Closely examining congressional actions and deliberations about the use of force in the modern period shows that political considerations, leadership choices, and partisan politics all affect Congress's decision making about whether to challenge the president's proposed policies.[34] But conventional politics played a similar role in the early republic as well.

So we should be cautious about characterizing entire time periods as fitting into an overarching synthesis. But at the same time, few question the fact that it is more common today than it was in the nineteenth century for presidents to take the initiative in using force and that Congress's assertions of authority today are weaker than they once were. Institutions, political exigency, partisan politics, and technology have shaped contemporary ideas about the constitutional text and the authority it confers on presidents. In particular, staff in the executive branch and former executive staff in the legal academy have been critical actors in developing, articulating, and defending the logic and ideas that defend presidential unilateralism.[35] In part as a consequence of their efforts, the ideas about authority articulated by political actors are different today than they were in the nineteenth century. The ways that modern actors construct authority today are shaped by ideas about security, interests, capitalism, race, threat, and American greatness that are embedded in multiple overlapping political orders. Earlier constructions of the constitutional text were similarly embedded in politics and ideas of the time.[36] If today's executive-led constructions of war powers authority are rooted in particular ideas and logics, it makes sense to ask whether and how congressionally dominated constructions of war powers were similarly grounded.

My research adds a new entry to these scholarly debates about when and how to define the emergence of the modern constitutional order for war powers. Focusing on the ideas and constitutional interpretations expressed in congressional debate, I argue that the groundwork for the modern constitutional order was laid after the Spanish-American War. The argument that emerged at that time was that the president represented the military, the flag, and the nation. This rhetoric displaced other congressional justifications for constrained presidential war power. The logic of congressional deference about a broad range of questions regarding war and peace that emerged around 1898 supplied reasoning and rhetoric to members of Congress who wished to support early acts of presidential unilateralism as the United States built its extracontinental empire in the early twentieth century.

While my research only shows a temporal association between the shift in available congressional logics and shifts in presidential governing behavior, other work suggests that such shifts in language may actually affect the distribution of constitutional and legal authority. John Dearborn shows that the argument that the president is the representative of the nation played an important role in congressional debates about domestic policy beginning around World War I. He shows that the argument that the president is "national representative" helped motivate Congress's construction of the president's domestic policy-making institutions, and that the weakening of that logic over time led Congress to assert more of its own authority over policy.[37] My observations complement Dearborn's argument and suggest that what Jeremy Bailey describes as cyclical presidential claims to be the best representative of the nation became critically important to constitutional development around the turn of the twentieth century.[38]

CONGRESS'S ROLE IN CONSTITUTIONAL CONSTRUCTION

Those who study American political development examine how institutions, politics, and policy interact to produce stability and change over time.[39] Like institutions, however, ideas can also be important to political stability and change, because widely held ideas define repertoires of legitimate moves for political actors.[40] Institutions and rules are embedded in ideas, and so changing patterns of thought and speech may be an important feature of institutional change.[41] Vivien Schmidt argues that political discourse within and about institutions legitimizes ideas and debates about political action in a particular institutional context according to a logic of communication.[42] The construction and evolution of war powers authority is unquestionably rooted in institutional capacity and shaped by ordinary politics. But the construction of constitutional meaning regarding war powers is also the creation and institutionalization of ideas.

While civics textbooks often say that only courts can articulate authoritative ideas about constitutional meaning, scholars make both normative and empirical arguments about the ways that the other branches also participate in constitutional interpretation. Keith Whittington has defined constitutional construction as a type of deliberation that can be practiced by any of the branches of government. Constitutional construction sits at a midpoint between policymaking based on assumed consensus about textual meaning and revolution that abandons the constitutional text. He argues that any branch, in moments of unsettled understanding, can consider fundamental political principles, examine textual meaning, and construct an interpretation of the Constitution's text that structures future political practice.[43] Given that definition, actions alone do not construct a constitutional order—ideas, language, and logical justifications are important as well. Indeed, scholars who have defined the modern constitutional order for war powers have looked to language and ideas expressed in presidential statements, legal memos, and Supreme Court decisions to explain how those institutions have constructed constitutional meaning and authority in the modern period.[44]

There is, furthermore, a growing interest in studying how Congress itself interprets and constructs constitutional meaning and authority.[45] Some legal scholars argue that, normatively, Congress should have a significant role in the construction of constitutional meaning.[46] Deliberation, ideas, and reasoning are ideally among Congress's institutional strengths. Some argue that Congress is well-equipped to participate in interpreting and constructing constitutional meaning because as an institution is has the capabilities to gather technical information and facts, to deliberate about them, and to include a wide range of voices and interests in that deliberation.[47] And indeed, historically, both Congress and the president have interpreted, reinterpreted, and made fundamental changes to the meaning and operation of the constitutional text, even outside of the formal amendment process. In modern times, Bruce Ackerman argues that political pressure emerging from the context of the New Deal and the civil rights movement, expressed by Congress and the president, fundamentally reinterpreted and effectively changed the Constitution's meaning and values, which the court eventually ratified.[48] Donald Morgan also chronicles various moments when Congress wrestled with and resolved constitutional dilemmas.[49] And David Currie notes that in the early Congresses, every new issue raised constitutional questions and most were decided by the Congress and the executive, with courts ratifying those decisions later.[50]

If language and ideas matter to political development, then the words members of Congress use to describe their understanding of constitutional authority are also an appropriate place to look for stability and changes in authoritative meaning over time.[51] War powers are an especially important area of constitutional law in which to look for nonjudicial construction of constitutional meaning, as it is an area where courts have ruled very rarely, leaving interpretation largely to the political branches.[52] With war powers as a case study, my research adds several contributions to scholarship on Congress's construction of constitutional meaning.

The coherence that I observe to be present in members' interpretations of the commander in chief clause supports scholarly claims that Congress can be a meaningful participant in constitutional construction. Observers today often find Congress's war powers deliberations to be purely deferential to the president and light on constitutional construction, which suggests to some that Congress might no longer have agency in interpreting constitutional war powers.[53] However, others argue that even modern congressional talk about foreign policy and war powers has been found to be nuanced and influential across the branches of government.[54] I began this project with an open mind about whether early Congresses would express any stable, widespread, coherent constitutional interpretations and was ready to accept a negative answer to that question. But fortunately, at least some nineteenth-century congressional debates about war powers were, as others have noted, rich and sophisticated in their constitutional reasoning.[55]

Scholars have articulated different standards for what constitutes sufficiently robust congressional deliberation in the constitutional construction of war powers. Some argue that the Constitution is clear about the breadth of Congress's constitutional war powers and that sufficient construction occurs only when Congress uses its war powers actively to authorize and regulate the use of force. These scholars tend to argue that the tendency of modern Congresses to defer war and foreign policy decisions to the executive branch results in constitutionally deficient authorizations of the use of force.[56] Others argue that the constitutional text does not necessarily have static meaning across varied security dilemmas and that the Constitution is adequately interpreted as long as the president and Congress articulate their collective view of how war powers should be applied in a given situation, regardless of whether Congress decides to act or defer to the executive in that moment.[57] These scholars argue that active deliberation produces the authority to act and helps to produce accountability by letting the other branches know that their interpretations of war powers authority are subject to review by a coordinate branch.[58]

My research informs these normative debates by describing what it looked like when Congress interpreted and constructed constitutional meaning of one particular clause over a long period of time. It offers new observations about how members of Congress interpreted the constitutional text and constructed constitutional war powers during a time when it is widely believed that Congress did a better job of deliberating about the use of force than it does today. In their conversations about the commander in chief clause in the nineteenth century, members of Congress did not turn to courts or presidents for authoritative interpretations of constitutional meaning. Instead, they confidently interpreted the Constitution on their own. In doing so, they relied on simple stories that synthesized constitutional text and familiar historical examples, sometimes referring to widely read textbooks. Across party lines and across many decades, they repeated these stories and rooted their arguments about policy dilemmas in these familiar logics and their assumptions. Members' repetition of these stories suggests that particular ideas about constitutional meaning were persistent across generations.

The content of these constitutional scripts contained an embedded logic about how much and what types of deliberation Congress should engage in. That logic supported what Griffin, Fisher, and others have characterized as the original constitutional order for war powers. Members who invoked these constitutional scripts did not always offer an elaborate justification for doing so. Rather, the scripts themselves seemed to offer a simple heuristic that invoked common knowledge about constitutional rules and principles. The scripts they used did not say that only courts could understand the Constitution or that presidents had a monopoly on foreign affairs authority. Rather, they said that the commander in chief was subordinate to Congress in making decisions about war and that narrative then made it obvious that Congress needed to make many decisions about war.

Even in that time period, when most agree that Congress was far more active in decision making about the use of force than it is in the modern period, not all references to the commander in chief clause involved drawn out, elaborate, thoroughly researched congressional deliberation. Often, references to the constitutional text and its meaning were brief, and so not all debates involving the distribution of war powers between Congress and the president reached the levels of engagement that Whittington would consider constitutional construction or that other scholars might consider constitutionally sufficient deliberation. But their brief references to often-repeated stories seemed to be useful heuristics that helped members interpret history and define when and how the Congress and the president should make decisions. Scholars studying modern congressional constitutional deliberation might want to look for other versions of constitutional scripts and to be attentive to what the content of those scripts tells members of Congress about their capacity to participate in decision making.

My analysis also contributes to scholarly literature about the role of precedent in constitutional reasoning. Legal scholars debate how much weight courts and political actors should give to historical precedents in understanding the balance of war powers. Bradley and Morrison argue that courts should not give much weight to historical examples of congressional acquiescence to executive unilateralism because of the structural difficulties of collective action by Congress, particularly given members' partisan ties to the president.[59] Zeisberg argues that because precedents that are cited may not be from relevant security dilemmas, and because precedential reasoning may lead to flawed and unethical decisions, deliberation across the branches and each branch using its political strengths should be prioritized over precedent in reasoning about war powers.[60] Spiro, on the other hand, argues that the historical accumulation of practice is how constitutional meaning is built.[61]

The chapters that follow show that while historical precedents were always important to members' reasoning about the commander in chief clause, their application of precedent was more partisan and less thorough than might be normatively desirable. Members in the nineteenth century, as today, did not carefully examine all of the conditions that might make a previous action relevant to their current policy dilemma but instead invoked precedent loosely, in support of their policy argument. Close reading of members' speeches about the commander in chief clause suggests that while members of Congress have always relied on precedents to understand constitutional meaning, prominent narratives help to highlight certain historical events over others and the logic of the narrative itself may make it easy for members to pick and choose among precedents. For example, George Washington's dutiful subservience to Congress was cited as relevant precedent for members of Congress who wanted to carefully regulate Lincoln's prosecution of the Civil War, but it was not relevant or persuasive to members who wanted to support executive led imperial policies during the Mexican and Spanish-American wars.

Obviously, the relevance of both precedents and constitutional scripts was intertwined with members' policy preferences, partisanship, and their partisan relationship to the president. Across every type of authority they discussed, members of Congress in the president's party and supporters of his policy goals tended to construct his authority more broadly than the opposition and tended to invoke a constitutional script that permitted presidential discretion. The evolution of the constitutional scripts that grounded members' reasoning was shaped by the push and pull of unified and divided government. During unified government, precedents were set that tended to interpret constitutional war powers in favor of more presidential discretion, a partisan context that later recollections of precedent often ignore. Investigations of constitutional construction by any of the three branches ought to grapple seriously with how partisanship limits each branch's independence from the other two and how politics affects the interpretive precedents set in particular historical moments. Scholars who think about how Congress constructs constitutional meaning should not ignore this dynamic.[62]

My research also suggests that shared stories about constitutional authority are applied, like common knowledge, within other moral and political frameworks, including racial orders. My dataset does not include congressional references to all uses of force in the nineteenth century—only those speeches that provoked members to refer to the commander in chief clause. One glaring omission from my dataset is that there are very few conversations about the commander in chief clause that deal with the repeated use of military force against indigenous Americans in the nineteenth century. My best explanation for the absence of deliberation is that the dominant logic at the time made it possible for members of Congress to determine how the commander in chief related to military force against Native Americans within uncontested constitutional understanding. Congress regarded the use of force against Native Americans in US territory to fall either under a constitutionally sound defensive presidential authority to protect American territory from attack, a constitutionally sound presidential responsibility to enforce treaties, or a constitutionally sound delegated legislative authority to repel invasions.[63] Those understandings did not require frequent reconsideration of the scope of the commander in chief's authority to deal with conflicts with Native peoples.

But there is an embedded racial order in this constitutional construction that also says that European white people have a right to "discover" Native lands, to own them, and to adopt policies that prefer white "civilization" over that of indigenous people. That racial order did not require that Congress fully authorize wars against Native peoples, although in other circumstances in the time period, Congress jealously guarded that authority. This racial order also framed early twentieth-century uses of force against nations in Asia and Latin America. Congress heatedly debated any use of force against France, Spain, or Germany but was content to rely on the president's implied authority to "defend" the nation and its citizens against perceived threats by "uncivilized," weaker, and nonwhite foes. The war in the Philippines was justified both by "laws of nations" interpretations of the commander in chief's authority to govern conquered territory and the "laws of (European) nations" doctrine of discovery, which said that when Spain surrendered to the United States, the Philippines were Spain's to cede to the United States. The speeches I collected for this project do not give me much purchase to unpack the relationships between racial orders and the distribution of war powers authority, but they hint at a rich research agenda on that topic. My data do suggest that members of Congress apply widely held beliefs about constitutional authority to policy and security dilemmas alongside and interaction with other widely held beliefs, and that those ideas about constitutional meaning may co-evolve in ways that deserve scholarly attention.

THE PROJECT

This book describes a unique collection of 2,823 congressional references to the commander in chief clause of the Constitution. It is important to be clear as to what can and cannot be learned by examining and describing these speeches. This dataset cannot answer every question we might have about the evolution of constitutional war powers in the United States. But it is a good dataset for answering some interesting questions that have rarely been asked before. I argue that this novel approach departs from and adds to the existing scholarly understanding of war powers in the American constitutional system in several ways.

First, my approach is relatively unusual in its focus on congressional, rather than presidential, construction of presidential war powers. My focus on this particular aspect of constitutional authority limits the conclusions that can be drawn about why war powers authority changed over time but also allows us to see the authority of the commander in chief from an important perspective. Congress is the key institution with which the president shares authority over war and peace. On the other side of the boundary from the commander in chief's implied authority is Congress's express and implied authority, which it can assign or delegate to the commander in chief through legal statutes or through political acquiescence. Therefore, congressional members' expressed beliefs about the scope of the implied commander in chief authority may be relevant to whether they act to grant, enhance, or limit that authority.[64] Although some scholars focus on individual aspects of congressional war powers authority, like congressional military spending, Congress's regulation of ongoing conflicts, or civil-military relations, very few efforts have been made to examine how these separate congressional war powers evolved alongside the president's authority as commander in chief.[65] Relatively little research focuses seriously on the commander in chief clause itself, and those pieces tend to focus on presidential claims, with less attention given to Congress's interpretation of the clause's meaning. Barron and Lederman, for example, describe the history of the commander in chief clause in two related articles in the *Harvard Law Review* published in 2008. In the first, they comprehensively describe its meaning at the Founding itself. In the second, they only episodically describe its meaning and development in the nineteenth century. Although they look for presidential invocations of the commander in chief clause and its appearance in court cases, scholarly works, and major debates of Congress, the list of congressional debates they identify is far smaller than I find in my more congressionally focused search. My work builds up that nineteenth-century record and more comprehensively examines the meaning of the clause in different political contexts throughout the pre–World War I era.[66]

Second, unlike other potential data sources like presidential pronouncements or court cases, there are several thousand congressional speeches in which members with different political orientations define the power of the commander in chief. These thousands of speeches offer more data points with which to sketch a picture of the multifaceted authority granted by the commander in chief clause. This variation also gives us a window into how Congress, as an institution, constructs constitutional meaning. Not every argument made by a member of Congress is historically important. However, to the degree that interpretations of implied commander in chief authority vary from person to person, individual-level information about the interpreters themselves, members of Congress, can help us to understand and explain why their interpretations vary in the ways that they do.

Third, my data are not limited to the outbreak of wars or the use of force, because when members of Congress speak about the commander in chief's authority, they speak about many different aspects of this question. This is a different approach than other studies of war powers issues take, as they often choose cases for study from lists of presidential actions, military actions, and major congressional debates.[67] Unlike other war powers research that focuses on the use of force itself, my focus on references to the constitutional text lets us see the use of force in context with the other aspects of the military authority of the commander in chief, as well as the ways that those different types of authority interact with and support each other. We can see how Congress understands its own powers and the president's in the regulation of the military, the occupation of foreign territory, the use of state militias, peacetime deployments, the regulation of the use of force during conflicts, and the initiation of the use of force, at least as they relate to this specific constitutional clause.

Finally, this analysis ends when World War I begins. For some readers, this may beg the question—how does Congress interpret and construct the president's commander in chief authority today? I would argue that there is no shortage of analyses of modern constitutional war powers. All make some argument about how war powers today are different than they were originally. In order to better understand and evaluate those arguments, it is also vitally important to understand exactly how they looked originally and what modern innovations have in fact changed. The speeches in this analysis pre-date both the era in which the United States was a world power and the time when the United States had a large military. By focusing on constitutional interpretation in that premodern period, we can highlight the ways that the president's inherent authority changed even before the growth of the presidency, the military, and American power in the twentieth century.[68]

There is a robust literature that attempts to explain changes in the distribution of war powers over time and this study only illuminates part of it. Members of Congress did not always refer to the commander in chief clause when war powers were used, and so this survey does not describe all aspects of congressional construction and action. In addition, I did not systematically examine presidential or judicial rhetoric, to see how it tracked with congressional usage. I did not systematically examine the use of the commander in chief clause in academic work, newspapers, or political party documents, to understand where members' understanding came from. I did not compare members' understanding of the clause to their understandings of any other important constitutional phrases, to look for interactions between them. There remains a large research agenda in trying to explain why constitutional war powers changed over time and what role congressional interpretations of war powers may have played in those changes. Hopefully the thick description of congressional understanding of the commander in chief clause and its relation to constitutional war powers helps inform other approaches to these questions.

Methods

The variable of interest that I track through time is how members of Congress interpreted the commander in chief clause.[69] What substantive powers did they ascribe to it? How far did those powers extend? Interpretive social science, in which a researcher tries to draw conclusions about what a text means, or what a historical figure was thinking, is notoriously hard to replicate and sometimes does not stand up to critical scrutiny. Because the central arguments of this book rely on interpretations of thousands of congressional speeches that no sane person would want to read on their own, I will be as transparent as possible about how I have gone about collecting, categorizing, interpreting, and presenting these texts. The goal of this discussion is to help the reader understand the reasons for the book's organization and the basis on which its conclusions are reached.

My first step in characterizing the use of the phrase in the congressional record was to identify all instances of its appearance in the congressional record. To that end, over the course of several years, my undergraduate research assistants and I attempted to find every congressional reference to the commander in chief clause prior to World War I.[70] To make sure we caught all of the references to the clause, we searched for any page in published congressional debates on which "commander" and "chief" both appeared. Over several years, we found more than fifty-eight thousand pages that include both the words "commander" and "chief" in the congressional record for this time period. We manually screened through those matches to screen out references to "chief clerks," "chief magistrates," and military "commanders," as well as references to military officers titled "commander in chief" who were not the president. We were able to identify a subset of 2,823 references to the president of the United States as commander in chief. Because we manually looked at every single one of the "commander"s and "chief"s found by the search function, we hope that we captured every reference to the president as commander in chief, even those in which one of the key words was misspelled or poorly scanned.[71]

Today, it is common to hear the press and public refer to the president interchangeably with the title commander in chief. On this mapping mission, one discovery we made was that prior to World War I, members of Congress did not refer to the president offhandedly in this fashion. Rather, when they used the phrase, they usually seemed to have in mind some kind of specific authority. These specific types of authority became the primary way that speeches were organized as data and will be presented in the chapters that follow.

In putting commander in chief references into categories, I coded according to the following criteria: Does the sentence in which the phrase "commander in chief" appears explicitly refer to a particular type of authority or power (regardless of whether the member of Congress argues whether or not such a power exists)? If the sentence itself is not explicit, does the speech's broader argument clearly and explicitly refer to a type of power or authority? If the answer to either question was yes, the speech got put into that category. If the answer to either question was no, the reference was categorized as "miscellaneous."

The categories themselves were constructed organically and iteratively. I simply looked for the most common types of speeches, and when I found a new type of argument, I created a new category.[72] Some of the speeches could have been categorized into two different types of authority.[73] Some references

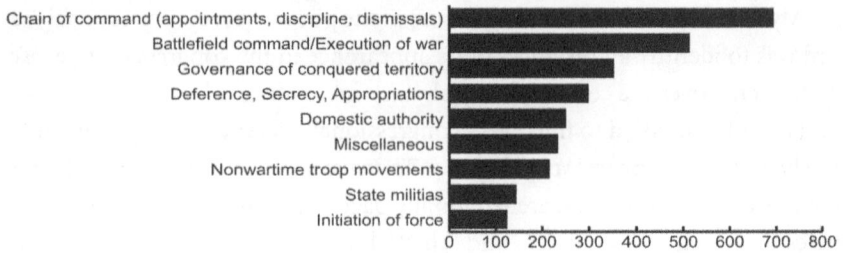

Figure 1.1

Chain of command (appointments, discipline, dismissals)
Battlefield command/Execution of war
Governance of conquered territory
Deference, Secrecy, Appropriations
Domestic authority
Miscellaneous
Nonwartime troop movements
State militias
Initiation of force

0   100   200   300   400   500   600   700   800

to the commander in chief might fall into one category if looking only at the few words around the clause itself (e.g., the member refers to the president's authority to direct troop movements), but a different one if understood in the conversation in which it took place (e.g., the member is participating in a debate about the governance of conquered territory). There were enough borderline coding decisions that I would not feel confident relying on this classification scheme for quantitative analysis. Nevertheless, figure 1.1 shows my best efforts to distill the substance of the members' of Congress comments about the commander in chief clause. Instead of relying on quantitative analysis, the substantive chapters of the book present representatives' own words in historical and political context, in a storytelling format.

There is a fairly long list of authorities that comprise the war powers of the United States government.

- raising and supporting armies,
- appointing officers,
- assigning officers to particular commands,
- writing rules about discipline,
- disciplining officers and troops,
- calling state militias into service,
- issuing orders for nonwartime troop movements,
- procuring weapons and supplies,
- interpreting treaties,
- interpreting unwritten international law and norms,
- initiating hostilities,
- issuing tactical battlefield commands,
- determining how prisoners will be treated,
- gathering intelligence about opposing forces,

- governing conquered territories,
- managing domestic affairs during a war,
- paying for war,
- making alliances,
- ending hostilities,
- making treaties,
- enforcing treaties,
- and others.

Some of these types of authority were not discussed in reference to the commander in chief clause at all, but others were mentioned frequently. In reading and categorizing these speeches, the first thing one notices is the precision with which members of Congress talked about the commander in chief clause. Today, "the commander in chief" is often used as a synonym for "the president." My data indicates that prior to the year 1900, members of Congress almost never used the "commander in chief" as a synonym for "the person who lives at 1600 Pennsylvania Avenue" or "the person who supports this tax bill."[74] Instead, they almost always talked about the "commander in chief" in reference to a particular type of military power or authority.[75] Members of Congress debated and discussed the "commander in chief's" authority over subordinate military officers in the chain of command and his authority to give battlefield commands to execute declared wars, to govern conquered territory, to direct nonwartime troop and ship movements, and to command state militias. They also debated and discussed whether his title gave him any domestic authority in wartime, whether there were types of information to which his title gave him privileged access, and his role in initiating the use of force.

Note that figure 1.1 *certainly does not show* that members of Congress always agreed about the scope of the president's authority in a particular category. Sometimes they agreed among themselves about how to interpret the commander in chief clause relative to a particular type of authority; often they did not. Nor does figure 1.1 imply that members of Congress ascribed broad powers to the president as commander in chief in regard to the topic in question. Often, the authority they ascribed was quite narrow.

Take, for example, the following two speeches that fall under the category of "battlefield command." These two members of the House are discussing the execution of prisoners during an ambiguously authorized invasion of Florida by Andrew Jackson (the details of which will be described further in chapter 1).

Representative Barbour of Virginia approved of the controversial executions by arguing that "the conduct of the war belongs to the President as Commander-in-chief, and under him to his commanding General, who is supposed to represent him. Is there any member of this Committee who denies that the mode of treating prisoners belongs to him who commands your armies?"[76] In contrast, Henry Clay denied "that any commander-in-chief, in this country, had this absolute power of life and death, at his sole discretion. It was contrary to the genius of all our laws and institutions. To concentrate in the person' of one individual the powers to make the rule, to judge, and to execute the rule, or to judge and execute the rule only, was utterly irreconcilable with every principle of free Government, and was the very definition of tyranny itself."[77] Barbour, here, argues that the commander in chief has broad discretionary authority to determine how prisoners should be treated, while Clay argues that the he has no discretion and must only enforce existing congressionally authorized law regarding the treatment of prisoners. Both are examples of arguments members of Congress made about the constitutional title, "commander in chief," and the authority it conferred on the president to give battlefield commands.

Thus, the categories in figure 1.1 do not imply agreement about any particular construction of authority. The figure simply shows that when they referred to the phrase, members of Congress meant something specific and constitutionally substantive. In their speeches, they referred to the commander in chief's ability to govern conquered territory without congressional permission (or not), or to the president's authority to discipline officers and troops (or not). The concrete, specific nature of congressional debates helps us to compare members' arguments and identify areas of congressional consensus and dispute in defining the boundaries of the president's constitutional power.

Figure 1.1 shows the number of congressional references that are reasonably related to each type of authority. It tells us that the majority of their comments can be coded into the categories that deal with the types of authority that are most closely related to the military origins of the commander in chief title. They most often mentioned the commander in chief in remarks about the chain of command, battlefield command, execution of war, and governance of conquered territory. Chapter 1 will show that there was fairly widespread agreement from the beginning of the republic that the president, as the highest ranking military officer by virtue of the title "commander in chief," had some legitimate and authoritative role in war-fighting—he could discipline and assign lower ranked officers, for example, and he could direct tactical decision making during wartime. However, the boundaries of each of those types of authority were contested in congressional debates.

The fact that members of Congress made hundreds of remarks about similar types of authority associated with the commander in chief clause makes it possible for us to compare members' sentiments on very similar questions across political conditions and over time. Figure 1.1 shows that more than 90 percent of the time prior to World War I, when a member of Congress talked about the commander in chief clause, they referred to an identifiable type of military authority or a specific aspect of the president's relationship to Congress.[78]

In addition, members of Congress usually mentioned the commander in chief clause in conversation with each other about some *substantive policy question*. Recall that prior to World War I, the United States fought four major wars: the War of 1812, the Mexican War, the Civil War, and the Spanish-American War. It also fought several serious undeclared wars, including the Quasi-War with France and the war in the Philippines, not to mention the centuries-long use of violence to conquer the Native Americans. There were, in short, plenty of opportunities for members of Congress to grapple with the extent of their own constitutional war powers and the extent of the president's. Though there were moments when only a single legislator mentioned the commander in chief clause in the course of a particular legislative debate, that was not the norm. Most of the time, when a member of Congress mentioned the commander in chief clause, he did so in a context in which other members were also doing so, and when the actual meaning of the commander in chief clause was relevant to the debate. Usually, if the clause was mentioned, it was mentioned more than once, by different members of Congress, while discussing some specific resolution, bill, or other real-time development.

Studying congressional constitutional construction requires more than identifying members' random comments. The questions of interest are whether the collective body deliberated upon constitutional meaning and whether the collective body agreed upon the authority conferred by the constitutional phrase. In the chapters that follow, I will describe both interpretations about which members of Congress broadly agreed and interpretations about which they disagreed.

Is it possible to use congressional speeches, coded as I have described, to identify a "congressional interpretation" of the commander in chief clause? I argue that the answer is yes but that some interpretations are more clear, bipartisan, and long-lasting than others and even the most durable interpretations are subject to change over time. The chapters of this book will describe the ways in which members of Congress used the commander in chief clause to construct arguments about war powers authority during the original constitutional order.

My data show that the original constitutional order for war powers, from the Founding through the Spanish-American War, was intertwined with a dominant constitutional "script" about the commander in chief clause.[79] That narrative was widely used and connected to multiple applications of the boundary between congressional and presidential war powers. The dominant constitutional script said that the commander in chief was a military title and so carried with it certain types of authority that would be held by any hypothetical high-ranking general or admiral, such as giving battlefield orders or directing troops from place to place. Like any high-ranking officer, he would be similarly prohibited from using the types of authority that would be prohibited for any high-ranking general or admiral—including and especially political decisions that would commit a nation to war. Members of Congress across party lines over several decades generally accepted the script's logic and consequently argued that Congress had both robust powers to make war policy and an obligation to do so. They also generally argued that presidents were constrained by hard limits to any authority implied by the commander in chief clause. Members behaved as though they believed these interpretations, and even when they took actions that seemed incompatible with the script, they defended themselves under its logic. As members of Congress and presidents abided by those limited definitions of the commander in chief clause repeatedly over the nineteenth century, those precedents helped to reinforce each other by supplying more recent examples to members of Congress who were searching for authoritative guidance on how to apply the Constitution to new situations.

This script was so dominant in congressional conversations about the commander in chief clause that it actually had two common subscripts, or repeated, reasoned justifications for how to further define the commander in chief clause in practice. The first subscript, which tended to dominate in congressional reasoning, encompassed the story of the American founding and the precedents set by George Washington as the first commander in chief. This repeated narrative recounted that Washington was willing to take orders from the Continental Congress during the Revolutionary War and that he was careful to adhere literally to the law governing the use of force and state militias as president. His example supported members of Congress for decades in their arguments to construct the commander in chief title narrowly, conferring authority that was similar to any high ranking military officer and therefore obviously subject to congressional law. According to this logic, Congress had broad authority to direct and micromanage the actions of the commander in chief, including during wartime.

The other subscript referred to a different set of precedents that came vaguely from European history that generally predated the Constitution but was stylized as the "laws of nations" by writers like Emmerich de Vattel. The "laws of nations," really a set of norms, defined certain actions that commanders on the battlefield could legitimately take, as part of an effort to create rules around ethical conduct in wartime. Members of Congress who wanted to support more expansive definitions of presidential power generally used arguments about the inherent authority of commanders in this uncodified international law to argue that the president, like any commander, had powers that Congress could not regulate after war had begun. It is important to note that even this broader argument was limited by the nature of the narrative itself. Neither subscript granted the president any implied authority to initiate hostilities against foreign nations.

The commander-as-general narrative was dominant enough, yet flexible enough, to ground vigorous partisan debates about the balance of constitutional war powers for more than a century. When members of Congress disagreed about what actions the country should take, they articulated their constitutional claims using one of the two subscripts—whichever one supported their position. Members of Congress in the president's party often favored the "laws of nations" interpretation that granted the president more discretionary authority in the direction of force. The opposition party often favored the George Washington subscript that gave Congress a dominant role in war policy. Members' references to the constitutional scripts were carefully intertwined with both partisanship and with the members' policy goals. For example, the subscript associated with George Washington, and narrower presidential discretion, was espoused by out-party Whigs during the Mexican War, and by Democrats and Unionists during the Civil War.

Congressional majorities passed laws authorizing and prohibiting particular actions that further defined the authority of the commander in chief and were consistent with the dominant narrative. Whichever party had a majority at any particular moment enshrined its interpretation, and the logic that supported it, into law. Those laws—and the particular subscript that justified them—were subsequently available to become part of future congressional discourse about how to define the commander in chief clause as the next set of policy questions presented itself. For example, during the Mexican War, the Democratic partisan majority, with some bipartisan support, agreed that under the law-of-nations logic, Polk as commander in chief could temporarily govern conquered lands.[80] A half-century later members of Congress consciously justified the imperialist war in the Philippines as rooted in that Mexican War era compromise. The inherited script, as interpreted and applied by members of Congress, said that once the territory was conquered from Spain, McKinley and Roosevelt as commanding generals had a responsibility under the laws of nations to "ensure order" in the conquered Philippines, sidestepping questions about whether the war against the Philippine people was a separate conflict that required congressional authorization.

Congressional discourse also evolved over time in the period I study in important ways that relate to debates about the evolution of war powers authority. Quite abruptly, around the year 1898, a new script emerged and quickly came to dominate congressional talk about war powers. Around the turn of the twentieth century, members of Congress in both parties started talking about their "responsibility" to "defer" to the president as commander in chief. This deference was acceptable in part because of the emergence of a brand new constitutional script that said the president as commander in chief represented the military, the flag, and the nation and so had legitimate authority to make policy about the use of force.[81] Instead of modeling their understanding of the commander in chief clause on the metaphor of a "general," legislators began to base their understanding of the president's role as commander in chief on the metaphor of a "national representative." They began to argue that Congress should be deferential to the president because of his electoral mandate. The introduction of this new constitutional script during the Spanish-American War organized a wider range of potentially legitimate congressional and presidential behaviors.[82] This new constitutional script was introduced at a precise moment when assertive presidents with overwhelming partisan support in Congress were eager to take advantage of that authority. Together, the new narrative and unified governments logically supported a range of new precedents that seemed to grant new presidential autonomy in war.

ROADMAP

In the chapters that follow, I attempt to do two things. The first is to share details from some of the rich constitutional debates about the commander in chief clause in the nineteenth and early twentieth centuries, without overwhelming the reader. The second is to organize those speeches and debates to highlight the themes that emerged as I analyzed them. An important strategy in my analysis was to compare like with like—to group speeches by the substantive arguments they made about the authority of the commander in chief and compare them to each other to look for stability and change across political and governing dilemmas. Thus, each chapter has two tasks. The first is to illuminate a theme that is important to Congress's interpretation of the commander in chief clause and the balance of powers. The second is to use a particular set of speeches, all dealing with a similar type of authority, to illuminate that theme.[83]

Members of Congress tended to agree across party lines, and at multiple points in time, about how the commander in chief clause applied to certain situations involving command and the initiation of hostilities. Chapters 1 and 2 describe the types of authority about which members of Congress developed this long-term consensus. These findings are consistent with what others have described related to the original constitutional order for war powers, and I contribute to that literature by demonstrating that members of Congress used the commander in chief clause specifically in predictable ways that conform to a limited definition of presidential war power prior to 1898.

Specifically, chapter 1 focuses on the commander in chief's "superintendence" authority—his superiority in the chain of command and his authority to give legitimate orders to state militias. In chapter 2, I discuss the consistent ways that members of Congress described the commander in chief's narrow authority to initiate the use of military force. In particular, I highlight the ways in which they referred to the line between offensive actions (which had to be authorized by Congress) and defensive actions (which presidents could take on their own). I also highlight the sometimes inconsistent ways those terms were defined and applied.

In chapter 3, I ask how members arrived at their constitutional interpretations. I describe the works and precedents they cited as providing authoritative advice about the meaning of the commander in chief clause. I conclude that they relied on constitutional scripts as shorthand when trying to understand how to apply the clause to novel situations in practice; I also provide some examples of bipartisan reliance on the same script at different points in time.

In chapter 4, I describe the moment when a new script was introduced. The chapter describes the set of speeches in which members of Congress talked about their own responsibilities to defer to the implied authority of the commander in chief. In the nineteenth century, talk about congressional deference was quite limited, but at the time of the Spanish- American War, the script changed and ideas about congressional deference were broadened as members began to talk about the commander in chief as a national representative rather than a military officer. I also show that the new constitutional script was quickly associated with many of the characteristics of the modern constitutional order for war powers. The "national representative" script supported members' arguments as they facilitated a broadening of the commander in chief's authority to unilaterally initiate the use of force in the development of the early twentieth-century American empire.

In chapter 5, I discuss the ways in which members of Congress both used and shaped historical precedents and how that informs normative debates about the role of historical precedent in constitutional interpretation. I show the interplay between the two competing interpretations of the "general in chief" constitutional script, partisanship, and policy preferences in the construction of important new precedents dealing with the governance of conquered territory. In the main case study in the chapter, I show how a bipartisan consensus during the Mexican War wove a particular version of the constitutional script into precedent that defined the role of each branch in the governance of conquered territory, as well as how those precedents were used in later similar governing challenges.

Chapter 6 focuses on a second important case study that shows how members' partisanship and policy preferences combined with constitutional scripts. I argue that in its discussions about battlefield emancipation, Congress was able to communicate an unlegislated consensus about the distribution of war powers authority, grounded in both constitutional logic and political coalitions. This example contributes to scholarly debates over the Emancipation Proclamation itself and also to debates over the relative roles that deliberation and legislation play in the expression of congressional war powers authority.

I conclude with some thoughts about the implications of the book's arguments for scholars who study war powers, the constitution outside the courts, and American political development.

CHAPTER 1

Stable Interpretations of
the Commander in Chief Clause

In many of their nineteenth-century debates, members of Congress disagreed about the authority implied by the commander in chief clause. Broadly speaking, they disagreed about the boundaries between congressional and presidential authority in directing the movements of the armed forces during declared wars, governing conquered territory, emancipating enslaved people, and other topics that will be described in later chapters. In this chapter, however, I discuss the congressional references to the commander in chief clause that displayed the most consistency from 1789 to at least 1898. I describe the several types of presidential authority for which all or nearly all members of Congress expressed the same opinions regarding its scope, in reference to different bills or legislative debates at different points in time.

These descriptions support several conclusions. First, the congressional discourse I describe is broadly consistent with other research about war powers in the early republic. Baron and Lederman, in their study of the preclusive powers conferred by the commander in chief clause, found that it conferred superiority in the chain of command, and little more that was not, in historical practice, regulated by Congress.[1] My survey of congressional references to the clause uses a novel dataset to confirm and reinforce Baron and Lederman's conclusions about the "superintendence" authority the clause confers; it also adds some additional nuances. Many scholarly accounts describe the operational uses of war powers in the original constitutional order as being "dominated" by Congress in law and practice. The speeches described in this chapter demonstrate that nineteenth-century members of Congress themselves used language that is broadly consistent with this interpretation. In addition, the debates and discussions I describe reveal details about the language that members of Congress repeatedly used to define the boundaries of their war powers authority and the logic by which they actively maintained it through legislation across party lines and policy dilemmas.

Second, the data from these speeches support the scholars who argue that

Congress is capable of engaging in meaningful constitutional deliberation and is capable of producing stable interpretations over time and across controversies.[2] In the modern era, it is widely assumed that courts, not members of Congress, are the sole and final interpreters of constitutional meaning.[3] Some legal scholars have explicitly argued that Congress does not have institutional or political capacity to engage in effective constitutional deliberation.[4] However, this chapter in particular shows that during the nineteenth century, members of Congress were able to deliberate and arrive at shared understandings of the constitutional text. They repeatedly considered alternative interpretations of the commander in chief clause, including considering possible future implications of those interpretations, and repeatedly arrived at widely shared, stable understandings of the distribution of war powers implied by that clause. They defined both positive actions that presidents could take on their own (preclusive authority) and the circumstances in which congressional authority superseded the president's.

METHODS: DEFINING CONGRESSIONAL AGREEMENT

Figure 1.1 (see introduction) shows that congressional references to the commander in chief clause can be grouped by the type of substantive authority to which they refer. Within each of those groups of remarks, there were varying degrees of consistency and agreement among members of Congress. When I claim that Congress has adopted a consistent interpretation of the commander in chief clause, I do so on the basis of five criteria. First, congressional agreement about the meaning of commander in chief clause must include repeated articulation of a particular definition of that type of authority over time. Second, congressional agreement refers to the absence of serious dispute about the scope of the commander in chief's authority.[5] (I also count as a point of agreement a long-standing consensus in which a dispute emerges but is short-lived and decisively resolved.) Third, congressional agreement refers to widely agreed-upon definitions of authority that were often expressed as unstated assumptions. Members, in their speeches, frequently relied on the assumption that a particular interpretation of the commander in chief clause was correct as they made offhand remarks or unrelated points. Fourth, members of Congress in both the president's party and the opposition party expressed that the authority in question existed and was conferred by the commander in chief clause. Finally, consensus implies that the words that members spoke were substantively meaningful. They were both consistent with and related to the specific bills, resolutions, and laws that they considered and passed.

For example, consider the proposition that the commander in chief clause of the Constitution confers upon the president *wide authority to give military orders*. One might say that such an interpretation is obvious and indisputable. But as this book will make clear, there are many potentially "obvious" interpretations of the clause and many of them have been hotly contested at various points in time. The evidence, however, shows that members of Congress broadly agreed that it conferred a vaguely defined "authority to give military orders" upon the president. That interpretation meets all five of the criteria described above.

First, members across many decades made statements that support that interpretation. As early as 1789, South Carolina representative Thomas Tucker moved to amend the Constitution to clarify that was precisely what the commander in chief clause meant. He moved to "strike out the words 'be commander-in-chief,' and insert, 'have power to direct (agreeably to law) the operations.'"[6] Although that amendment did not pass, members of Congress throughout the nineteenth century commonly expressed a similar understanding that the clause was synonymous with "having the power to direct the operations of the military consistent with the law."[7]

Second, there was no disagreement or serious debate that the commander in chief had at least a general authority to issue military commands. Congress surely debated the specific types of orders that might be issued unilaterally (see chapter 6 for a discussion of the Emancipation Proclamation, for example) and how much authority Congress had to regulate the types of commands that could be given, but it was widely assumed that some authority to give orders was conferred along with the commander in chief title. I found no remarks that seriously questioned the president's authority to issue at least some commands to the military, generally.

Third, in addition to members' explicit statements, their *implicit* arguments also convey a consistent support for an implied authority to issue orders. Sometimes, they just referred to the president's role as commander in chief in passing. For example:

> I understand those troops never were mustered into the service of the United
> States . . . never subjected to the command of our forces, never subjected to the

authority of the Commander-in-Chief of the Army of the United States.[8] (Senator Howe [1863])

I charge it home upon the policy of an Administration that makes it necessary for the boys of this country . . . who out of love for their country or patriotism and devotion to its flag have followed it across the-ocean to the distant isles of the sea-to obey the Commander in Chief of the Army and the generals and officers who command them."[9] (Representative Bartlett [1902])

These members of Congress are speaking decades apart (in 1863 and 1902), about entirely different issues. The first is talking about a Civil War–era Missouri regiment that was never called into service. The second is offering a critique of the US occupation of the Philippines after the Spanish-American War. But in both comments, it is possible to discern that the speakers *assume* that rank-and-file soldiers are legitimately commanded by the president as commander in chief.

A generic authority to issue military orders was frequently an unstated assumption when members talked about the commander in chief clause. For example, Congress twice debated whether it was unconstitutional for members of Congress to serve concurrently in Congress and in the US Army or a militia. In both cases, the debates were really about the credentials of specific members of Congress, and in both cases, they resolved the debate in favor of concurrent service. However, members of Congress on both sides of the question took it as given that the president could issue binding orders to the armed forces that would be binding on even a member of Congress (indeed, that was the concern).

The following are two brief excerpts from a debate in 1870 about the wisdom of having an army officer serve concurrently in the army and as the (Republican) senator from Mississippi. This speaker (a Democrat) objects to the appointment on constitutional grounds and bases his objection on the assumption that the commander in chief could give binding orders to a member with a dual role:

The Constitution intended that the President should have no power to control the action of Congress in any respects[;] that it should be perfectly independent. Now, suppose that every member of Congress were a colonel in the Army in the service of the United States, and the President, who is by the Constitution the Commander-in-Chief of that Army, should come into the Halls of Congress and order each individual member to retire immediately, under the penalties inflicted for disobedience of orders, to his post in the Army, what would become of Congress? . . . To allow those two offices to be held by the same person would utterly destroy the independence of Congress and convert the country into a military despotism."[10]

The following speaker (a Republican) argues against the threat to Congress's power—but also makes the same assumptions, namely that the commander in chief can give orders to a member of Congress:

I agree that so far as his bodily movements are concerned he is subject to orders. If the Commander-in-Chief says "Go," he must go; if he says "Come," he must come. So far, then, as his corporal movements are concerned he is not sui une, as the term has been used here; it is not at his volition that he goes hither or thither, but it is in obedience to orders. But was it ever held that because an officer of the Army of the United States is subject to obey orders in the line of his duty, that fact trammels him mentally; that he has not just as good a right as you or I have to form his conclusions as to whether he will have his home here or there, and those conclusions once formed are just as good in his case as they are in yours or mine?[11]

Often, partisan and policy concerns comingle with constitutional interpretations. But that's the point—members of Congress were arguing about something else, and no matter the position they took, both sides assumed for the sake of that argument that the commander in chief clause grants the president an implied, unquestioned power to issue at least some binding orders to active duty members of the military.

It is especially noteworthy when *many different members of both political parties* articulated similar views about a particular presidential power. At different points in time, and even at the height of Civil War animosity, both Republicans and Democrats agreed about the commander in chief's right to issue orders.

It is clear from the congressional record that while members agreed that the commander in chief clause granted some powers to the president, they also believed that power was also limited. One way that we can see the limits to that authority is in the *laws they passed*, in which Congress granted the president authority to take actions that they collectively believed he could not take on his own. Those laws also illuminate the types of implied authority members of Congress did not believe they needed to grant through statute.

In even the earliest laws organizing the armed forces, or empowering the president to use the militia or the armed forces, there is never a congressional grant of specific authority to the president to issue orders. In the Declaration of War against the United Kingdom in 1812, for example, Congress declared a state of war and said that "the President is hereby authorized to use the whole and naval forces of the United States to carry the same into effect."[12] Congress did not statutorily empower him specifically to give orders. In his "use" of the armed forces, the power to give commands was assumed.

QUALIFIED AUTHORITY GRANTED BY THE
COMMANDER IN CHIEF CLAUSE

Members of Congress repeatedly said that the clause conferred specific, narrowly circumscribed military authority on the president. Across decades and party lines, they expressed the belief that the clause conferred superiority in the chain of command, the ability to appoint and assign officers, and the authority to command state militias. Even in dealing with hard cases and partisan controversies, members of Congress enforced consistent definitions of the commander in chief clause through the words they spoke and the actions they took—like creating new military ranks—and refused to take, for example, rejecting legislation that would grant important appointment powers to a general instead of the president. This finding reinforces and adds detail to other scholars' characterizations of the original constitutional order for war powers, by documenting some debates and moments of congressional constitutional construction of presidential powers that other scholars have overlooked.

Members of Congress consistently defined and policed the boundaries between the commander in chief's authority and congressional war powers. Moreover, they did not only repeat statements in which they argued that the clause conferred authority. They also reliably repeated interpretations of the clause that defined limits to the authority it conferred. For example, they consistently said the clause conferred the ability to execute military discipline but agreed that Congress had the authority to prescribe the discipline that was to be executed. Members of Congress also consistently said that the commander in chief clause gave the president authority to direct the movement of troops and ships but repeatedly defined the limits to those movements to defensive positions only unless an offensive posture was specifically authorized by Congress. Policing the limits to presidential power was difficult for members of Congress, who sometimes had partisan and policy reasons to support broader authority for the commander in chief. But in the cases I describe in this chapter, the language they used to define the commander in chief's authority is quite consistent across time and policy questions.

In this section, I describe five types of authority that, across many decades, members of Congress seemed to agree were conferred upon the president by the commander in chief clause. In the next section, I describe two types of authority that members of Congress agreed were *not* conferred by the commander in chief clause. In the next chapter, I discuss the third type of authority that members of Congress agreed was not conferred by the commander in chief clause, the authority to initiate the use of hostile force.

Superiority in the Chain of Command

Members of Congress prior to World War I regularly talked about the commander in chief in relation to those serving in the armed forces. More than a quarter of the speeches I collected referred to the commander in chief clause in reference to the chain of command, including the president's superiority within it, his responsibility in the appointment and assignment of officers, and his role in enacting military discipline. These speeches tend to make very similar statements about the president's place in the chain of command and articulate that the constitutional clause conferred some inherent authority. Members of Congress throughout the nineteenth century agreed that no matter the rank of an army or navy officer, the president, as commander in chief, outranked them all. Legislators supported the president's authority to command subordinate officers and troops, at the most basic level, because it ensured civilian control of the military. For example, one Civil War–era representative noted that "the Constitution of the United States made the President Commander-in-Chief of its army and Navy for the purpose of asserting and maintaining the great principle which lies at the foundation of our Government, that the military should ever be subordinate to the civil power; and it is as the civil head of the nation that the President is Commander-in-Chief of the Army."[13] Members of Congress, like others then and now, were especially sensitive to the possibilities that a rogue military commander could pose a threat to democratically elected government. Assuring that the president out-ranked all other officers reduced that potential.

Throughout, members of Congress reiterated the commander in chief clause's grant of superintendence authority while recognizing Congress's own role in overseeing the military. Recall that Congress has the constitutional authority to raise and support armies and navies, "to make Rules for the Government and Regulation of the land and naval Forces," and to create particular ranks in the army and navy through legislation and appropriation of salaries.[14] During some debates over whether Congress should create positions for high ranking generals, members asked themselves whether by creating such positions, they threatened the supremacy of the president in the chain of command. In both parties, and across decades, Congress weighed these concerns and repeatedly concluded that no military officer could possess authority that superseded that of the president as commander in chief. Similar conversations from the 1840s, 1860s, and 1900s illustrate this consensus.

During the Mexican War (1846–1848), President Polk requested that members of Congress create a new rank in the army above all others: the position of lieutenant general. Although there had been a tradition of a single high-ranking general having supreme command over the army, no general since Washington had held that particular rank. At the time of the 1847 debate in question, Major Gen. Winfield Scott, who had commanded the army before the war, and who was a prominent Whig who would be the Whig nominee for president in 1852, was one of three major generals in the army. Members of Congress in President Polk's party (the Democrats) and the opposition party (the Whigs) generally agreed with each other that it was appropriate for Congress to create such a position because it would still obviously be subordinate to the president in the chain of command.[15] They agreed about the supremacy of the commander in chief in the chain of command—but not on Polk's specific request for the new rank, which they denied.[16]

In 1864 the question of creating the rank of lieutenant general resurfaced. Across party lines, there was support for Congress's ability to create the position, with the expectation that it would be filled by Ulysses S. Grant, "in subordination, of course, to the Commander-in-Chief under the Constitution."[17] Though there was a little bit of disagreement from Democrats who distrusted Grant, again the majority agreed that creating the position was not a threat to the president.[18]

Having the votes to do so, the Republicans created the position of lieutenant general, to which Grant was appointed.[19] In 1866 Congress created the higher rank of general of the army, to which Grant was also appointed.

Similar arguments were made when Republican president Theodore Roosevelt and his secretary of state Elihu Root asked Congress to create a general staff and a chief of staff in 1903. John Hull, Republican of Iowa, argued that structuring the upper ranks of the military would not diminish the commander in chief's ability to rely on other aides and reassured his colleagues that the authority of the commander in chief could not be undermined by a general.[20] Democrat representative James Hay similarly argued that the new staff officers would be no different than a commanding general, because "that officer has no powers except such as may be conferred upon him by the Commander in Chief of the Army, the President of the United States."[21] There were no significant constitutional objections from either Republicans or Democrats.[22]

In these repeated debates, as well as in implicit assumptions in unrelated arguments, members of both the president's party and the opposition party affirmed that they believed that the commander in chief clause conferred supreme military rank upon the president. True, there was one episode in which the president's supremacy in the chain of command was challenged. The challenge—three provisions of the Reconstruction Acts (see chapter 6)—deviated from that norm, but the acts were short-lived and did not overturn the nineteenth-century consensus.[23]

To Appoint Officers to Command

At various times, Congress considered creating new officer ranks and positions while discussing the merits of particular candidates for those commands. During those discussions, there was bipartisan agreement that Congress could not by law tell the president whom to appoint to particular commands.[24] For example, as already discussed, during the Mexican War, Congress explicitly refused to create the lieutenant general position because the congressional majority disapproved of whom President Polk might appoint to that position— implying that if the position was created, the choice was his. During the Civil War, there was ample criticism of President Lincoln's appointments but no real question that he had the authority to appoint officers to particular commands. At the same time, Congress maintained its right to confirm officers' nominations.

Even during Reconstruction, when the president's command authority was being limited by law, there was still deference to the president's implied authority over the assignment of particular commands. The first draft of the First Reconstruction Act, proposed on February 2, 1867, created five military districts in the South. It proposed to give General Grant, rather than President Johnson, the power to appoint the generals in command of the Reconstruction districts.[25] Opponents argued that this provision would strip the commander in chief, the president, of his rightful authority to appoint officers to command.[26] Though Republicans controlled the Congress and acted to limit Johnson's authority in several other ways, the opponents succeeded in deleting the appointment provision. The final version of the Reconstruction Act did not give General Grant the power to choose the five generals to govern the military districts in the South, instead leaving those decisions to President Johnson. This outcome seems to indicate that in both parties, there was agreement that the president's constitutional appointment power was connected to his commander in chief authority.

To Discipline and Dismiss

Congress consistently reasserted its authority to "make rules governing the land and naval forces" while conceding that the commander in chief had some practical discretionary authority to execute those rules in specific cases. For example, the legislators repeatedly acted upon their constitutional obligation to write specific laws governing discipline in the armed forces.[27] In 1800 they even sanctioned a member of the House for suggesting that the president could discipline troops without express congressional authorization to do so.[28] They maintained and exercised congressional statutory authority over retirements and dismissals during various episodes of military downsizing.[29] At the outset of the Civil War, they explicitly gave the president statutory authority "to dismiss and discharge from the military service . . . any officer for any cause which, in his judgment, either renders such officer unsuitable for or whose dismissal would promote the public service."[30] After controversial firing decisions during the Civil War, in 1865 the Republican Congress wrote legislation that said that presidents could only dismiss officers in peacetime after a court martial, or in wartime by presidential order.

In general, members of Congress also argued that such laws were to be administered by the commander in chief. Some argued that his authority over discipline was actually absolute, and unreviewable. But many, even in heated debates, argued that his authority over discipline was limited by law. So while the consensus position was that the commander in chief clause conferred some authority to administer military discipline, the boundaries to that authority, and Congress's power to review his actions, were politically contested.

Congress found it to be a complicated challenge to enforce its role in rulemaking for military discipline when presidents took controversial actions that demanded congressional oversight over the commander in chief's execution of those rules. On two notable occasions, questions about the administration of military discipline were controversial enough that Congress investigated and publicly debated the specifics of the commander in chief's authority. In such moments, the questions about the commander in chief clause revolved around whether Congress, as a superior branch, had the power to review decisions about discipline as they were administered by the commander in chief or subordinate officers—or whether his authority to administer military law was so complete that Congress could not interfere. These two debates each ended the same way, with a subtle agreement. In each instance, Congress reaffirmed that the commander in chief was bound to execute military discipline as prescribed by Congress. Congress asserted its right to oversee the execution of those laws. But Congress was also deferential to the commander in chief in its oversight of those decisions.

Two debates, already alluded to, illustrate this tenuous agreement.

One major debate over Congress's role in overseeing military discipline took place in 1818, after General Andrew Jackson had prosecuted a legally ambiguous war against the Seminoles in the Florida Panhandle. In the course of the conflict, he had ordered the executions of two British citizens who were accused of helping the Creeks and the Seminoles fight the United States. Alexander Arbuthnot, a Scottish trader, was accused of selling arms to the Seminoles. Robert Ambrister, a former lieutenant in the Royal Marines, had tried to convince the Seminoles that he was a representative of the British government and promised the Seminoles an alliance. When captured by Jackson, Arbuthnot and Ambrister were tried by a military tribunal. Ambrister was first sentenced to death but then threw himself on the mercy of the court and was sentenced to a year at hard labor. Jackson overruled the second decision and had him killed by firing squad.[31] Arbuthnot was hanged. The Seminole War itself raised several different questions for Congress (the invasion itself is discussed in chapter 2) but the executions posed questions specifically about who has the final say about how military law is applied. They posed potentially important questions for Congress because Congress is specifically granted the power to "make rules concerning captures on land and water" and because those prisoners who were executed were British citizens, which raised foreign policy concerns just a few years after the end of the War of 1812. The president had not punished Jackson, and some in Congress questioned whether that lack of response was appropriate.

Critics of the executions, and of Jackson, argued that Congress's authority to define the law of war regarding prisoners is absolute and that General Jackson had applied that law incorrectly and so was open to congressional sanction if the president was unwilling to discipline him. Henry Clay argued that

> the Legislature had not left the power over spies undefined, to the mere discretion of the commander-in-chief, or of any subaltern officer in the Army. . . . [Clay] denied that any commander-in-chief, in this country, had this absolute power of life and death, at his sole discretion. It was contrary to the genius of all our laws and institutions. The assertion of such a power to the commander-in-chief was contrary to the practice of free Government and was the very definition of tyranny itself.[32]

Others, however, argued that there is a zone of purely military authority between the commander in chief and his subordinates. They claimed that the application of congressional laws to particular cases, and any punishment for misapplication, was outside of Congress's jurisdiction. Some, such as Virginia Federalist Charles Fenton Mercer, opposed Jackson's raids as wholly illegal but argued that the application of discipline and proceedings of a court martial were not subject to congressional oversight.[33] Other members of Congress simply argued Congress did not have an appropriate oversight role in the application of military law in the field. Rep. Philip Barbour, Republican of Virginia, said that "our inquiry is not whether the commanding General obeyed the orders of the Commander-in-Chief—that question is between themselves."[34] Supporters argued that regardless of the law, a general in the field, acting on orders from his commander in chief and administering a court martial, could dispense justice that was not subject to oversight.

Congress did not, in the end, sanction the popular General Jackson. In 1821, however, he was forced into retirement by the downsizing of the army.[35] The important point here is that there was disagreement about the boundaries to the commander in chief's authority over discipline.

A prominent second case nearly a century later was hotly debated but was resolved with a similar conclusion. In July 1906, during peacetime, an African American army regiment (the Twenty-Fifth) was stationed at Fort Brown, near the segregated southern Texas town of Brownsville. Many whites in the surrounding community were openly hostile to the presence of the Black soldiers. On the evening of August 13, 1906, someone (history does not tell us who) shot and killed a bartender and a police officer in Brownsville in the middle of the night. Although the fort commanders (who were white) said that the soldiers had all been in their barracks at the time of the shooting, the townspeople argued that the Black soldiers had perpetrated the murders. President Theodore Roosevelt summarily discharged the Black soldiers from three companies, denying them a court martial, and causing them to forfeit their pensions and any civil service employment in the future. The affair caused a major political uproar and eventually Congress would create a commission to allow soldiers to prove their innocence, which allowed a few of the soldiers to reenlist. Further historical research has generally concluded they were wrongly discharged.[36]

In the Brownsville case, the commander in chief clause was interpreted by both supporters and critics of the president's actions in their public remarks. Supporters argued that the clause conferred unilateral implied power to discipline soldiers accused of wrongdoing, including the power of summary dismissal. As Republican senator Philander Knox put it, the power to discipline troops

> inheres in the office of the Commander in Chief and is part of his power, unless it is, if it can be, taken away by statute. Not only is this power or function not taken away under the laws of the United States, nor qualified by any positive enactment, but, on the other hand, it is distinctly recognized by statute law, by judicial decisions, and by Army regulations, which have the power of law.[37]

Critics argued that as commander in chief the president was bound by the law, which Roosevelt had not followed. Roosevelt's chief opponent, Republican senator Joseph Foraker, specifically denied that the president has any implied power to discipline those under his command. He said,

> What he derives directly from the Constitution is his constitutional power; what he derives from the Congress of the United States is his legal power. . . .

In prescribing these rules the Congress can say "The President may have power in certain contingencies to dismiss men from the Army which we have raised;" but, without such a provision, if the Congress should have spoken upon it at all, the President would not have that power, except in conformity with the law of Congress.[38]

In the closing days of the congressional session, as Senator Foraker was leaving office, he got the Republican Congress to pass a watered down version of a bill creating a commission to allow the dismissed soldiers to apply for reinstatement. By instituting the commission, albeit with terms favored by Roosevelt, through a Congress controlled by the president's party, Congress seemed to acknowledge that the dismissals without trial violated the law and to affirm that the president's implied authority over discipline and dismissals is rooted in, and can be modified, by law.

These cases show that linguistic norms and understanding of the president's superiority in the chain of command chafed against similarly common language broadly defining Congress's authority to prescribe the rules of military discipline. In moments of political disagreement and unsettled constitutional understanding, members of Congress had to weigh their received understanding of the constitutional text against their partisan and personal attitudes about the president and his actions, and in these specific cases, their racial sympathies as well. Studying these debates can tell us about the range of interpretations of the commander in chief clause that were articulated. Notably, there was no consensus about Congress's right to oversee the commander in chief's military decisions. But nor was there consensus that his authority was absolute. In their deliberations, members of Congress reached complicated middle positions that upheld shared authority over military discipline.

To Command the Militia When Called into Service

Fewer than 10 percent of the speeches referring to the commander in chief clause primarily discussed the commander in chief's relationship to state militias. In general, members of Congress did not dispute the president's authority to command state militias. Both explicit statements and offhand remarks in unrelated debates, from the 1820s to the 1910s, concede that when properly called into service, state militia officers are bound to obey orders from the president as commander in chief.[39] Throughout the nineteenth century, the congressional consensus held that the president's implied constitutional authority over the state militias was limited to command only, and that his authority to call troops into service was a congressional power delegated to him by statute.[40]

The president's right to command militias was an unstated assumption for both sides in one of the major debates that referenced this type of authority. The most contentious nineteenth-century debate referencing the commander and chief and militias regarded the Civil War–era Conscription Bill. Opponents (Democrats) argued that the bill would enable the commander in chief to conscript men who were not already in service, and that the bill therefore undermined the states' Second Amendment militia rights.[41] Even in making these arguments, they conceded that once legally mustered in, militias were bound to obey commands from the president.[42] Republicans supported the bill but did not make arguments about the commander in chief specifically. In the end, the bill was supported by nearly all Republicans, with both Democrats and Unionists opposing, mostly for reasons related to conscription itself but not to the constitutional authority of the president over militias.[43]

Members of Congress did consider the commander in chief's implied authority over militias in other contexts—they debated whether the president had to issue orders to state militias by going through state governors, and whether the states should really get to appoint their own officers if the president was in command.[44] But they did not debate his right to command per se. Instead, most of the time, when members of Congress talked about the commander in chief's authority over state militias, they talked about the fact that such command was constitutionally conditional on Congress' statutes that defined and regulated his authority to call those militias into service.

To Direct Troop and Ship Movements

Throughout the pre–World War I period, whenever members of Congress spoke of command, they often referred explicitly to movement. Many of these were offhand remarks. Members of Congress spoke matter-of-factly about the president's constitutional authority to move troops from one place to another during peacetime within US territory and in both American and enemy territory during wartime.[45] In 1862 one senator said his job is "in the command of the army" to assume "control of the army in the field."[46] In 1898 a senator said that the president had "control of all military and naval operations there on the part of our ships and our troops in his hands."[47] In 1907 another senator described his authority as "limited to command; the same power as . . . would belong to the Admiral of the Navy or the first General of the Army."[48] Members of Congress described his authority to order a regiment forward, to "send troops now in service," to "conduct" and "control" the army's "movements."[49] They said that the commander in chief alone could determine "where" and "how" the army "shall march."[50] They further referred to the commander in chief's authority to "direct campaigns" and to "urge" and "recommend" military advances and retreats.[51] His will, "in conducting a war, carrying on its field operations, was to be paramount."[52] Members of Congress, in keeping with that definition, rarely tried to regulate the president's orders about the movement of troops.

However, members of Congress in all political parties consciously distinguished this authority to direct movement and two closely related types of authority. First, they distinguished orders about movement from decisions about the overall direction and execution of a declared war. In the Mexican and Civil Wars in particular, many members of Congress maintained a right to direct the commander in chief's purposes and overall strategies.[53] They also distinguished between the movement of troops for training, management, or defensive purposes and a separate authority to put troops into foreign territory in ways that in Alexander Hamilton's words "might give cause of war to a foreign power."[54] They repeatedly articulated an understanding that moving troops from place to place was not synonymous with prompting or initiating hostilities with adversaries. They similarly constructed a boundary between defensive and offensive movements and the line between offensive congressional and defensive presidential authority, which will be discussed more in the next chapter.

AUTHORITY *NOT* GRANTED BY
THE COMMANDER IN CHIEF CLAUSE

Close reading of congressional debates indicates that members of Congress did assume that the commander in chief clause granted some authority: to physically direct troops, to maintain rank superseding that of other officers, to appoint officers, to enact military discipline according to the law, and to command state militias. However, similar analysis reveals, consistent with what other scholars characterize as a congressionally dominated constitutional order for war powers, that members also believed that the commander in chief clause did *not* confer certain types of authority on the president, discussed in what follows.

Calling forth the State Militias

In their remarks and their actions, members of Congress repeatedly demonstrated an understanding that their own constitutional mandate empowered them "to provide for calling forth the Militia to execute the Laws of the Union, suppress Insurrections and repel Invasions." They repeatedly recognized that any presidential order to call out the militia depended upon congressional statute. Congress was also cognizant of the limitations upon its own power to call out the militia—for the itemized purposes of repelling invasion, putting down insurrections, and executing the laws of the union.

Beginning during the first Congress, and several times within the first decade of the republic, Congress wrote laws that empowered the commander in chief to call up the state militias to ensure domestic security and tranquility. Those laws specified and regulated the conditions under which he could use that discretion.[55] When Congress first authorized presidents to use the militia, it granted the president broad statutory discretion to call up the militia in cases of invasion or imminent invasion but only granted him limited authority to call up the militia in the case of insurrections. The Militia Act, as passed in 1792, said that in cases of invasion or imminent danger of invasion, the president may call up as many members of state militias "as he may judge necessary to repel such invasion."[56] However, that 1792 law used the courts to constrain the president's decision making in cases of insurrection. Congress only allowed the president to call up the militias to combat lawlessness once a district judge notified him that ordinary judicial proceedings were insufficient to put down the rebellion. George Washington followed this legal procedure exactly, including referring to the judge's conclusions, and referred to the Act of 1792 as the source of his authority when he called out the militia to suppress the Whiskey Rebellion in 1794.[57]

In 1795 Congress revisited the Militia Act, making it easier for the president to call upon the militia in cases of insurrection by removing the requirement that presidents get judicial certification of a rebellion. The 1795 law left it up to the president to determine whether law enforcement in a state was sufficiently obstructed to call the militia into service. Members of Congress were aware of that law and frequently referred to it throughout the nineteenth century.[58] Interestingly, despite there being later versions of the Militia Act, members over many decades and in different situations rooted the president's command over the militia in "the law of 1795."

Readers might recall that the War of 1812 was at least in part a (failed) war of conquest in which American troops were sent into Canada to fight the British. Democratic-Republicans, who preferred closer relations with France and war with Britain, saw no problem with the commander in chief sending state militias into Canada.[59] Representatives from the Federalist strongholds in the Northeast, on the other hand, generally favored ties to England and objected to sending their own state militiamen into Canada on a mission of conquest.[60] They particularly latched onto the constitutional and statutory language that said that Congress could only empower the commander in chief to use the militia to protect *against invasion.* Invading another country to conquer its territory was not, in their view, within the letter of the law in the Militia Act or the Constitution. Initially, the governor of Massachusetts refused to summon his state's militia to respond to the president's orders, although eventually, the orders were obeyed.[61] The Supreme Court later ruled in *Martin v. Mott* (1827) that under the 1795 Militia Act, the commander in chief *by law* legally commanded the militias during a declared war, and when he judged that invasion was imminent, he could send them anywhere he deemed necessary, including into foreign territory.[62] That decision effectively ended questions about whether the commander in chief clause included the power to command state militias. Presidential discretion to deploy state militias for purposes of his choosing, codified by Congress, and strengthened by the language of the Supreme Court, became a generally accepted *statutory* power of the president after this incident.

Members of Congress consistently recognized Congress's right to authorize and regulate the conditions under which the president could call state militias into service. For example, in 1818 (as noted above), Congress was grappling with the legality of actions taken by General Andrew Jackson in Florida. When Rep. John Holmes of Massachusetts (no party) made broad arguments in favor of executive discretion, he was careful to note that the president's authority to call up the militia derived from Congress.[63] In 1826 members debated a bill to reimburse states for expenses incurred during the War of 1812. Adams' party representative Peleg Sprague of Maine noted that "by the Constitution, the President has no power to call forth the militia, in any event whatever, but to

Congress, and Congress alone, belongs the power to provide for calling them forth."[64] In a separate, wide-ranging argument on the same bill, Rep. Henry Dwight also referred to the "the law of 1795" regulating the use of the militias.[65]

As time went on, Congress revised the "law of 1795" but continued to empower the president by statute to call up the militias under conditions regulated by Congress. These bills passed without partisan conflict about constitutional authority. In the early twentieth century, Congress wrote several bills overhauling the relationships between the federal government and the state militias, including redesignating them the National Guard. In 1903 a new law granted the president the statutory authority to call up the National Guard for up to nine months. The Organized Militia Law of 1908 eliminated the nine-month service time limit and permitted the president to call up militia troops to send them out of the country if necessary.[66] Congress then replaced the provision with the "Volunteer Army Bill" in 1914, which provided that in time of actual war or imminent war, the president could issue a call for volunteers, and state militias could volunteer as a unit.[67] In 1916 Congress considered and passed a major overhaul of the military and its relationship to the guard and militias in the National Defense Act, which granted greater control over militias to the national government in exchange for greatly increased federal funds.[68] It also required militia members to take an oath to obey the president and allowed the president to draft them into federal service. The provision allowing the president to call the guard into federal service without permission of the governor was the most controversial, though the bill passed.

These Militia Act(s) and Congress's clear awareness of the authority they confer have important implications for our interpretations of nineteenth-century uses of force. Though presidents called out the militia repeatedly in the nineteenth century to enforce laws or protect borders, such actions were not considered by members of Congress to be exercises of the president's constitutional authority as commander in chief. Instead, they were understood to be legally authorized by the congressional acts that gave the president discretion to do so. In employing the state militias, in Congress's eyes, presidents acted under statutory authority, not under the commander in chief clause itself.

Domestic Use of Force in Wartime

During wartime, Congress sometimes considered whether the commander in chief clause conferred any special authority on the president to restrict civil

liberties or to seize private property. In the nineteenth century, Congress repeatedly agreed that the clause did not give the president the power to declare
martial law, and he could only take such actions as executive enforcement of
congressional statutes.

For example, in 1798, on a nearly party line vote, Federalists passed the
Alien and Sedition Acts. The debates on those bills focused on their policy
substance, but members did question whether legislation was necessary, or
whether the commander in chief possessed the power to "apprehend, restrain,
secure, and remove" alien enemies. They concluded that the law was necessary,
because the president did not have that power.[69] Most Federalists believed that
such a power might be useful in wartime, but by codifying it, they conceded
that it was not a power the president already had.

In January 1862 Congress considered passing the Railroad and Telegraph
Bill, which authorized the president to take control of the railroads and telegraph lines of the United States whenever he deemed it militarily necessary to
do so.[70] In the debates, they considered whether the commander in chief clause
granted him unilateral authority to take such action. On the final vote, the majority of Republicans voted for the bill, and the Democrats and Unionists were
divided, mostly on the merits of the bill itself.[71] The law's passage suggests that
most members of Congress, including those in the president's party, believed
that the commander in chief clause did not grant implied constitutional authority to take control of the rail lines on his own.

By far the most contentious debates over the domestic authority of the
commander in chief surrounded President Lincoln's suspensions of the writ
of habeas corpus during the Civil War. Article I of the Constitution provides
that the writ of habeas corpus, or the right to be charged with a crime upon
arrest, can be suspended "when in cases of rebellion or invasion the public
safety may require it." Its presence in Article I, with other powers of Congress,
has led many observers in history to believe that only Congress could suspend
it. However, during the Civil War, President Lincoln unilaterally suspended
habeas corpus on several occasions. The first time, with Congress out of session on April 27, 1861, Lincoln suspended the writ and ordered General Scott
to arrest suspicious persons anywhere along the military supply lines from
Philadelphia to Washington, DC.[72] Other suspensions followed. Lincoln himself insisted that the public safety required the suspension of the writ and that
the Constitution was not clear that it was a power only Congress could wield,
especially when Congress was out of session.[73]

During the first two sessions of Congress during the Civil War, Congress repeatedly considered but could not agree about how to construct legislation to regulate the suspensions of the writ. When the final debate over habeas corpus legislation began in December of 1862 and continued through the winter of 1863, the commander in chief clause came up repeatedly. Many Republicans supported Lincoln's claim to unilateral authority, but Democrats and third-party Unionists insisted that if the writ was to be suspended, Congress had to do it.[74] As Unionist Henry Grider argued, the commander in chief could not suspend habeas corpus because like other military officers he acted only "in subordination to the laws of their country, from which they derive their authority."[75] In the end, the Republican-controlled Congress did stake its claim to the constitutional authority to suspend the writ, while granting the president discretion to do so. In March 1863 Congress finally passed, and Lincoln signed into law, "An Act Relating to Habeas Corpus, and Regulating Judicial Proceedings in Certain Cases."[76] The law authorized the president to suspend habeas corpus "whenever, in his judgement, the public safety may require it," as long as the rebellion continued. It also regulated his use of that power, making rules requiring that the names of detainees be made public and prescribing conditions for court proceedings and release.

DISCUSSION

One important observation presented in this chapter is that Congress was able to consistently interpret an important constitutional phrase over more than a century. This evidence supports those who argue that Congress can and should have a role in interpreting the Constitution. In our system, any constitutional interpretation of a grant of authority is theoretically unstable, because any of the three branches of government, the states, and the public all have the ability to contest that particular interpretation.[77] Because instability in interpretation, and instability in whose interpretation is authoritative, invites instability in the political process and in government control, legal scholars debate the best pathway to stable, authoritative constitutional interpretations. Some argue that only courts can provide such a final and authoritative settlement of constitutional debates.[78] The political construction of judicial supremacy in constitutional interpretation evolved to supply some of that stability.[79] In the case of twentieth- and twenty-first-century war powers, the courts have adopted a deferential posture toward the political branches, especially the presidency.[80] Additional stability in interpretation of modern war powers has then been supplied by the executive branch, which has crafted and enforced a distribution of war powers that enhances executive authority.[81] Some have suggested that Congress's collective action problems, when set next to the president's authority to issue orders, always advantaged the president.[82] But in the nineteenth century, both of the political branches, including and especially Congress, played a more important role in constitutional interpretation and construction than they do today, despite the same collective action problems. The cases in this chapter supply evidence that Congress was actually able to supply consistent interpretations and stability in construction of the authority associated with the commander in chief clause.[83]

Moreover, Congress was able to do so over time, even given acrimonious political disagreements about when and how to regulate the armed forces and use force. The disagreements that referenced the commander in chief clause included members of Congress engaging in substantive deliberation, reasoning collectively about the text's meaning and how to apply it to a contemporary dilemma. Scholars who study constitutional construction outside the courts argue that to effectively interpret the Constitution, presidents and members of Congress (and courts) must actively deliberate, articulating and explaining constitutional rules and principles to each other and to the public.[84] They emphasize that it is important that authoritative interpretations be well-articulated and that all of their implications be considered when they are adopted.[85]

Such robust deliberation does not happen all the time, for every decision that involves constitutional interpretation. Whittington calls the routine application of widely agreed upon norms simple "policymaking," and he distinguishes that routine process from more meaningful and significant deliberation when novel circumstances arise, which he calls "construction."[86] The descriptive findings I present in this chapter (and others) include many examples of Congress as a body interpreting the constitutional text and applying it to political controversies about the distribution of power, and many of the conversations I describe can probably be characterized as examples of deliberative "constitutional construction." However, these data also include offhand remarks, and scholars may want to consider that these definitions may also play a role in reiterating constitutional definitions and norms, perhaps contributing to collective understanding, even outside of deliberative constitutional moments.

CHAPTER 2

Constructing the Authority to Initiate the Use of Force before 1898

This chapter describes members' of Congress references to the commander in chief clause that fall into the category "the authority to initiate the use of force" before the year 1898. This category comprises about 120 speeches and in them members overwhelmingly articulate the norm that the commander in chief clause confers some authority to defend the nation from sudden attacks and no authority to initiate hostilities. Because the initiation of the use of force is at the heart of modern debates about the division between legislative and executive authority, I present these cases in a bit more depth. The following debates are the only ones in which Congress considered whether the commander in chief clause conferred any authority upon the president to initiate the use of force before the year 1900. I consider cases after the year 1900 separately, in chapter 4, as these norms do change over time.

When they discussed the initiation of the use of force alongside the commander in chief clause, members of Congress often invoked the difference between offensive and defensive force. The importance of the concept of defense raises the important question: Can "defense" be constitutionally defined? That boundary between the branches' constitutional authorities is not present in the constitutional text, though it does have roots at the constitutional convention of 1787.[1] James Madison's language at the convention makes clear that he believed the president had the authority to "repel sudden attacks." Michael Ramsey argues that "in eighteenth century writing, 'defensive' war arose when a nation was actually attacked or war was formally declared against it. Wars undertaken to defend national interests, such as trading rights, treatment of citizens and or ambassadors by foreign powers, etc., were "offensive" (though justified), not defensive."[2] Scholars who have examined the evolution of war powers note that prior to 1900 the "decision to mount offensive actions remained with Congress" and describe repeated episodes in which presidents themselves obeyed that distinction.[3]

But defining defensive and offensive actions may not always be so simple.

Mariah Zeisberg argues more broadly that defense may not be limited to direct attack but rather can be defined at any given time by the national security priorities jointly set by Congress and the president. She argues that provocative US actions could be categorized as defensive or offensive not based on the simple location of the troops but within the jointly developed national security orders of their time.

In repeatedly articulating a dividing line between the commander in chief's authority to defend the nation and Congress's authority to initiate hostilities, my data show that members of Congress used language that is broadly consistent with the division of authority that scholars describe as characterizing the original constitutional order for war powers, largely tracking a literal definition of defense.[4]

However, though members articulate a consensus interpretation of the commander in chief clause, their language also presents some important puzzles. Some of the most consequential presidential military orders of the nineteenth century, such as President Polk's offensive troop movement that provoked the Mexican War, objectively violate the dominant interpretation that only Congress could authorize offensive actions. Notably, Polk's actions, which he publicly claimed were an act of defense, were both literally an act of offense and also lacking in legitimacy according to Zeisberg's broader, politically constructed definition of national security.

My dataset of speeches invoking the commander in chief clause shows that, prior to 1900, even members of Congress who voiced approval of presidential overreach like Polk's displayed a strong (almost universal) tendency to rearticulate the dominant norm that the commander in chief's implied authority was limited to defense. Many members of Congress supported Polk's actions, but most did so by creatively twisting the facts about the president's offensive actions (by arguing, for example, that plainly offensive actions were actually defensive) in order to justify them. Polk's stated fiction was useful to members of Congress who wanted to support his policy of expansion but were not eager to argue for broad presidential power to do so. Only a tiny handful of speeches prior to 1898 argue that the president had any flexibility to initiate military force without express prior congressional authorization. In the case studies that follow, I describe how members of Congress talked about the commander in chief clause. In the subsequent discussion, I highlight the discrepancies between some of their actions and their words.

QUASI-WAR: ARE NAVAL CONVOYS DEFENSIVE?

In the 1790s, Britain and France were at war. After the United States signed Jay's Treaty with Britain, France felt offended by its terms, which seemed to violate its own treaty with the new American state. France then broke off normal diplomatic relations with the United States and began to harass American shipping, capturing 316 US ships in 1795 alone.[5] By 1797 the situation had become serious enough that President Adams sent a message asking Congress to put the country "in a posture of defense." Congress responded by passing bills to increase the size of the navy, regulate the arms trade, authorize construction of harbor fortifications, and prohibit American privateering.[6]

In summer 1798 Congress authorized the building of three additional frigates: the *Constitution*, the *Constellation*, and the *United States*. As they discussed building up the small navy, they talked about where the commander in chief could send those ships and what he could order them to do, with and without specific congressional authorization. (Such questions would become even more important with the growth of the military, and military technology, in the twentieth and twenty-first centuries). Across party lines, they agreed that the commander in chief clause granted the president authority to issue defensive orders and to direct troop movements *within American territory*. Rep. Albert Gallatin (Republican from Pennsylvania and an opponent of President Adams) thought the president needed specific guidance for how to use the navy ships but conceded that "within our own territory, it is in the power of the President to grant escorts, or convoys, for the exportation of any provisions from one part of the United States to another."[7]

Collectively, led by the president's party, Congress interpreted the commander in chief clause slightly more broadly. Lawmakers concluded that the clause conferred implied authority on the president to order US Navy ships to act as a protective convoy for the country's commercial vessels on the open seas. Rep. Harrison Otis, Federalist from Massachusetts, articulated the average opinion in Congress. Like many in his time period, he thought that moving ships from place to place within the lines of defense was an implied presidential power.[8] Similarly, like others, he said that Congress could regulate the ships' uses when they were beyond the line of defense. But he also said that in the absence of congressional direction, the commander in chief could order them into international waters to act as defensive convoys:

> The President is Commander-in-Chief of the Army, and of the Militia when
> called out, but Congress might, nevertheless, direct the use of them. [I believe],
> therefore, it would be equally proper to leave the employment of these vessels
> wholly to the President, or to direct them to be employed as convoys.[9]

Jonathan Dayton, speaker of the House and Federalist from New Jersey, stated on the floor of the House that he was willing to leave it up to the discretion of the (Federalist) commander in chief whether the ships could be used as convoys. Dayton "was not prepared to say the frigates should or should not be employed as convoys; nor was he ready to say they should be confined within the jurisdiction of the United States. [I am] willing to leave this matter to the President of the United States, as commander-in-chief."[10]

At the same time they concluded that directing protective convoys fell within an implied defensive commander in chief power, members of even the president's party agreed that only Congress could take the nation from a defensive to an offensive posture and that Congress could regulate the use of force. Samuel Sewall (MA-Federalist) agreed that by the nature of "command," the president should have some discretion to direct the naval ships. But Sewall also noted that it would be an abuse of power to use them in ways that contradicted congressional statutes or unilaterally initiated hostilities with a foreign power:

> These frigates were to be considered as the public force, as the navy of the United
> States. It was true, it was a small one; but it was such as Congress had thought
> proper to raise, and put in the power of the President. And why should this power
> be limited? It seemed as if they supposed, from his natural disposition, or from
> some other cause, he would abuse it, by employing the vessels contrary to law,
> and thereby involve the country in war.[11]

Congress acted consistently with this construction of the commander in chief clause during the Quasi War with France. Members considered and then deleted the sections of a bill specifically authorizing the president to employ the ships as convoys without recorded vote, an action that recognized an implied presidential authority to direct the movements of American naval vessels in defensive operations.[12] However, that implied authority did not, in these conversations, encompass the offensive use of force that might "involve the country in war."

The authority to employ offensive force was broadly believed to derive from statutory, not constitutional, authority. During the summer's debates over the preparations for the Quasi War, Congress passed laws that specifically authorized the commander in chief to intercept and capture French ships on the high seas and prescribed how the crew and goods on the ship were to be treated.[13] Additionally, the courts held the president to a literal interpretation of those very specific laws, upholding the congressional power that members of Congress believed to exist.[14] In conversations like these, members of Congress helped to define the boundaries of the president's implied constitutional powers and then acted in accordance with those definitions to help establish congressionally dominated war powers, even in undeclared wars. But this very early debate also foreshadowed the practical difficulty of defining the boundaries between defense and offense when the president can give orders that put troops and ships in harm's way.

FIRST SEMINOLE WAR: CAN AN INVASION
BE AN ACT OF DEFENSE?

As described in chapter 1, at the end of the War of 1812, Maj. Gen. Andrew Jackson was left in charge of protecting the southern border of the United States, which included the border with Spanish Florida. He used that authority to prosecute an ambiguously legal war against the Seminoles.

Andrew Jackson's intervention in Florida prompted serious debate in Congress.[15] On the question of whether Jackson (and by extension the president) had legitimate right to initiate hostilities as he did, members of Congress across party lines agreed that he had no constitutional right to do so. Therefore his opponents argued that he had behaved unconstitutionally and deserved sanction, while his supporters argued that he had followed congressional *law* and therefore behaved appropriately. Even Jackson's supporters did not argue that the president, and by extension, a general under his command, had a broad right to invade Florida without prior congressional authorization.

In the early 1800s, across southern Georgia's border, Spanish Florida was populated by several tribes of Native Americans, a few Spaniards, and some people who had escaped slavery. Florida was nominally Spanish territory but was only weakly held. Some Native Americans living there had been driven out of the Southern states by American expansion and by the departure of their

British allies at the end of the War of 1812. There were serious land and border disputes between white Americans and some Native peoples about exactly what territory had been ceded to the United States at the end of the war. Ongoing white settlers' raids in Seminole territory in Georgia and Florida prompted some retaliatory attacks on white settlements in Georgia. In the midst of that turmoil, Jackson wrote a letter to President Madison informing him that it would only take him sixty days to wrest Florida from Spain. Madison did not respond. Secretary of War John C. Calhoun sent orders to Jackson and his subordinates granting them authority to cross the Georgia border into Spanish-held Florida to fight the Seminoles but told them that they were not authorized to fight the Spanish.[16] Jackson drove into Florida and brutally attacked Seminole villages. In defiance of his orders, he also captured the Spanish fort at St. Marks, and while there, executed two British citizens accused of collaborating with the Seminoles. He then moved to Pensacola and captured the Spanish Fort Barrancas, even though the Spanish governor there publicly read to him part of President Monroe's message to Congress that had stated that Jackson was to attack the Seminoles and not the Spanish.[17]

In the ensuing congressional debate, most speakers tended to be skeptical of the legality of Jackson's attacks on the Spanish, which were clearly offensive actions (because all agreed that the Spanish had not attacked Americans). Their criticisms were wide-ranging, although only a few specifically referred to the commander in chief clause. The critics that did refer to the clause argued that Jackson's actions against both the Spanish and the Seminoles were constitutionally illegitimate because they lacked congressional authorization.

One critic, James Johnson, Republican of Virginia, argued that since the Spanish had not attacked the United States, the actions Jackson took against Spanish forts were unjustified by both the Constitution and international norms. He carefully drew a line between the commander in chief's authority to take limited defensive actions and Congress's authority to initiate offensive hostilities.[18] To Johnson, Jackson's actions were illegitimate because they seemed to be aimed at conquering Florida territory, a clearly aggressive action that was within Congress's powers rather than the president's.

Others questioned whether Jackson's actions were illegitimate not because they were aimed at conquering Spanish territory but because they were retaliations against the Seminoles, an action that fell under Congress's broader power over the use of force. Henry Clay referred to acts passed during the Quasi War that had specifically authorized the navy to retaliate against French ships that had harassed or attacked American ships. He argued that those laws demonstrated that Congress, not the president, had the authority to authorize retaliations against foreign aggressors.[19] Clay's argument may have held some weight with other members, given his stature as speaker of the House.[20]

The discourse in support of Jackson's actions is most illuminating about the collective understanding of the scope of the commander in chief's authority at the time. His supporters tended to carefully delineate the reasons why Jackson's actions were appropriate, often distinguishing his actions against the Seminoles from those against the Spanish. Given Americans' racial and territorial attitudes at the time, it should not be surprising that there was widespread approval of Jackson's actions against the Seminoles. However, most members justified Jackson's actions by making arguments that narrowly interpreted the implied authority of the commander in chief clause.

Specifically, they argued that Jackson's attacks on the Seminoles were justified based on laws which had been authorized by Congress. One advocate argued that in the 1795 Militia Act, Congress used its own authority to authorize the president to repel invasions. He said that "statute gave to the President a discretionary power to employ the forces of the United States and to call forth the militia to repress Indian hostility; and gave it to him properly, on the principles of the Constitution."[21] Similarly, Joseph Desha of Kentucky agreed that

> by the second section of the second article of the Constitution, the President of the United States is Commander-in-Chief of the Army of the United States, [and] consequently is entitled to all the prerogatives and privileges necessarily attached to so high a command. You have had a law in operation, he believed, ever since 1795, authorizing the President, in case of invasion, or imminent danger of invasion, to call out the forces of the country to repel invasion. The question is, was there an invasion? No gentleman will deny but what our territory was invaded, and our citizens murdered: there, then, was not only an invasion, but war was actually declared against this Government by the Seminoles.[22]

Ballard Smith of Virginia justified the actions that started the conflict as enforcement of the treaty with the Creek Indians that had been negotiated at the end of the War of 1812. He argued that "the President is charged with the duty of asserting the rights of the nation, and he is furnished with the means. He is Commander-in-Chief of the Army; and it is his duty to see that the laws (which include treaties) be faithfully executed. . . . He may do beyond the jurisdiction of the United States whatever the law of nations or treaties authorize the United States there to do."[23] By Smith's logic, when Native Americans violated the treaty with the Creeks, the president, and by extension, Jackson, were legally authorized to attack the Seminoles in enforcement of the treaty.

It is noteworthy that members of Congress who were predisposed to favor Jackson's actions did not ascribe to the commander in chief a broad constitutional authority to initiate the use of force. Rather, they carefully circumscribed the legal authority of the commander in chief and found ways to rationalize Jackson's actions within those bounds. That they did not make broader arguments about the authority of the president suggests that such arguments were not familiar enough, or not legitimate enough, to be articulated in congressional debate, even by members who were motivated to look for legal support for Jackson's actions.

This debate also highlights that questions about the use of force require members of Congress not only to interpret constitutional text but also to interpret actions on the ground, like whether skirmishes along the Georgia-Florida border constituted an "invasion" or an "attack" on American territory, and whose interpretation of treaty boundaries were most valid. Members' sympathies for white Americans, as well as their definition of "offense" and "defense" were integrated into their interpretations of constitutional authority.

THE MEXICAN WAR: CAN A PRESIDENT PROVOKE A WAR?

Members of Congress did not agree about whether Polk's actions at the outset of the Mexican War were appropriate. But even his supporters did not argue he had an inherent right to provoke a war. Rather, his critics argued he had initiated the use of force illegally, while his supporters accepted the fictional account of the war's origins so that they could argue he was using commander in chief authority in self-defense. The Mexican War was initiated under famously murky circumstances. When Texas was admitted to the Union in 1845, the official border as recognized by the Mexican government was the Nueces River in Southeastern Texas. Texans, and expansionists like President Polk, however, argued that the real border was the Rio Grande, 150 miles to the South. In 1846 Polk began negotiations with the Mexican government to move the border southward and simultaneously to purchase California. When those talks failed, he ordered General Zachary Taylor to move his troops south of the Nueces River toward the Rio Grande. After the Mexicans in that disputed territory fired on the advancing American troops, Polk reported to Congress that Mexico had "shed American blood upon the American soil" and asked Congress to declare war, which it promptly did. As word later came to Congress about the misleading information upon which Congress had based its declaration of war, legislators who opposed the obviously expansionist purposes of the war seized upon the false information and excoriated President Polk for effectively initiating the war without Congress's permission by ordering troops to cross into disputed territory.

Members of the opposition party, the Whigs, who referred to the commander in chief clause, almost uniformly argued that the commander in chief had no authority to initiate hostilities, that (Democrat) Polk had initiated hostilities without authority, and that as such he had violated the Constitution. Rep. Joshua Giddings, Whig of Ohio, professed shock to have witnessed "the commander-in-chief of the army and navy, as well as the militia, invade a foreign soil, plant the American standard there, subverting the rights of a foreign people, and extending a military despotism over them."[24] His fellow Whig representative from Ohio Alexander Harper said that "the wise and patriotic men who framed [the Constitution] never intended that the President of the United States, although constituted, in virtue of his office, commander-in-chief of the army and navy, should possess the high and tremendous power of making war."[25] Seaborn Jones of Georgia quoted Justice Joseph Story's *Commentaries on the Constitution* to argue for limited authority for the commander in chief.[26] Rep. Albert Smith, Whig of New York,

> could not but regard this conduct of the Executive as unparalleled in the history of this country, and entirely indefensible . . . What, he would ask, became of this high constitutional prerogative of Congress, if the Executive may, with impunity, and of his own mere will as commander-in-chief of the army, send our troops, far beyond our, actual jurisdiction, into the country of a neighboring nation, under any pretence [*sic*] whatever, and thus bring on war?[27]

Many Whigs insisted that Polk "yield a respectful attention to the advice of Congress, and to govern himself as commander-in-chief of the army at the direction of Congress."[28] Whig Garrett Davis expressed the frequent nineteenth-century assertion that anyone could have been the constitutional commander in chief, and whoever it was would still be clearly subservient to Congress. He said, "If the Constitution had not created the office of commander-in-chief, it might have been done by act of Congress, and then General Scott, or some other person, would have filled it, . . . and had he, as such commander, undertaken what Mr. Polk has, Congress would at once have brought him up as a sort of knight De la Mancha."[29] Whigs often accused the president of personal imperialism.[30]

Democrats generally defended the president, not on the grounds that he had a right to initiate war, but on the grounds that the commander in chief had a responsibility to defend against Mexican aggression. They generally accepted Polk's original reasoning for the war—that American blood had been spilled on American soil—and did not want to look more closely at the circumstances that led the first shots to be fired. Sen. Isaac Pennybaker, Democrat of Virginia, said of the commander in chief, "If the country be invaded, what is his duty? It is to defend it. His duty as commander-in-chief requires him to defend it. When he does defend it, therefore, does he act without authority from the sovereign power of the State? He acts but in pursuance of his constitutional duty, and when he so acts he represents the sovereign power of the State."[31] John Tibbatts (D-KY) said that if Mexico invaded American territory, "the President of the United States, in the exercise of his constitutional duty, should repel that invasion by the military power which is under his control, as the commander-in-chief of our military and naval forces, then this country is in a state of defensive war, without any declaration of war on the part of Congress."[32]

Democrat representative Samuel Lahm argued that Polk's order to Taylor was legal under the Militia Act of 1795, which had authorized "that whenever the United States shall be invaded, or be in imminent danger of invasion, from any foreign nation 'or Indian tribe,' it shall be lawful for the President to call forth such number of the militia of the State or States most convenient to the place of danger or scene of action as he may judge necessary to repel such invasion." He also argued that Story's *Commentaries* had declared that the "command and application of the public force to execute the laws, to maintain peace, and to resist foreign invasion, are powers . . . obviously of an executive nature."[33]

William Yancey (D-AL) was the Polk supporter who went the farthest toward a presidentialist argument, as he argued that the president had authority to enter disputed territory to defend against an imminent attack.[34] Unlike many of his colleagues, he acknowledged what Polk had actually done and tried to craft a justification for it. He said that the president "did what he had a right to do as its commander-in-chief-what he was bound to do President of the Republic. If, then, the 'Rio Grande ought to be our boundary,' the President 'ought to be' no subject of censure. If Mexico was in arms, and in hostile attitude, it did not become a prudent Executive to wait until the country was invaded before he used the means given him by the nation for its defence."[35] Though the logic of preemptive war is familiar in the post-9/11 era, Yancey was the only member Congress to explicitly interpret the commander in chief clause so broadly in the nineteenth century.

This episode of constitutional construction suggests support for a few conclusions. First, despite policy disagreements about whether the war should be fought, and partisan variation in members' willingness to believe Polk's description of the war's origins, nearly every speaker on both sides conceded that the authority to initiate offensive hostilities was outside the constitutional authority conferred by the commander in chief clause. That their language about the constitutional text is consistent with the dominant norms of the nineteenth century is noteworthy, particularly because so many members actually supported the war.

The second point raised by this example is how members' words and actions varied. Members overwhelmingly interpreted the text of the constitution as prohibiting the action that Polk plainly took. Nevertheless, the United States, with congressional support, fought the Mexican War and conquered an enormous amount of territory in doing so, forever shaping the future of the continent. So what do we make of that conflict between words and actions? On the one hand, it suggests that members' interpretations of the constitutional text matters less to them than their policy preferences, a point that will resurface in other chapters. So perhaps members' understanding of the Constitution doesn't really matter. On the other hand, as the saying goes, "hypocrisy is the tribute virtue pays to vice," and members' refusal to echo Yancey's broader arguments about presidential power was itself a reinforcement of a constitutional norm that might have affected members' and presidents' behavior in other ways. That members' language about the Constitution did not change to more logically support expansionist policy points to friction between ideas, which some suggest is a source of institutional development over time.[36]

THE UTAH WAR: DEFINING THE LINE BETWEEN
LAW ENFORCEMENT AND ACTS OF WAR

In 1857–1858, the United States fought the "Utah war," a series of standoffs and small skirmishes between Mormon settlers in the Utah territory and army units sent by President James Buchanan to install a new, secular, Washington-appointed territorial governor. Again, members of Congress and the president agreed that the president could not initiate the use of force against foreigners. Critics of the president argued he had illegally started a war. Supporters argued he was just enforcing the law in American territory.

Though Utah was American territory, opponents of the action defined it as an illegal initiation of the use of force. Free Soil representative Edward Wade argued that Buchanan should have gotten permission from Congress before sending the army to Utah because by committing "the nation to war deliberately, [he] has violated the Constitution as flagrantly as he could do it in any other way."[37] Republican Benjamin Stanton argued that by declaring war, Congress could confer broad powers on the president. In the absence of a declaration, however, "the power of the President to commit acts of hostility upon anybody, except in repelling an invasion, is at once extinguished. He has no power in time of peace to 'make war,' either upon a foreign nation, or any portion of the American people."[38] Democrat John Quitman, a member of the president's own party, agreed that the commander in chief's powers were limited and subservient to Congress's and that his role was "to present the facts to Congress; and then for Congress to say what shall be the character of that force, and for how long a period it shall be mustered into service."

In spite of those criticisms, Congress did not act to stop the operation. Buchanan framed the resistance in Utah not as war but as rebellion covered by the Militia Act and reported to Congress about the actions he said justified sending the army units to the territory. Congress appropriated money for supplies.

THE CIVIL WAR: WHAT JUSTIFIES
PRESIDENTIAL USE OF MILITARY FORCE
AGAINST REBEL STATES?

Members of Congress who spoke about secession and the commander in chief clause in 1861 generally agreed that the president had legal authority to respond to Southern attacks, whether considered acts of war or acts of rebellion covered by the Militia Act. After Abraham Lincoln was elected president by the Electoral College, but before he was inaugurated, six Southern states seceded from the Union, formed a new government, elected a president of their own, and began organizing an army.

While Democrat James Buchanan was still president, members of both parties argued that the commander in chief clause granted him the authority to keep the states in the Union. Republican Thaddeus Stevens argued that the government had sufficient authority to make sure states obeyed the law and stayed in the Union.[39] Republican William Conkling argued that the commander in chief had authority over national defenses and "for the complete exercise of this power, he needed no courts to issue process and no marshal to execute it. Nothing was needed but firmness and integrity."[40] Democrat William Holman agreed that we "must consider it nothing more than the ordinary case of the President, as commander-in-chief of the Army and Navy of the Union, employing the latter in the discharge of his duty to 'take care that the laws be faithfully executed.'"[41]

Abraham Lincoln, of course, acted more boldly than Buchanan. He was inaugurated on March 4, 1861, and the first shots of the Civil War were fired on Fort Sumter, in South Carolina, on April 12. Lincoln did not call Congress into special session until July 4. Between April and July, Lincoln ordered a blockade of the South, called up the militia, and suspended habeas corpus along the rail lines through Maryland that were needed to supply union forces around Washington, DC.

In supporting Lincoln's actions in the early months of the war, even his own partisans tended to support a very narrow view of the implied authority of the commander in chief. Sen. Jacob Howard, Republican of Michigan, supported Lincoln's actions as falling under the category of self-defense, previewing arguments that would be made by the Supreme Court in the *Prize* cases. As he did so, he argued that Lincoln's authority was limited to self-defense and was otherwise completely controlled by Congress, with or without a declaration of war:

> It is, of course, folly to pretend that the nation may not be actually engaged in war unless by and under a declaration of Congress. Such a declaration is not essential to the existence of belligerent rights, nor to the actual existence of public war. The [declare war] clause seems rather intended as a restriction upon the President's

authority as Commander-in-Chief of the Army and Navy, preventing him from
performing any aggressive act leading to war with a foreign Power. . . .
The [declare war clause] does not, in fact, contribute one iota to the quantum
of power [Congress] possesses. It was plainly intended as a caution-yes, I must
go further-as a prohibition to the President, whether acting as Commander-in-
Chief of the Army and Navy, or in forming treaties with foreign Governments
against any assumption by him of the right, the power, or the duty of involving
the nation in war with another nation, leaving the whole right, the whole duty of
initiating a national war for any purpose except that of self-defense, to Congress,
to the law-making power.[42]

Garrett Davis (Unionist-KY) conceded that Lincoln had the authority to take
actions against the Confederacy, but only due to his statutory authority from
Congress and not any implied constitutional power. He said,

Congress has the power, either to recognize all cases of resistance to the execution
of the laws, of insurrection, of invasion, or domestic violence in a State, and to
call out the militia to meet them, by suitable provisions in laws passed as such
occasions might occur; or it could pass a general act, as that of 1795, providing for
all cases, and confer the power, both to ascertain the particular occasion, and to
call out the militia to meet it, either upon the President, the courts, or any other
agency it might choose to select. When there was a recognition of either case by
any proper authority, and armies were raised for it, the President became their
"Commander-in-Chief" by the Constitution; and then, but not before, his right
to act as such in the premises commenced.[43]

Members of Congress, mostly Republicans, generally spoke approvingly of
Lincoln's actions, in part by arguing that his actions were not the type of offensive force that required congressional approval. They either argued that the
commander in chief clause gave the president authority to defend the nation
from foreign adversaries or that Congress had granted him statutory authority
to suppress insurrections in the Militia Act. Nevertheless, they voted retroactively to approve of his actions, to erase any doubt.

THE DOMINICAN REPUBLIC: IS A DIPLOMATIC
DEPLOYMENT AN ACT OF HOSTILITY?

In May of 1870, invoking the Monroe Doctrine, President Ulysses Grant submitted to Congress a treaty agreeing to the United States' annexation of the
Dominican Republic. Sen. Charles Sumner, Republican, for a variety of reasons, ultimately killed the treaty.[44] Grant had sent the Navy to the Dominican
Republic (Santo Domingo) to potentially protect it from invasion by its neigh-
bor, Haiti, during treaty negotiations. Grant "did not seek theoretical justification in the commander in chief power" but rather relied on his authority
as chief diplomat in doing so.[45] Members of both parties seemed to concede
that in the absence of congressional direction, nonviolent deployment abroad
might be legitimate, but they disagreed about whether Congress could regulate
that deployment. The president's most ardent supporters made the broadest
arguments about his implied constitutional authority. They tended to define
Grant's actions as simple "direction" of troops and ships that resembled the
"general" model of military authority.

In December 1870 Carl Schurz (R-MO), who would go on to oppose the
treaty on policy grounds, offered a resolution asking the commander in chief
to divulge whether American naval vessels were in the waters of the Dominican Republic, and if so, to withdraw them.[46] Democrat Eugene Casserly of
California, a partisan opponent of the president, argued in favor of congressional oversight and control over the deployment of the navy. In his view, "The
direction to withdraw the ships of war, [is not] undue interference with the
prerogative of the Commander-in-Chief. Whether a ship of war shall be stationed here or there is a matter which Congress may regulate or may leave to
the Secretary of the Navy."[47]

Many Republicans, predictably, supported Grant's deployment. Republican senator James Harlan of Iowa made a broad argument in favor of implied
command authority to deploy ships into the territorial waters of foreign nations as an act of peace, not a use of force:

> Surely no member of this body as intelligent as the honorable Senator from
> Missouri would undertake in this way to control the official action of the
> Commander-in Chief of the Army and Navy of the United States or direct by
> statute the movement of our squadrons at sea . . . The citizens of the United
> States may have- interests of great value, which would be greatly endangered or

destroyed by the violent overthrow of [The Dominican] Government. In such
a supposable case would it not be the duty of the President to protect those
interests by the presence of an armed fleet, to lend the existing Government,
with which we are in peaceful relations, the moral support of the presence of our
flag?[48]

The Senate ultimately rejected the amendment that requested that the administration report upon and withdraw the navy from Dominican waters. Twelve
senators supported the motion, including all of the Democrats and the dissi-
dent Republicans Sumner and Schurz. The remaining thirty-two Republicans
supported Grant by voting against the motion.

The navy's presence in the Dominican Republic was questioned again
during debate over the treaty itself. Republican senator Frederick Frelinghuysen broadly interpreted the commander in chief's implied authority not in a
military or law enforcement function but in his role as a diplomat. He said:

Nobody denies this right in the President to negotiate. If this be so, it must be
admitted that the Administration usurped no power by sending a fleet to Samana
Bay pending the negotiations. . . . Mr. President, this is a nation; and that it may
have a vigorous life among the nations of the earth we have an executive who is
entrusted with all our foreign relations, subject to the provision that a treaty must
be ratified by the Senate to be valid. The President is the Commander-in-Chief of
the Army and the Navy, and he is so all the time, that he may be able to preserve
the dignity and interests of the nation.[49]

Because, in Grant's view, annexing the Dominican Republic was in the nation's
interests, Frelinghuysen argues that it was therefore lawful to move the navy
into Dominican waters during treaty negotiations. The logic that the "executive is entrusted with all our foreign relations" would become normalized
in the twentieth century but it was unusual to connect such an idea to the
commander in chief clause prior to this point. As noted above, the president's
annexation treaty itself was defeated in the Senate, by Democrats voting with
part of a divided Republican party.

It should be noted that Grant was, by most accounts, using the navy as
described, not to forcefully coerce the Dominicans to agree to an annexation
treaty or to depose its leadership. A bipartisan group of Republican defectors
and Democratic opponents of the administration relied in part on a narrow

construction of the commander in chief clause to argue against the deployment and the treaty. Republican supporters of Grant's treaty relied on arguments about treaty negotiations to construct justifications for the president's peaceful employment of the navy during those negotiations. Debates about annexation were also fused with arguments about race.[50]

Note that although Grant was a legitimate war hero, members of Congress did not make claims that he was owed special deference as commander in chief because of his expertise, accomplishments, or constitutional authority. Yet, even in similar geopolitical circumstances, congressional debates sounded quite different after 1900, as will be seen in chapter 4.

THE SPANISH-AMERICAN WAR: CAN A PRESIDENT INTERVENE WITHOUT CONGRESSIONAL AUTHORITY?

During the lead-up to the Spanish-American war, the press and members of Congress drove the discussions about going to war with Spain and helping the Cuban revolutionaries. Both Democratic president Grover Cleveland and Republican president William McKinley publicly held back from instigating war with Spain, and both faced Congresses who talked about how the commander in chief had to fight a war if Congress told him to.

When Cleveland was president, the question was whether Congress could force a reluctant president to fight a war. Members of Congress who raised that issue argued the commander in chief had to initiate hostilities if Congress told him to do so. In 1895 Cuban independence fighters left Florida to start their insurgency against Spanish colonial rule on the island. As the rebels began their insurrection, President Grover Cleveland expressed an unwillingness to intervene and threatened to veto a declaration of war against Spain if Congress were to pass one. He also issued a proclamation warning American citizens not to violate neutrality laws to help the revolutionaries.[51] Sen. John Tyler, Democrat of Alabama, argued vociferously in 1896 that if Congress decided to go to war with Spain, the president could not veto or resist that decision. In a clear contrast to the arguments presidents make today, Tyler went so far as to suggest that because the commander in chief must execute the decision, he should not even participate in Congress's initiation of the use of force.

I never have thought that the Commander in Chief of the Army of the United States could refuse to go into the field and lead the armies because he did not want to fight, if we ordered him to do it . . . if we concede to him the power to declare war, or by the application of his veto to defeat war, when he holds the commission of Commander in Chief of the Army of the United States, we acknowledge the principle that the military is superior to the civil power.[52]

Cleveland was unwilling to risk relations with Spain over the Cuban insurrection, and Congress did not, at that time, decide to declare war. Congress did, however, in March of 1896, debate and pass a resolution stating that it was the opinion of Congress that there was a war in Cuba between revolutionaries and the Spanish government and that both sides should be allowed access to American ports as neutral parties.

When Republican William McKinley became president, the question was whether the commander in chief could suppress a full-scale war by fighting a limited one of his own initiation. Again, members of Congress defined the commander in chief clause narrowly. McKinley, also reticent to declare war on Spain, expressed an interest in "intervening" to help the Cuban revolutionaries, short of declaring war. Members of Congress, especially Democrats, argued that Congress had to sanction any use of force and that all such interventions in foreign territory fell under Congress's powers. Democratic senator Edmund Pettus referred to both the Constitution and court rulings from 1798 Quasi-War with France to argue that the president could not initiate even minor "interventions" without congressional support and declaration. He argued,

Mr. President, this is not a monarchy, where the king can use the army and navy to make war or to "intervene" whenever and wherever he desires to do so. . . . The President, though he is Commander-in-chief of the Army and Navy, and of the militia when called into service, cannot "declare war." Neither can he make war until the Congress has declared war. This is so plainly written in the Constitution that no one has or will contradict it. And the Supreme Court of the United States has many times decided that the Congress alone has power to "declare war." . . . The Congress must order what the war shall be. And it is the duty of the President, as Commander in Chief, to carry on the war as Congress has declared it, and not otherwise.

After the destruction of the USS *Maine* in Havana harbor, public opinion in the United States as well as in Congress, supported going to war. Alongside diplomatic actions taken by President McKinley, and at his request, Congress declared war with Spain on April 25, 1898.

EXCEPTIONS

It is important to remember that my analysis here only extends to congressional debates in which at least one member discussed the commander in chief clause. That largely excludes the conquests of Native American lands, as well as Hawaii. It also excludes other episodes that some scholars argue contributed to the growth of presidential war powers in the twentieth century. Victoria Farrar-Myers notes more than a dozen deployments during this time period, most lacking formal congressional approval but often defended under the guise of "protecting Americans abroad" and connected to the idea of the commander in chief's defensive authority.[53] Naval interventions in Samoa in 1888, Hawaii in 1893, and in the Boxer Rebellion in 1900 and others were relevant to the definition and use of commander in chief authority, but members of Congress did not discuss the clause in relation to the initiation of force during those episodes. There are a handful of references to Hawaii among the speeches I collected, but not to the US military's actions there in 1893. Nor does my dataset include many of the Latin American interventions that occurred after 1900.

Another case that is notably missing is the bombardment of Greytown, Nicaragua. The most serious unauthorized presidential intervention in Latin America in the nineteenth century took place in 1854, when the administration of President James Pierce authorized an American naval ship to force local authorities in Nicaragua to make amends for offending an American diplomat. In questionable enforcement of that authority, the navy bombarded and burned Greytown. Afterwards, President Pierce defended the naval commander's actions (on questionable grounds) and Congress ordered an investigation.[54] Congressional discussions of this particular event did not refer to the authority of the commander in chief, so do not appear in my dataset. Members of both parties, including secretary of state and future president James Buchanan, publicly rebuked Pierce for the incident. The Supreme Court did weigh in on the side of expansive presidential power, but the case was not cited by members of Congress in later arguments about the powers of the commander in chief prior to World War I.[55] Importantly, members of Congress did not incorporate that incident into redefinitions of the commander in chief clause in subsequent years.

Four years later, another incident in Nicaragua did provoke discussions of the commander in chief clause. In that case, President Buchanan, in the same party as Pierce, rejected executive unilateralism. American mercenary William Walker had previously attempted to set up a pro-slavery government in Nicaragua.[56] A navy commodore landed there to arrest Walker. President Buchanan then overturned the authority for the landing.[57] Democrats in Congress supported their partisan ally Buchanan, agreeing that any interventions abroad required advance congressional approval and that Buchanan was right to overturn the commodore's decision.[58] They proposed a resolution stating that the arrest was "in violation of the territorial sovereignty of a friendly Power, and not sanctioned by any existing law, Congress disavows it."[59] Republican opponents in Congress argued the commander in chief should be able to use the navy to prevent Americans from carrying out "lawless war" against other countries (and that therefore, the commodore's arrest of the pro-slavery mercenary Walker was legitimate).[60] They proposed a resolution that said that "no further provisions of law are necessary to confer authority on the President to cause arrests and seizure to be made on the high seas, for offenses committed against" an 1818 neutrality act. Neither party's resolution passed.[61] Both parties construed Buchanan's actions through the lens of their own preferences about slavery, and stalemate about those preferences prevented them from acting on one of the competing resolutions. But both parties also construed the commander in chief's authority to take unilateral action in Latin America quite narrowly, grounded in statute, and far more narrowly than Pierce or the Supreme Court had just a few years earlier.

Like the questions about "defensive" naval convoys during the Quasi-War and the unclear nature of the Utah War, the cases discussed here were not easily characterized according to the traditional offensive/defensive dichotomy associated with the commander in chief clause. What those episodes also have in common is that traditional ideas about "offense" and "defense" did not capture what Theodore Roosevelt would popularize as "gunboat diplomacy," the projection of military force as a clear threat to another nation, but without the gunshots that might more clearly signal the "initiation of hostile force." The text and history of the commander in chief clause did not tell members of Congress which branch could authorize threats of force that might be either nonviolent or use minimal violence but were nevertheless coercive.

DISCUSSION

Members of Congress prior to 1900 often repeated the argument that the commander in chief had only limited defensive authority to initiate the use of force. Cataloguing those arguments helps us to understand how policymakers articulated the overall worldview that supported the original constitutional order for war powers. Scholarship on the role of ideas in political development suggest that rhetoric may even help to legitimate certain political actions and help to sustain institutions like the original constitutional order.[62] With their words, members restated norms about congressional dominance of war policy and limited legitimate presidential action to defense. It is possible that their repetition of narrow constructions of the commander in chief clause even affected presidents' choices, and perhaps affected Congress's view of its own responsibilities. Other scholarship suggests such rhetoric can affect political behavior. Dearborn, for example, argues that congressional rhetoric about the president as a national representative after the turn of the twentieth century affected members themselves, as they created institutions to support a stronger presidency. Kriner shows that in the modern era, presidents themselves listen to the words spoken by members of Congress about war powers authority.

Except that members' words and those norms didn't *actually* constrain President Polk from waging offensive war against Mexico, or many presidents from waging undeclared genocidal war against Native peoples in North America. Perhaps, those repetitions simply forced enterprising presidents to justify aggressive actions with other reasoning. As we will see in later chapters, partisan and policy preferences also shape what Congress does (if not what members say). Such mismatches between language and action highlight that when members of Congress interpret a constitutional phrase and apply it to a political controversy, they do not merely interpret the phrase itself. Although members were quite consistent in the ways that they defined the commander in chief's authority, especially related to the initiation of hostilities, they were much less consistent in the ways that they defined "defense" and "offense." Other concepts like these interact with members' interpretations and how they apply them in the laws that they write and choose not to write. Offensive and defensive force are two important and interrelated terms in the interpretation of constitutional war powers. But so are "American interests," "protection," "civilization," "threat," and others, each of which must also be understood in the context of dominant racial orders and international legal regimes.

Definitions of those interrelated concepts were important to some of the constitutional constructions discussed here, including the way that Congress reacted to Gen. Andrew Jackson's offensive actions against Spanish settlements and Native Americans in Florida, and to Polk's initiation of the Mexican War.

Focusing on congressional debates about the commander in chief clause shows that while members consistently articulated some particular interpretations of the clause, there were also challenges to the dominant interpretation. Identifying those logical and rhetorical discrepancies helps us understand how congressional politics and received understanding of the constitutional text interact. On several occasions, members continued to repeat the same interpretation of the constitutional text, even when by their actions, they defied those words. Members who supported Jackson's incursions into Florida could presumably see that his actions were constitutionally questionable (and if they couldn't, their fellow legislators pointed it out to them). But they found creative ways to justify his actions within existing rhetorical frameworks rather than articulating a broader definition of presidential power.

Such mismatches, though rare during the period under study, took place more often when members of the president's party were responding to examples of executive overreach. Such mismatches between action and rhetoric help us see the cases where the dominant rhetoric and logic came into the most conflict with political pressures, and cases where alternative rhetoric and logic might be more likely to emerge.

With data only on congressional rhetoric, we are not able to definitively address the question of whether and how members' words influenced anyone, either members themselves or presidents. We can say they repeated those norms, and mostly legislated consistently with them. But how were members of Congress able to maintain such a consistent set of interpretations, and one that is quite different from the one that Congress has constructed in the twentieth century? To answer this question, in the next chapter, I describe how members went about the rhetorical and logical process of constructing their constitutional interpretations.

CHAPTER 3

Authoritative Sources and Constitutional Scripts

Constitutional interpretation is not an easy task. Figuring out the scope of executive power is hard for everyone—members of Congress, scholars, the public, and even judges. If you spend any time reading about war powers in the American constitutional system, you'll probably read Supreme Court Justice Jackson's concurrence in the 1952 case *Youngstown Sheet and Tube v. Sawyer*. In that case, the Supreme Court told President Truman that he couldn't seize privately owned steel mills to protect steel production during the Korean War. Arguing in favor of that decision, Jackson eloquently described how hard it is to figure out what powers belong to the president and what powers belong to Congress. As he put it,

> A judge, like an executive adviser, may be surprised at the poverty of really useful and unambiguous authority applicable to concrete problems of executive power as they actually present themselves. Just what our forefathers did envision, or would have envisioned had they foreseen modern conditions, must be divined from materials almost as enigmatic as the dreams Joseph was called upon to interpret for Pharaoh. A century and a half of partisan debate and scholarly speculation yields no net result but only supplies more or less apt quotations from respected sources on each side of any question. They largely cancel each other. And court decisions are indecisive because of the judicial practice of dealing with the largest questions in the most narrow way.

Courts have established processes for interpreting texts and for passing those interpretations to others in stable arrangements. Legal scholars have entire schools that teach students the norms for interpreting and receiving authoritative interpretations of laws and constitutions. But members of Congress have no such special training for determining when and how to authoritatively interpret the Constitution. Researchers, especially those who normatively prefer that all three branches of government participate actively in interpreting and constructing constitutional meaning, seek to understand when, how, and why Congress can participate meaningfully in such deliberations.

Scholars in the modern period have investigated how members of Congress perceive their role as constitutional interpreter by surveying members themselves. Members generally report they have an institutional responsibility to examine constitutional issues genuinely, and thoroughly, though today they report giving little attention to constitutional questions about foreign affairs. Decades apart, Donald Morgan and Bruce Peabody were able to ask members of Congress what they thought about Congress's capacity to interpret the Constitution and their role in doing so.[1] Specifically, Peabody replicated a survey of members of Congress originally conducted by Morgan in 1959. Along with continuities, he found that between 1959 and 1999, fewer members expressed confidence in their capacity to reach constitutional interpretations. A plurality of members shifted from thinking they had an independent authority to deliberate on constitutional principles to which the courts should defer to believing they had such an independent authority but that courts need not necessarily defer to it. Peabody finds that today's congressional lawmakers, who frequently rely on cues from courts and presidents about constitutional issues, may not believe they have a responsibility to participate in war powers and foreign affairs decisions. There is some evidence that the modern Congress engages in constitutional deliberation mostly in response to court decisions that review and overturn laws it has recently passed. J. Mitchell Pickerill finds that members of Congress are simply interested in passing popular laws, and they do not often consider constitutional issues because their legislative work builds on previous laws that members presumed were already within their constitutional authority to pass.[2] Generally, members of Congress are thought to prioritize policy outcomes when legislating, and so they consider constitutional issues only when the court or the president might be reasonably expected to overturn their actions.[3] Hendrickson also found that Congress's modern decisions about how and whether to assert its constitutional war powers are affected by partisan calculations and the sometimes-idiosyncratic political choices made by congressional party leadership.

Such decision making is not unique to the modern period. As we saw in the previous chapter, some of the times that nineteenth-century Congresses considered the commander in chief clause were in response to unorthodox presidential uses of command authority. In those cases, Congress often reacted by legislating to reestablish its dominant interpretation of constrained commander in chief powers, even while sometimes letting presidents achieve some policy outcomes through statutorily granted discretion. But Congress also interpreted the war powers granted by the Constitution, and asserted its right to do so, in the course of ordinary legislation as well.

We saw in the last chapter that members of Congress in the nineteenth century routinely discussed the constitutional text and its meaning in war powers contexts and arrived at consistently broad interpretations of the legislature's own authority. How did members of Congress across a century's time, motivated, as they are today, by wildly different partisanship and policy preferences, arrive at consistent and similar interpretations of the commander in chief clause?[4] How did they construct war powers in ways that favored their own policy preferences, without giving in entirely to a president's broad interpretation of his powers? Because of the passage of time, we cannot ask members from this time period how they arrived at their ideas, or the reasons they might have wanted to deliberate about them. But we can use their own words to look for clues about why they arrived at the conclusions that they did.

In what follows, I describe how members of Congress in the nineteenth century talked about their process for constructing constitutional authority. As they made political arguments about policy, they also made arguments about why the Constitution supported their favored policy and specified the sources that supported their constitutional interpretation. They referred to presidential actions and court decisions, as they do today, but they also referred often to history in broader terms. In my reading of congressional debates, I found repeated references to the same constitutional-historical arguments about the authority conferred by the commander in chief clause.

A particularly dominant constitutional-historical argument, which said that the commander in chief is a military title and that history dictates that his authority is comparable to that of a military officer, is present in many of Congress's debates about the commander in chief clause. This often-repeated argument is consistent with many specific interpretations conferred by the clause, both in offhand remarks and engaged debates. When political actors publicly share and defend their constructions of constitutional meaning, that discourse can fall into patterns that are similar to what Victoria Farrar-Myers calls constitutional scripts.[5] Such scripts are repeated summaries of how authority is distributed and why that distribution is justified. Members do not invent or construct these scripts but refer to them as if they are already familiar to all. Sometimes, in moments of uncertainty, the scripts themselves are subject to debate and their application to a particular situation is contested. At other times, scripts can be used as simple rhetorical shorthand that substitutes for deliberation but refers to its legacy. These constitutional scripts seem to be an important part of congressional construction of the commander in chief clause and the authority it confers. They supply an accessible and easily understandable description of constitutional authority, draw attention to relevant precedents, and allow members to reason from outside their current political situation.

In the first section that follows, I describe the sources of authority that members of Congress referred to as they struggled to define the commander in chief clause and the scope and boundaries of the powers it conferred. In the second section, I describe the role that constitutional scripts seemed to play in their reasoning.

WHEN MEMBERS OF CONGRESS CITE THEIR SOURCES

Today, people often discuss the founding debates and documents when trying to understand the meaning of the constitutional text regarding war powers (or any other topic).[6] In the nineteenth century, however, members' remarks in the congressional record indicate that the Founding itself offered little guidance about how to interpret the commander in chief clause. Of the more than two thousand references to the commander in chief in the pre-WWI congressional record, only about three dozen (about 1 percent) are simple recitations of the text of the Constitution. These references sound like this excerpt from a speech by Representative Duncan in 1840: "Our Constitution provides that 'the President shall be Commander-in-Chief of the Army and Navy of the United States, and of the militia of the several States, when called into the actual service of the United States.' The power to declare war, raise armies, and to maintain them, belongs to Congress, and not to the President."[7]

A handful of others reference the constitutional convention, the Federalist papers, or specific Founding Fathers, including James Madison or Alexander Hamilton.[8] These references are fairly randomly scattered throughout the record and are used to support a variety of different arguments about the commander in chief—sometimes the same source is used by opposing sides in the same argument.[9] But the founding documents do not actually appear as often in the congressional record as one might imagine and do not dominate members' discussion of the phrase's meaning. In fact, as noted by Justice Jackson in 1952, the debates about the drafting and ratification of the Constitution offered only vague guidance about presidential power and were utterly silent about the commander in chief clause and so couldn't have been much help.[10]

Nor did members of Congress look to British history. Specific British laws and precedents were invoked extremely rarely as a legitimate guidepost for defining the authority of the commander in chief. That is ironic since the commander in chief title itself also originated in English law, in 1639.[11] Members did refer to political theorists like William Blackstone, John Locke, and Montesquieu in their own speeches in passing, but not in close connection with the commander in chief specifically.[12] The actions of British commanders were very rarely cited as valid precedents for understanding the commander in chief clause.[13] When English law and history was mentioned, it was as a foil, or in reference to the British origin of democratic norms, such as the illegitimacy of martial law or Parliament's control over the king's war spending.[14]

Congress also did not appear to take its constitutional construction from either presidents or courts. That members of Congress had a significant amount of agency in how they interpreted their constitutional war powers should not be that surprising. Scholars have also observed that even in the modern era, there are important feedback loops between presidents and members of Congress in their decisions about war powers. Congressional partisans do not necessarily do what presidents want them to do.[15] Court decisions touching on war powers are written after the facts on the ground have been resolved and courts tended to ratify whatever the political branches already decided.[16]

Congressional lawmakers' speeches about the commander in chief clause prior to 1900 do not suggest that presidents at the time directed Congress's interpretation of war powers. If following presidential definitions fully explained members' behavior, we would expect to see more references to the contemporary president's arguments about his authority in the congressional record—yet legislators discussing the clause in the period studied very rarely referred to the wishes of the person who was president at that moment. Members of Congress also legislated about the military and its uses without public leadership from the president, which was, in any case, rare in this era. In addition, modern scholarly research gives us reason to believe that presidents listen carefully to Congress when defining and using their war powers, so there is probably some circularity in Congress's receptivity to presidential arguments, whether prior to 1900 or today.[17] Certainly, there is some evidence that members' partisan connection to presidents significantly shaped their interpretations, which will be discussed in detail in chapter 6. Senators and congressmen did refer to the presidencies of Washington, Adams, Jefferson, Madison, Jackson, Polk, Buchanan, Lincoln, Grant, McKinley, and Roosevelt after their administrations had passed.[18] In short, presidential leadership might account for some, but certainly not all, of the stability in Congress's construction of the commander in chief clause.

Importantly, members frequently also called back to acts taken by prior Congresses. Laws passed by Congress in the past were seen as authoritative guides to how to define the commander in chief's role relative to Congress in the present. As discussed in chapter 1, the law that received the most attention in this time period was the Militia Act of 1795, which members repeatedly cited as controlling precedent for both congressional supremacy and (delegated) presidential discretion in repelling invasion, border protection, and suppressing domestic unrest.[19]

Nor was Congress's construction of the commander in chief clause entirely dependent upon court decisions. Members' speeches show some deference to court opinions, especially regarding particular types of authority where the court spoke clearly. The Supreme Court and its specific decisions were cited fairly often.[20] In my dataset of speeches related to the commander in chief clause, the cases that received the most attention were *Martin v. Mott* (1827), *Cross v. Harrison* (1853), the *Prize* cases (1863), *Ex parte Milligan* (1866), and *United States v. Eliason* (1842).[21] Each came up in congressional discussions on questions closely related to those cases—the use of state militias, the governance of conquered territory, the recognition of a rebellion, and the disciplining of troops.

Some scholars argue that Supreme Court decisions helped to shift war powers authority from the Congress to the president. But congressional speeches in the period studied here, from 1789 to 1917, do not necessarily support that claim, at least prior to World War I. Not every case that might seem relevant to understanding the power of the commander in chief clause was mentioned in conjunction with the clause during the time period studied here. Most of the cases that dealt with war powers were narrowly focused, supported robust congressional power, and were cited by members of Congress in defense of bills and resolutions that codified congressional war powers.

One outlier case was *Durand v. Hollins* (1860), in which the court seemed to grant the president broad rights to use the military to intervene in other countries' affairs when American citizens were in danger. This case might have, in theory, caused members of Congress to adopt a broader view of presidential war powers. But legislators did not cite the *Durand* decision in connection with the powers or rights of the commander in chief during the half century following that decision. The justices in that case had used the language that the president is the "only legitimate organ of the general government" in communication with foreign governments, language that had previously been used to justify broad executive power by Alexander Hamilton in his *Pacificus* letter and by British jurist William Blackstone describing the foreign policy authority of the king of England. It is also used by proponents of broad presidential power today. However, in all of the nineteenth-century congressional discussions of the commander in chief clause, the sole "organ" language appears fewer than ten times, and none in reference to *Durand* or the right of the commander in chief to use the military to protect Americans abroad.[22] The *only* use of the language and logic of the "sole organ" in foreign affairs to defend presidents' active assertion of commander in chief authority before the first World War came during Theodore Roosevelt's administration, when his ally, Republican senator Henry Cabot Lodge, used the phrase to argue in favor of Roosevelt's use of the navy to intervene in Colombian politics and win the United States the rights to build the Panama canal. Despite using the "sole organ" language, Lodge did not explicitly cite the *Durand* decision. Lodge's reference to the case is also not the only explanation for Congress's deference to Roosevelt's Panamanian intervention. And in the second half of the nineteenth century, Congress repeatedly cautioned presidents not to "intervene" without congressional authority.[23]

Although the court's decision in *Durand* might have led to the growth of presidential war authority, the absence of specific congressional citations and the delayed timing of early twentieth-century presidents' assertions of rights to employ the military seems imprecisely connected to that forty-year-old court case.[24] In most legislative debates in this time period, members of Congress operated without direct and specific guidance from the court. Moreover, the court decisions that seemed most important to members of Congress almost always ratified the definition of the commander in chief's authority that had already been constructed by Congress and the president.[25]

Just as Justice Jackson noted that judges struggle to define the boundaries of executive power, a close examination of legislators' interpretation of the commander in chief clause shows that Congress struggled as well. Members of Congress clearly grappled with competing definitions of what the clause might have meant in the particular circumstances that confronted them. They argued about it. Through those arguments, as a body, Congress synthesized several streams of information about the meaning of the Constitution. Like judges, when they referred to the constitutional text, members generally did not reason only from their personal or political preferences but instead often referred to externally authoritative foundations, and a particular set of sources served as those authorities.

One such authoritative source, repeatedly cited by lawmakers, was a popular nineteenth century textbook, Joseph Story's *Commentaries on the American Constitution.*[26] Since books transmit historical detail and authoritative historical narratives from one generation to the next, it is perhaps unsurprising that members of Congress also invoked well-regarded legal and historical texts in their arguments about how to interpret the commander in chief clause. Story's *Commentaries* gave considerable attention to both the division of war powers between the two branches and the reasons for it. His description of Congress's power was comprehensive. He argued that Congress's legislative power extends to authorizing all uses of offensive force, in both declared and undeclared wars.[27] Story did not discuss whether the commander in chief clause implied any particular powers, though he alluded to an implied authority to use defensive force, at least in the extreme case of resisting foreign invasion.[28]

However, the most durable touchstones that genuinely seemed to guide members' interpretations of the distribution of legitimate war powers authority were a set of widely known historical precedents. Legal scholars have noted that courts and presidents have a tendency to rely on historical practice to determine boundaries in the separation of powers system, and so it should be no surprise that members of Congress do so as well, and for similar reasons.[29] As Bradley and Morrison note, relying on historical practice can enhance the credibility of the decision maker by providing a reasoned explanation that "is not dependent on the political valence of the controversy in question."[30] Members of Congress referred most often to historical precedent that incorporated actions by presidents, congresses, and courts, and that, most importantly, were easily summarized by known scripts.

The mixture of references itself was often important. For example, both historical and legal precedents during the War of 1812 combined to clarify for members of Congress after the war that the president could rightfully issue orders to state militias, following congressional delegation of that authority. As described in chapter 1, some states in the Federalist Northeast resisted the president's order to send state militias to invade Canada as part of the War of 1812. The troops were eventually deployed, and after the war the Supreme Court recognized the president's authority to send militias anywhere he deemed necessary during a declared war, including into foreign territory. Members of Congress who subsequently referred to the president's authority to deploy state militias could have referred to a variety of sources. But rather than referring to the *Mott* case in subsequent years, they were more likely to refer to the "Act of 1795" as the controlling historical precedent when they talked about the commander in chief's command of militias.

Not every relevant historical example became enshrined in a repeated, persuasive narrative about war powers the way the Militia Act did. Those precedents that were repeated were often summarized in a constitutional script that connected the text, history, and constitutional authority into a simple story. Through their repetition and invocation of relevant historical precedents, these "constitutional scripts" seemed to be recognized as legitimate sources of authority by members of Congress. The dominant narrative during the nineteenth century was that the commander in chief, by virtue of his title, was akin to "a general," who had authority to command troops, but not to make deliberative decisions about war and peace. There were two competing versions of this narrative that will be discussed further in chapter 5. But the overall constitutional script dominated in part because it was backed by the historical precedents set by George Washington during the Revolutionary War.[31]

THE POWERS OF A GENERAL

The constitutional script invoked most often was the one backed by the historical precedents set by Washington, the first and most revered commander in chief. Other scholars have noted that the Framers and others in the founding generation relied on their experience with Washington during the Revolutionary War to frame the authority of the constitutional commander in chief.[32] In a developing nation whose citizens had mostly local loyalties and attachments, the memory of Washington was one of only a few widely regarded national symbols.[33]

Recall that upon declaring their independence from the king, the

American colonies proceeded to operate as a fledgling nation through the Continental Congress. The Continental Congress possessed and used the powers to raise an army and navy, designate their commanders, issue orders to those commanders, permit private citizens to act on behalf of the state (grant letters of marque and reprisal), create alliances, pay soldiers, buy or take supplies from citizens, and negotiate treaties.[34] The congress famously hired George Washington as commander in chief of its army and defined his mission and the scope of his powers—sometimes granting broad authority, as when it gave him authority to "use every endeavor" to keep troops in the Army and to take supplies from citizens unwilling to sell them.[35] Sometimes, however, the congress gave Washington very specific instructions, as when it ordered him on October 5, 1775, to intercept two particular British vessels.[36] At several points in the war, the Continental Congress specifically ordered General Washington to move forces to particular places and Washington complied. The Continental Congress unquestionably possessed the power to hire and fire generals and define the scope of their actions on the battlefield—after all, it hired George Washington (and others). Most of those wartime congressional powers were subsequently codified as powers of Congress in the Articles of Confederation and then copied directly into Article I, section 8, of the Constitution of 1787.[37]

Members of Congress in the nineteenth century repeatedly referred to that historical lineage as a guide to resolving disputes about the proper balance of power between the president and Congress on matters of war and peace, lines of argument that supported broad power for Congress and narrow independent authority for the commander in chief.[38] In repeated arguments during the Mexican, Civil, and Spanish-American Wars, congressional lawmakers grappled with the degree to which Congress could direct the commander in chief in how he should execute a war. The Revolutionary era echoes loudly in the arguments of both proponents and opponents of presidential discretion, and in the arguments made by members across party lines. The strongest proponents of the "Washington as general" model argued that Congress had the power to govern—even micromanage—the execution of a declared war, just as the Continental Congress had done. But even weaker or competing versions of that argument agreed to the basic premise that "a general" was the correct metaphor for the president's wartime powers. The "commander in chief as general" narrative, reinforced by widely read textbooks as well as by Washington hagiography, supported the broad authority for Congress, real but limited authority for the commander in chief, and the sharp distinction between the branches' authority over offensive and defensive force (see chapter 2).[39]

When members of Congress invoked the "Washington as general" model for the commander in chief, they ascribed to the president certain limited powers. He could, according to this reasoning, do what generals could generally do—during peacetime, move units from one fort to another and train and discipline troops, and during wartime, give orders to take territory and kill the enemy. But this archetypal general could not start a war and could not violate orders from his civilian authorities, at least not while maintaining the supremacy of civilian over military power. This general was also not constitutionally special—certainly, the Constitution designated that the president was commander in chief, but just as with Washington when he commanded the Revolutionary Army, the title granted by the Constitution granted the president only the power of command, narrowly conceived. No policymaking power came with it.

As will be seen in the chapters that follow, the script was ubiquitous—so much so that it was even occasionally used to make opposing arguments. For example, even though Democrats and Whigs disagreed about the actual merits of the Mexican War and talked about the powers of the Congress and the president quite differently, members of Congress on both sides repeatedly argued that the commander in chief is a purely military title that confers no policymaking authority, even during wartime. They recalled Washington's subservience to Congress when making these arguments.

In 1847 members of Congress raised these questions while debating a military appropriations bill. The following exchange from the House features two Kentuckians from opposing parties, Whig Garrett Davis, who opposed the Mexican War and spending on it, and Democrat John Tibbatts, who favored the war and war spending. Both used the "general-in-chief" metaphor and made strong arguments against the discretionary authority of the commander in chief, but one used that argument to support war spending while the other used that argument to oppose it.

Davis, who was a frequent speaker on presidential power during both the Mexican and Civil Wars, made several related arguments that invoke the "Washington as general" model. First, he argued, like many others at the time, that the Constitution might have made anyone the commander in chief, and if it hadn't, Congress would have had to name one, as it had named George Washington during the Revolution. In either case, the job came with "the authority of a general" and no policymaking authority whatsoever. He referred to the "command and direct" functions that were commonly associated with the commander in chief but defined them as narrow and subordinate to Congress. Davis said:

> If the Constitution had not created a commander-in-chief, the law of Congress might have established such an officer[40] . . . [o]ur commander-in-chief being then statutory and not constitutional . . . how preposterous it would be to say that it was his right and function, and not that of Congress, the exclusive war-making power of the Government, to decide how long and for what objects and end this war, or any other, shall be prosecuted[41] . . . But the Constitution having appointed the President commander-in-chief of the army and navy of the United States, what are his powers and duties in that capacity? Precisely the same that attached to that officer under the old Confederation: not a particle larger than if he were now any other individual and appointed by the President and the Senate, or elected by Congress. The extent of the powers of a commander-in-chief in no kind or degree depend upon the manner of his appointment, and that the Constitution devolves this office on the President does not, cannot enlarge its authority. He cannot, constitutionally at least, make war; he cannot raise, appoint, or supply armies, or build or put ships in commission; he is merely our first military and naval commander, and as such the entire aggregate of his authority is to direct and control the operations of the army and navy. He is the mere agent of Congress in its exercise of the sovereign war power of the nation; not appointed or removable by it, but wholly subordinate to it.[42]

Davis opposed the war and its goal of acquiring additional territory, and as a Whig generally espoused limited arguments about presidential power. Fellow Kentuckyan John Tibbatts, on the other hand, was in the president's party and a supporter of the war's aims. Yet he also invoked the "Washington as general" model of presidential war power. In defending Polk from congressional criticism, he argued that once Congress had declared the Mexican war, President Polk bore no more responsibility for it. He said that Polk merely "assumes his new position of commander-in-chief, and acts under the authority of the laws of Congress, just as any other officer or soldier engaged in the war, and is at all times under the control of Congress."[43] Tibbatts was rhetorically incredulous that Whigs could argue that president was taking an inappropriate role in the war beyond what Congress defined for him. He argued:

Do not gentlemen, then, see, that the moment the country is engaged in an offensive war the relation of the President in regard to the war is changed? – that he no longer acts as President of the United States, but only as commander-in-chief of the army and navy? – that he has no power whatever in relation to the war derived from the Constitution merely? – that his directions must all proceed from Congress? – that he is subject entirely to our action, when we choose to act? – that in fact he is no longer responsible for the existence of the war? – that we have taken that responsibility upon our own shoulders? – that we can look to him as responsible only for the proper use of the means we may place under his control, and obedience to the rules we may prescribe to him?[44] . . . When the President acts as President, he derives his powers from the Constitution; but the Constitution confers no powers upon him as commander-in-chief. When he acts in that capacity, he derives his powers from the laws of Congress. Congress, it is true, cannot create an office superior to his; but Congress can at all times prescribe laws to govern and control him, and extend or limit his power.[45]

Both critics and supporters of Polk conceded the premise that the commander in chief under the Constitution of 1789 was fairly compared to the commander in chief under the Articles of Confederation, both of them subservient to Congress.

SCRIPTS AS GUIDEPOSTS

In the nineteenth century, Congress articulated and enforced limits to presidential war powers, an arrangement to which presidents mostly acquiesced. This relatively stable arrangement, contrasted with an equally stable arrangement that favors the president today, has been called the original "constitutional order" for war powers. As Congress maintained that order through its actions, its members referred to historical examples and texts that justified their actions and their interpretations of the constitution's distribution of war powers authority. They did so using repeated shorthand like the "Act of 1795" to refer to congressional authority and the constitutional script that said that the commander in chief's authority was limited "like a general's." These two observations raise some important questions about the relationships between rhetoric, ideas, and authority. Do constitutional scripts simply summarize a constitutional order? Or do they help to give it order? What role do language

and ideas play in the construction and the development over time of constitutional authority?

Those who study American political development often talk about path de-
pendence, self-reinforcing or positive feedback processes in a political system.
In the historical institutionalist tradition, those processes are often embedded
in institutionalized and durable interest group arrangements that shape politics.[46] Historical institutionalists would generally say that a group of bureaucratic structures like the national security state, a set of congressional committees with established practices, or organized veterans' groups would constitute
institutions that would perpetuate a stable political order. They tend to exclude ideas from their definition of institutions that drive political stability
and development.[47]

Other scholars, however, argue that ideas help to construct governing authority as ideas justify particular arrangements of power. The justifications
offered for a particular conception of authority can shape how that authority
is understood over time.[48] For example, the arguments written into *The Federalist Papers*, which justified replacing the originally dominant ideas about the
union and federalism, became part of Americans' understanding of constitutional authority itself.[49] There is a sense in which constitutional scripts may be
thought of as a self-reinforcing idea, weaker in holding constitutional authority constant than institutions, but potentially important at any given decision
point. Through their repetition, logic, and utility in crafting justifications for
policy, constitutional scripts may help to produce stability in the distribution
of authority.[50]

A constitutional order may have a special relationship to ideas because the
text, and interpretations of it, are especially meaningful to political actors as
they decide whether and how to use their power in novel situations. And the
institutions that perpetuate the constitutional order are also maintained and
shaped by the people who inhabit the branches of government. But words and
ideas are not simply received institutions and do not supply the same constraints as bureaucracies do. Political actors may have real autonomy in gener-
ating ideas different than those they inherit, and those ideas, when embedded
in political coalitions, might alter developmental trajectories.[51]

The evidence presented here suggests that members of Congress actively
debated the meaning of the constitutional text and how it applied to novel
situations that confronted them. But these legislators were not necessarily especially sophisticated folks. They were neither historians nor legal scholars;

neither did they have expert staff to inform them. They were politicians, and they reasoned about the Constitution from common forms of knowledge—widely received histories, very widely read textbooks. They used their own reasoning skills, shaded by political motivations, to interpret and apply the histories and constitutional theories they had learned. Their reasoning was appropriate both to whom they were as people and to whom they were speaking—other similarly situated members of Congress and the public at large. Their use of constitutional scripts and invocation of relevant history was an accessible tool that seemed to be useful to them as they debated how to define the boundaries to presidential authority.

The narrow scope of the consensus reading of the commander in chief clause described in chapters 1 and 2 fits neatly within the metaphorical "general's" authority. He was superior in the chain of command and could execute discipline. He could move troops on the battlefield but not start wars. Without being able to ask them, we cannot know whether this script influenced senators' and congressmen's thinking about constitutional war powers. However, the metaphor itself told members of Congress when it was time to police the boundaries between congressional and presidential authority, both proactively without presidential input and reactively when presidents seemed to step over the line. Members both repeated the script and often behaved consistently with it. At a minimum, the "general in chief" script helps modern observers to understand how members of Congress talked about the original constitutional order for war powers. Its logic may have also helped them think about the Constitution.

CHAPTER 4

Hail to the Chief

A New Script for a New Century

By examining congressional rhetoric about the commander in chief clause as a continuous time series, it is possible to see that after about 1898, presidents who were looking to Congress for signals about how to construe their war powers would have heard new types of rhetoric. With the beginning of the Spanish-American War, members of Congress began to conflate the commander in chief with the military, the flag, and the nation itself. They began to repeat arguments about Congress's duty to defer to the president, rather than scripts that required congressional supremacy in decisions regarding the use of force. The "president as general" narrative model, repeated often throughout the nineteenth century, now faced competition from a script that described the commander in chief as "representative of the nation," who deserved respect and obedience from Congress.

The idea that presidents represent the whole American public did not originate at the turn of the twentieth century.[1] Debates about who—which geographical unit, which party, which branch of government—empirically or normatively best represents the nation are as old as the nation itself and continue in both scholarly literature and in political discourse today.[2] Jeremy Bailey shows that even at the time of the Founding, there were conflicting ideas about whether the president was responsible to the law or to the people, to what degree his selection by the electoral college represented the popular will, and to what degree popular selection was a source of his executive authority. Bailey argues that although prominent progressives like Theodore Roosevelt clearly articulated the theory that the president is the best representative of the people, and that a president's election was a source of policy authority, that argument was neither novel nor decisively won in the early twentieth century. However, scholars of American political development have often noted that around the turn of that century, a confluence of historical changes began to change the election of the president, his relationship to the public, the professionalism of the bureaucracy, and the United States' role in the world.[3] This chapter adds to those arguments by showing that the turn of the twentieth century also brought about a new kind of presidential nationalism that had not been widespread in previous congressional references to the commander in chief clause.

Rhetoric that conflates the presidency with national unity and with war powers authority is familiar to us today. We routinely refer to the president as commander in chief and use his military title as a simple synonym for his office. We also associate special political authority with the commander in chief title, and at times systematically conflate the president with the flag and the nation. For example, based on modern public opinion data, political scientists have identified and modeled the "rally around the flag effect," a sudden uptick in a president's public approval ratings in response to dramatic international events like the use of military force.[4] The rally phenomenon has particular characteristics. It involves rhetorically and emotionally associating the president with the whole nation, a conflation that allows both elites and the public to equate support for the president with patriotism. Public rally effects have a complicated relationship to congressional support for the military action, the president, and his policies. Members' of Congress words and actions seem to affect a rally's existence and duration.[5] At the same time, members seem to be affected by wartime nationalization of politics and when they are, they offer more support to the president and his policies.[6]

Though rally effects had not been documented in scientific ways in the eighteenth century, members of the founding generation were wary of the possibility that war might cause the people to lionize the commander in chief, to the peril of constitutional and representative government. They worried that if the executive was given the authority to begin wars that would give him heroic status, the possibility of accumulating fame and power might tempt him to start wars that were not in the public interest.[7]

In the nineteenth century, members of Congress did not rhetorically conflate the "commander in chief" with the nation itself. There are a handful of exceptions, in which members of the president's party impart to the president, as commander in chief, an exalted status, and suggest that criticism of the president is unpatriotic. But prior to the Spanish-American War, such comments neither dominated the rhetoric of the president's party nor were accepted by members of the opposition party.

At the turn of the twentieth century, however, lawmakers from both parties began to routinely refer to Congress's *patriotic obligation to be deferential to the president as commander in chief* about a range of issues in foreign, military, and even domestic policy. They justified that deference by rhetorically conflating the president as commander in chief with the nation and the flag, which in turn led to conflating their support for his position with patriotism. They also begin to associate the president with military expertise, using language that they had not used even when prior presidents had significant personal military service records.

Scholars note that the president's relationship to the public began to undergo an important transformation at the turn of the twentieth century.[8] Presidents' relationships with their political parties changed over time, as did the norms that had restricted earlier presidents from actively running for office and speaking to the public.[9] Historians and political scientists have long noted that Theodore Roosevelt and Woodrow Wilson changed the presidency in a number of ways. They began to make more domestic policy proposals, to publicly advocate for their proposals, and to claim the right to speak to and on behalf of the public.[10] Around the same time, they began to connect the public's support for them personally to their authority to persuade Congress and their authority to act unilaterally.[11] Finally, they began to reach out to a newly nationalizing press, which in turn fed on the personalized narrative about public affairs that presidents could provide.[12]

The growth of presidential speechmaking at the turn of the twentieth century was also related to a growing movement towards more active self-promotion in presidential campaigns. In the nineteenth century, presidents abided by antidemagogic norms that prevented them from making public appeals for votes or support. After nearly a century of "standing" rather than "running" for office, presidents beginning in the late 1800s began to inch their way into active campaigns for the presidency.[13] Both McKinley's "front porch" campaign of 1896 and his rival William Jennings Bryan's extensive, losing campaign against him accelerated changes to those norms. These more direct public appeals made it easier for presidents like Roosevelt to claim a "mandate" to govern.[14] John Dearborn shows that by the second decade of the twentieth century, the idea that the president was elected to represent the whole country, whereas members of Congress were only parochial representatives of their own communities, had gained widespread traction in and outside of government.[15]

The president's role as chief executive was also changing. His main job in prior decades had been handing out party patronage in the form of federal jobs. Beginning in the 1880s, civil service reforms placed the president atop a professionalizing bureaucracy that helped to service and regulate the nationalized economy.[16] The army also became more professionalized at this time.[17] All of these reforms came during a wave of institutionalization of expertise that also encompassed professions like medicine and law. Presidents in this time period had more experience working in the bureaucracy in their early careers and perhaps were able to make claims that Congress owed deference to the expertise of the bureaucracy that prior presidents would not have made.[18] The rise in congressional deference to the "expertise" of the executive branch, and the army, conflated with the president as commander in chief, is plausibly related to these other institutional developments.[19] Interestingly, such deference had not accompanied rhetoric about presidents like Washington, Taylor, or Grant, who had actually been successful military generals. Later in the twentieth century, presidents also gained material war powers resources (like executive staff, or a large standing army and navy) that could facilitate their exercise of expanded constitutional authority.

In addition to these changes in the institutional presidency, historians also note changes in the public's relationship to the nation and the rise of nationalism. Scholars in various fields have delineated the prevalence of patriotic and militaristic nationalism in public discourse between 1876 and 1900.[20] Though many groups contested the nature of patriotism during this time, national symbolism itself became widespread. The Pledge of Allegiance, for example, was written in 1892. In the 1890s flags became ubiquitous in schools, political campaigns, and commercial advertising.[21] Conflation of patriotism and militarism also appeared in local state legislatures and news sources at the time of the Spanish-American War.[22] For example, the day after Congress declared the war, the New York state legislature "instructed the state superintendent of public instruction to prepare a program providing for a salute to the flag at the opening of each day of school."[23]

Among the public, those patriotic and nationalistic impulses were connected to fallen soldiers and veterans. In the late 1800s prominent veterans' groups like the Grand Army of the Republic conflated patriotism with military service as a strategy to achieve pensions and other policy benefits; in doing so, they helped to connect the nation, the military, and the flag in the national discourse. In the end, this rhetoric helped to erase slavery as a cause of the Civil War and to bring the white "North and South together through memory."[24] Members of Congress, however, may have played an important role in connecting those diverse patriotic and nationalistic impulses to the powers of the president as military commander in chief.

Scholarship about the powers of the president also began to change in this period. Members of Congress began to refer to new books when they argued on the floor about the commander in chief's role. New textbooks, such as John Norton Pomeroy's 1883 constitutional text, described the president's war powers in more expansive terms than earlier ones had and were cited by members of Congress as they discussed the commander in chief clause.[25] Moreover, Admiral Alfred Thayer Mahan, president of the Naval War College in the 1890s, wrote two influential books arguing for the use of naval power as a tool of national defense and economic expansion, which members of Congress cited as they argued for a larger and more professional military.[26] References to these books do not dominate members' arguments, but they do represent a changing body of general knowledge and appear as references in support of broader authority for the commander in chief.

Arguments in favor of a nationalist conception of the presidency also supported the new imperialism that took hold in American foreign policy in the late nineteenth and early twentieth centuries.[27] Driven in part by economic uncertainty, a perceived need for markets, rhetoric about the decline of the internal frontier and some policymakers' self-conscious imperial aspirations, the United States slowly began to build a navy and to construct foreign policy goals around property rights and trade interests abroad. Ideas crafted by historians like Frederick Jackson Turner helped to justify an outwardly expanding empire as a capitalist solution to domestic economic problems.[28] There was a conscious connection among elites between these ideas, social Darwinism, and conceptions of white racial superiority.[29] In line with these theories, presidents at this time began using the military more often to "protect Americans and American interests abroad."[30]

In sum, the turn of the century was a time when several aspects of the public's conception of national identity, its relationship to the military, and the role of the presidency were all in flux. It is perhaps unsurprising, then, that we see those changes reflected in how members of Congress talked about the president's role in war powers. Around 1898 new arguments for presidential representation become routine in congressional rhetoric about the commander in chief clause. A confluence of events—institutional changes that made the president more prominent and gave him more resources, growing elite foreign policy interests in "opening markets" abroad, symbolic changes in political discourse that emphasized white national unity under one flag—were reflected in a new constitutional script that seemed to disrupt Congress's confidence in its own war powers.[31] Beginning during McKinley's administration, we see in members' talk about the commander in chief at least some acceptance of that individual as a special representative of the people. Note the reference to the president's election in Senator Pettus's exhortation to support McKinley during the Spanish-American War:

> We ought to support the Army and the Navy, and the President, who is the Commander in Chief. He is our Commander in Chief. And who is he? He is a loyal citizen of the United States, *elected to the highest office* in the power of the people to confer, and he is no doubt acting patriotically, so far as he is allowed by his unconstitutional advisers, and, I believe, in a great degree better.[32] (Italics mine.)

McKinley returned the compliment when he thanked the Congress for their patriotism in funding the war, although he does not seem to have led a charge to conflate himself with the flag.[33]

Such language seems to replace Congress's confidence in its own status as the best representative of the people of the United States. During the Mexican War, members of both parties had articulated the sentiment that "the people of the United States have placed [the war] power in their own representatives, in the Congress of the United States, simply providing that the President shall be Commander-in-Chief of the Army."[34] In the mid-nineteenth century, members of Congress defined the commander in chief as one who executes the will of the people embodied in *Congress's* dictates regarding the use of force. It was the legislature's actions that best represented the nation. By the early twentieth century, however, senators and congressmen began to commonly articulate the argument that the president was the primary representative of the nation, both through his relationship to the patriotic soldiers under his command and because of his status as the only nationally elected official. With that status, it became logical to defer to his judgment about war rather than their own.

SPECIALIZED DEFERENCE PRIOR TO 1898

Throughout this book we have been considering specific types of authority (to command, to defend US territory) that members of Congress attributed to the president via the commander in chief clause. Most of the time, when members of Congress talked about the commander in chief clause before World War I, they referred to one of these specific authorities. In this chapter, we examine a separate class of references to the commander in chief clause, in which members of Congress debated whether they owed the president *deference* because of his role as commander in chief. In this section, I describe the limited ways that members argued for congressional deference to the commander in chief in the nineteenth century. In the next section, I will describe how that changed after 1898.

Examining congressional language over time shows that prior to 1898, even members of Congress in the president's party who argued for broad presidential power tended *not* to argue that Congress owed deference or allegiance to the commander in chief. When they did make arguments that Congress should defer to the president, such arguments fell into three specific categories. First, as we have seen in other chapters, some members of Congress argued that a *specific* type of commander in chief authority (such as the authority to discipline officers) should be construed broadly in a particular situation. Second, members of Congress mentioned congressional deference as they made arguments that the president was specifically entitled to request military appropriations from Congress. Third, they mentioned congressional deference in situations where they considered whether the president was specifically entitled to keep some specific types of military secrets from Congress. The very rare claims for broader, generalized congressional deference were greeted with skepticism across party lines. After 1898, however, members of Congress across party lines argued that the president, due to his expertise, or his public mandate, or his identity as representative of the nation was owed congressional loyalty, allegiance, and favor. This deference was afforded presidents in both parties who took major military actions like supporting Panamanian secession and bombarding and invading Mexico. It was a striking change.

During the nineteenth century, there were a few very particular types of conversations in which members of Congress across party lines argued that they should defer to the judgment of the commander in chief. Like their other conversations about the commander in chief clause, the scope of presidential discretion was defined narrowly and members relied at least in part on the constitutional script that defined the commander in chief's authority as similar to any other "general." The pervasive narrative that the president was akin to a "general" implied particular answers to questions about congressional deference. Namely, the general consensus was that it was the president's responsibility to be deferential to Congress, with very few, widely agreed upon exceptions—battlefield tactics, superiority over subordinate officers, a right to give orders to those officers, etc. This model, again informed by the model of George Washington as commander in chief, also implied that presidents had a right to request funds for the military, and that Congress really ought to listen to those requests, but not that Congress had any special obligation to grant requested funds. Washington's experience also set a tenuous precedent that Congress ought to let the president keep some military secrets, though Congress had a right to demand most types of information related to the military.[35]

Limited Deference before 1898: Patriotism and Deference during the Mexican War

Thus, during the nineteenth century, it was extremely rare for members of Congress to argue that the commander in chief had an exalted status that demanded patriotic deference from members of Congress. This tracks with what historians have seen when looking at other sources. As noted by Cecilia O'Leary, "the chauvinist variety of patriotism—associated with 'my country, right or wrong'" not widespread among the public prior to World War I.[36] In the congressional record, the major exceptions were remarks made by a handful of partisan supporters of President Polk during the Mexican War.

Polk explicitly promoted such reasoning. Facing questions about his actions to provoke war with Mexico, the president accused his critics of lacking patriotism and helping the Mexican cause. In his Second Annual Message in December 1846, Polk complained that critics of the war were unpatriotically giving "aid and comfort" to the Mexican enemy:

> The war has been represented as unjust and unnecessary and as one of aggression
> on our part upon a weak and injured enemy. Such erroneous views, though
> entertained by but few, have been widely and extensively circulated, not only
> at home, but have been spread throughout Mexico and the whole world. A
> more effectual means could not have been devised to encourage the enemy and
> protract the war than to advocate and adhere to their cause, and thus give them
> "aid and comfort." *It is a source of national pride and exultation that the great
> body of our people* have thrown no such obstacles in the way of the Government
> in prosecuting the war successfully, but *have shown themselves to be eminently*

patriotic and ready to vindicate their country's honor and interests at any sacrifice.[37]
[Italics mine.]

Polk specifically implied that members of Congress who criticized him were aiding the enemy and that members of Congress who supported him were patriotic. A handful of Polk's fellow Democrats in Congress echoed his language. Rep. John Smith Chipman said that anyone who argued that "the Commander-in-Chief of the military and naval forces of the country, is an aggressor" is "a man as much a traitor at heart as that man who commits an overt act of treason."[38] William Brown said that "the Democratic party voted for the war-helped to place on the head of the President the burden and responsibility of its prosecution; they have in good faith, in word and deed, stood by, and cheered on the commander-in-chief of the armies and navy of the country in the conflict." The Whigs, he implied, had not.

The rhetoric conflating support for Polk with support for the war, and support for both with patriotism itself, was inflammatory enough that many Whigs remarked upon it.[39] Most Whigs, however, weren't cowed by such accusations. They laughed off the accusations that they were unpatriotic and continued to attack Polk. One noted, in contrast, that "it is base treason to our institutions to resign our right of thought and speech."[40] Sen. Thomas Corwin excoriated Polk for suggesting that by criticizing his illegal initiation of the war, he was "giving aid and comfort to his enemy." Referring to Polk's Message, Corwin said he was speaking for the people, while the president (sarcastically referred to as his "master") was illegally waging war for himself:

> I find it written in this message that this war was not sought nor forced upon Mexico by the people of the United States. I shall make no question of history or the truth of history with my master, the commander-in-chief, upon that particular proposition. On the contrary, I could verify every word that he thus utters. Sir, I know that the people of the United States neither sought nor forced Mexico into this war, and yet I know that the President of the United States, with the command of your standing army, did seek that war, and that he forced war upon Mexico.[41]

Erastus Culver (Whig-NY) argued that Polk's words were plainly autocratic and demanded that his colleagues consider the implications of the president's argument. He imagined another scenario by which Polk could have illegally provoked a war and asked if criticism would be just as "unpatriotic":

Suppose Mr. Polk had desired to promote a marriage between some branch of his
family and that of the Governor of Canada. The proffered nuptials are declined.
Mr. Polk is offended; deems himself insulted; and, as commander-in-chief of the
army, he orders six regiments of infantry to the city of Toronto, in Upper Canada;
they invest it, plant their cannon; cut off the supplies; they are ordered off by
Canadian authorities; they refuse; a fight ensues; war follows; Congress recognises
[*sic*] it. Would that war on our side be just or unjust? If unjust, would the people
be-guilty of treason, of "giving aid and comfort," if they "represented it unjust
and unnecessary?" Out upon such an autocratic doctrine from the pen of the
Chief Magistrate. If every sentiment or avowal which technically can "give aid and
comfort to the enemy" is treason, moral or political, then, sir, I arraign James K.
Polk as guilty of that crime.

Once the conflict started, there was sufficient support in Congress for the
Mexican War to be waged to its conclusion. Polk certainly tried to invoke patriotic support for himself in his role as commander in chief, and such claims
were echoed by a few of his own partisans. However, his party also lost thirty
seats and control of the House in the fall of 1846. In 1848 the Whig-controlled
House passed an amendment that censured Polk for illegally starting the war.
Members of the opposition party were not swept up in his suggestion that to
support his proposals was to support the flag itself.

Limited Deference before 1898: Patriotism and Lincoln during the Civil War

Unlike the Democrats during Polk's presidency, Republican members of Congress only rarely invoked deferential patriotic language when referring to Lincoln as commander in chief.[42] Republicans certainly supported broad interpretations of his specific authorities, as described in other chapters, but they
did not routinely argue that as commander in chief, Lincoln deserved patriotic
loyalty or blanket congressional deference. They did, however, occasionally
speak about "cooperating" with the commander in chief.[43]

During Reconstruction, some Republicans expressed faith that the commander in chief deserved the benefit of the doubt because his intentions were
good. Sen. James Doolittle, for example, argued that Lincoln's actions to appoint military governors were not "a military usurpation" but rather "an attempt on the part of the President to lay down his military power; and . . .

the President is endeavoring in good faith to do it."[44] His fellow Republican, Sen. William Fessenden, said he would have preferred a longer military reconstruction, "to have kept all those States under his own power as Commander-in-Chief of the Army of the United States," but though he disagreed with the decision, "I had no disposition to complain, for I believe he acted with good motives and good intentions."[45] Again, this language demonstrates respect for the president as commander in chief but does not conflate fealty to his title with patriotism.

THE RISE IN GENERALIZED DEFERENCE AND NATIONALIST LANGUAGE AFTER 1898

At the turn of the twentieth century, as already indicated, this status quo changed. Figure 4.1 shows the number of patriotic or nationalistic words members used in speeches discussing the commander in chief clause (per year) both before 1898 and afterward. It shows that while Congress occasionally used patriotic language to talk about the commander in chief in the nineteenth century, it was only after the turn of the twentieth century that they frequently used that language in order to argue for congressional deference to the president.[46]

In congressional debates spanning the century between 1789 and 1898, members used the word "patriot" in connection with the "commander in chief" fewer than two dozen times. They made the connection more often just in the twenty years between 1898 and 1917. Between the Founding of the United States and 1898, they talked about the commander in chief along with the flag fewer than ten times. After 1898 they used it more than twice as many times in just two decades. The word "duty" was used often prior to 1898, but on an annual basis, it was used far more frequently after that year than before it.

In addition to increasing frequency, there were also dramatic changes in the ways they used that language. In the nineteenth century, when members of Congress used the word "patriot" in the same paragraph as "commander in chief," they tended to say that soldiers and sailors in his service were patriots.[47] When they occasionally referred to the president as a patriot, they did so in a complimentary, not deferential way. For example, consider the following from the Civil War:

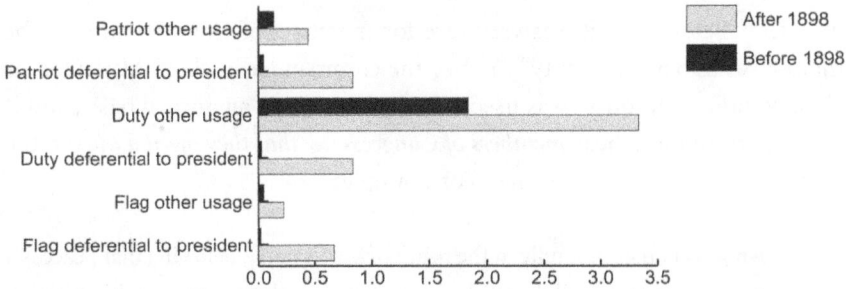

Figure 4.1

> Our President may act, our Commander-in-Chief, within his province, and the officers under him in command may act, and I believe are called upon to act, by every consideration of humanity and of patriotism.[48]

That reference to Lincoln (and battlefield emancipation) implies that Lincoln's and other officers' actions are patriotic, but the remark is not obsequious. After 1898 members of Congress began to argue that *because* the president was a patriot, therefore Congress needed to do what he said. As in the following:

> How many men shall constitute the Army is a matter to be left to the discretion of the President. Who shall object to the exercise of that discretion? Does anyone, in view of his record, distrust the judgment or the patriotism of our President?[49]

Or

> He is, under the Constitution, the Commander in Chief of the Army and Navy. He knows the diplomatic situation. He knows the demands which should be promptly met, and I believe he is prompted by patriotism and the highest and best motives and the Senate of the United States should comply with his recommendation.[50]

Similarly, at the turn of the century, members of Congress substantially changed the way they used the word "duty." In both centuries, duty was a term frequently used when talking about the commander in chief. Mostly, in the nineteenth century, it was used to describe the *president's duty* to enforce the laws or to win a war, to supervise servicemen and officers under his command, or other specific functions.[51] It was also used to describe soldiers' duty to the commander in chief and *Congress's duty* to pass laws directing the commander in chief.[52] Before 1898 it was very rare for members of Congress to describe themselves as having a "duty" to obey the commander in chief. After 1898, as already indicated, "duty" was used far more often, on an annual basis, and it became common to hear *members of Congress say that they owed a duty* to the president as commander in chief. For example:

> Believing, as I do, profoundly in the peace of our country, believing that peace is for the best interests of all the world, I have felt it my duty to present this question to the Senate, and I feel it *my duty* to vote to sustain the President of the United States as Commander in Chief of the Navy in his appeal to Congress to give four battle ships instead of two as "a measure of peace and not of war."[53] (Italics mine.)

Similarly, before the Spanish-American War, there were only seven speeches that connected the commander in chief to the "flag." After 1898 members of Congress began to more commonly refer to the commander in chief's relationship to "the flag" as a reason for Congress to defer to the president's judgement. For example:

> I will say that there is no Senator on this floor who will go further than I to uphold and sustain the President of the United States, the Commander in Chief of our Army and Navy, in this present difficulty. There is no Senator who has more love for the American flag than I have.[54]

There had always been certainly partisan, and at times bipartisan, support for presidential actions during wartime. But the conflation of the president, the military, and the nation emerged around the time of the Spanish-American War. The year 1900 gives us the first deferential conflation of the commander in chief and military glory on the floor of the Congress.[55] Members of the president's party, to be sure, used that language more than their opponents, at least at first. But the usage soon spread to both parties and a variety of issues.

RALLYING AROUND THE FLAG

After 1898: The Rise of Generalized Deference

At the start of the Spanish-American War, Americans felt good about the justice of their cause as they understood it (at least initially helping to free

Cuba from imperial Spain and to retaliate for the sinking of the USS *Maine*), and many speeches about the war were infused with optimistic nationalism.[56] Within this context, Republicans in Congress began fusing nationalist and patriotic rhetoric onto support for the president as commander in chief. The Republican party had also moved considerably to court veterans in the previous decade, which may have affected their adoption of patriotic rhetoric.[57] Not all criticism of the war by the opposition party Democrats, especially of the war in the Philippines, was muted by Republican efforts to conflate the commander in chief and the flag. However, Republicans did try to use the flag to silence dissent.

For example, Republican representative Marlin Olmsted complained that "day after day we hear echoing through these Halls charges against the Army, . . . against the President as Commander in Chief of the Army . . . all in the hope of destroying the efficiency of the Army."[58] From the same party, Rep. Henry Spooner argued that to criticize the president, the commander in chief, "is an ugly and unfit prelude to the roar of cannon, the rattle of musketry, the roll of war drums, and the groans of the wounded and dying."[59]

For his part, Republican congressman George Foss said that "the American[s] . . . stand a solid phalanx behind their President to sustain him in this trying hour. . . . the American people have such an abiding confidence in the character, the statesmanship, and the patriotism of William McKinley, Commander in Chief of both Army and Navy."[60] His fellow Republican representative Romulus Linney noted that destroying the Spanish fleet was "itself enough to shed glory upon the Commander in Chief of the armies of these United States."[61] He brushed aside questions about the Philippines and Puerto Rico, saying that "in my humble judgment it ought not to be discussed. When the earth is drinking the warm blood of American heroes . . . that which is fit to be done, is to stand by the flag of our country and by the Commander in Chief of the American Army—our President." The *Congressional Record* notes that his remarks were followed by applause.[62]

Members of other parties were not as vociferous in their rhetoric but did seem to be caught up in the patriotic logic. Silver party senator William Stewart argued that Congress should not blindly accept the president's recommendations, saying, "I deny that it is the duty of Congress to authorize such an outrage because the President is Commander in Chief of the Army and Navy."[63] Even so, he conceded that there was something about the commander in chief's role as military commander that demanded a certain amount of deference. He said he would support the president's actions on the battlefield, but not his policy recommendations. Stewart continued,

> when his duties are prescribed and he is executing them in his capacity as President or in his capacity as Commander in Chief, he is my President. I would follow him, but I will not follow him in dictating laws inconsistent with honor and justice, inconsistent with patriotism, inconsistent with right, inconsistent with anything that is sacred to liberty and to man. I will not follow him there.[64]

Stewart received a mild rebuke from Democratic senator Arthur Gorman, who agreed with Republicans that criticism of the president was inappropriate: "In this hour when we ought to have calm deliberation, our Commander in Chief has been taunted and criticized . . . I regard denunciation of him at this time, when I believe we are on the verge of war, as injudicious and unwise."[65]

Throughout the war, Democrats were predictably less effusive in their praise of the president than Republicans. Democrat Thomas Ball chafed at the Republicans' rhetoric and noted the similarities between some Republican criticism of Democrats' opposition to the Philippine expansion of the war and the accusations made against Whigs during the Mexican War. He said, "How history repeats itself. In many respects the situation then was not unlike the situation now, so far as the men are concerned who venture to criticise [*sic*] the war begun and carried on by this Administration without constitutional right or authority."[66]

Nevertheless Democrats adopted a patriotic frame when describing their support for military appropriations and other aspects of the war and the occupation of the Philippines. For example, Rep. Rudolph Kelberg argued that while Congress should engage in "a sober and deliberate discussion," "we are now ready and willing to uphold the Executive as Commander in Chief of the Army and Navy of the United States and to give him all the forces necessary to prosecute this war successfully and vigorously."[67] Similarly, from the same side of the aisle, Rep. Joseph Crowley said that he was "willing to give the Commander in Chief of the Army every man necessary to put down a rebellion" in the Philippines.[68]

*After 1898: Deference on Military Appropriations and a Large
Standing Army*

As Congress adopted this new constitutional script, it also took actions that
helped construct the institutions of the modern constitutional order for war
powers. At this time, and with support from the "representative of the nation'"
script, the Congress greatly expanded the size of the standing army. Some scholars argue that this process fundamentally changed the balance of war powers
in American history, granting to the president consistent ability to put the
armed forces into harm's way without express congressional authorization.[69]

As Congress expanded the army, members debated the commander in
chief's changing role as the head of that army. That creating a large standing army (or more precisely, a hundred-thousand-man limit to the size of the
army, with the actual size to be determined at presidential discretion) was a
departure from prior practice did not go unnoticed in Congress. But supporters of the measure infused their arguments with nationalist and patriotic references to the president as commander in chief. They told their colleagues that
they needed to defer to him via a traditionally congressional function (appropriations) in a way that could predictably expand the president's authority
over war and peace.

Republicans, who favored granting discretion over the size of the army to
the Republican president William McKinley, argued that he could be "safely
trusted" with such discretion.[70] They lauded the "discreet, courageous, and patriotic" president who prosecuted the war with "an earnestness of purpose, a
vigor, and a success which were worthy of the high office that he holds as Commander in Chief of the Army and Navy of the United States."[71] They accused
Democrats of "espousing the case" of the enemy and trying to obtain "cheap
party advantage by an assault on our troops 10,000 miles across their water"
and upon "their Commander in Chief at the White House."[72] They claimed
Democrats wanted to leave the "Commander in Chief of our Army and Navy
alone in the field without a sufficient army."[73] On the question of the "safety"
of a large standing army, Republican representative Romulus Linney argued
that Americans "need not fear the presence of a reasonably large standing
army" because

> President McKinley does not stand at the head of the Army as do the despots of
> Europe. He does stand there as Commander in Chief under our laws and under

our Constitution. He stands there not as a despot, but as a great citizen of the Republic, conservative in character, and chosen by his country-men; and by reason of his high office and the selection of his people he holds ex officio the position of Commander in Chief of the armies of the United States. Under the Constitution he has duties to perform. He owes allegiance to the people; is bound by the solemnity of his oath to every principle embodied in the Constitution; is under the lynx-eyed control of the House of Representatives and of the Senate, the former with the power under the Constitution to prepare and present articles of impeachment and the latter to try them.[74]

Democrats, for their part, were clearly on the defensive as they tried to stand up for the founders' preference against a large standing army. They said that they would happily authorize any number but preferred not to authorize him to choose it. One critic argued that "we have no desire, no disposition, no intention whatever, to withhold from the President, as Commander in Chief of the Army and Navy of the United States, any amount of money or any number of soldiers necessary for all possible contingencies in the future."[75] Another echoed that there was no need for a large standing army "when we say to you that we will give you all the men that the Commander in Chief of the Army may think necessary to suppress the rebellion in the Philippine Islands or to maintain peace in Cuba and Porto Rico, and that when those cases shall have been adjusted the Army must resume its normal condition."[76] What is especially notable in Democrats' response is that even their policy objections are framed around enormous deference to the president, conceding to the political power of the conflation of the military power of the nation and the president as commander in chief. Despite the Democrats' objections, the bill, unsurprisingly, passed the Republican-dominated Congress.

THE PATRIOTIC COMMANDER IN CHIEF AND
THE INITIATION OF MILITARY FORCE

Prior to the year 1900, representatives in both parties subscribed to a rigid distinction between offensive and defensive force. When they spoke about the authority conferred by the commander in chief clause of the constitution, members of both parties agreed that the commander in chief clause granted limited authority to use defensive force and that offensive force required congressional authorization. When presidents used force that seemed to cross a line between offense and defense, members who supported questionable actions were careful to define them in terms of prior congressional authorization and laws. There was bipartisan agreement that only Congress could authorize the initiation of offensive force. After 1900, those lines were not as clear, and members of Congress across party lines did not insist on vigorously (at least rhetorically) policing the boundaries of the commander in chief's authority. The "president as representative" constitutional script did not reference defense and offense. Instead it implied that what was important was that the people like the president's action. So when presidents took plausibly offensive actions in the early twentieth century, members of Congress did not debate whether they were offensive or defensive; instead, they argued that the criterion for legitimacy was that they were *popular*.

Panama

Throughout the nineteenth century, developers and speculators in the United States and abroad looked for routes across Central America to shorten the distance between the Atlantic and Pacific Oceans. In the late 1880s, the country of Colombia had negotiated with a French company to build a canal across the Panamanian isthmus. When the project fell apart, President Theodore Roosevelt negotiated a treaty with Colombia to give the US government the rights to build the canal and control the land surrounding it. The Colombian senate, however, rejected the treaty in August of 1903. On November 3, 1903, proponents of building the canal organized a revolt to separate Panama from Colombia.

Without congressional authorization, Roosevelt immediately sent the navy to protect the Panamanian revolutionaries. Roosevelt recognized the independence of Panama on November 6 and negotiated a new treaty within two weeks, which was quickly ratified by the new government of Panama and submitted to the US Senate at the end of 1903. Ostensibly, by using the navy to back up the revolutionaries, the president was enforcing a fifty-year-old treaty guaranteeing peaceful access to the isthmus. The action was later deemed illegitimate and the United States paid reparations to Colombia in 1922.

As Congress began debate on the treaty, members did not often refer to either the commander in chief clause or the legitimacy of Roosevelt's use of his commander in chief authority. In the few speeches that did reference that source of constitutional authority, the president's supporters connected his role as commander in chief to public opinion. For example, Republican senator Platt argued that because the action was popular, it would be inappropriate for Congress to try to reverse it and order the president to help Colombia get its isthmus back.

> I do not think [the American people] would be satisfied that the Congress of the United States, issuing its directions to the Commander in Chief of the Army and Navy, should require the withdrawal of those vessels from those waters. . . . Would [the Senator] say . . . that we, the United States, prevented Colombia from putting down its revolution, that we should right that wrong, or so-called wrong, by going there and helping Colombia to recover the Republic of Panama?

Partisan opponents still relied on traditional arguments about the commander in chief's limited authority to oppose the treaty. Sen. John Morgan, Democrat of Alabama, criticized the treaty with Panama and Roosevelt's use of the military to secure it.[77] He said that the treaty unlawfully made

> the Government a party to a war with Colombia that is already waged by the order of the President as Commander in Chief of the Army and Navy. It is, moreover, the distinct purpose of the President in making this treaty to gain the support of two-thirds of the Senate for the ratification of his illegal acts already committed, and to obtain a declaration of war against Colombia, for which he is unwilling to ask Congress.[78]

Morgan argued that it was illegitimate for the commander in chief to initiate hostilities in order to create conditions Congress would have to agree to. That criticism notwithstanding, two-thirds of the Senate approved the treaty on February 23, 1904.

Roosevelt's action on Panama fell into a category of the use of force that members of Congress might have had a hard time categorizing, even if they had been trying to apply the standard that the president's authority to use force was only defensive. Roosevelt offered the fig leaf of treaty enforcement as legal authority. But Platt's combined references to the commander in chief clause, congressional deference, and public opinion point to a different story about when and how Congress should step up to evaluate and regulate presidential uses of force.

Nicaragua

From 1909 to 1912, Nicaragua was engaged in a civil war, and the United States government repeatedly intervened in order to support American business interests in that country. Marines landed and engaged in hostilities in 1909, 1910, and 1912. In August 1912 Congress finally debated whether the commander in chief could send the navy into another country's waters. When the question was raised, Republicans defended President Taft, and the only constitutional criticism was offered by a Democrat.

Specifically, Democrat Augustus Bacon proposed an amendment that prohibited the use of funds for the military in any deployment into foreign lands that was not explicitly and previously authorized by Congress.[79] In a long speech describing the dangers of congressional acquiescence to the unilateral deployment of military personnel into other countries, he said,

> I deny the assertion of the Senator that the great office of the Commander in Chief of the Army of the United States clothes him with any power except in cases of emergency. I speak of sending armed forces into a foreign country without the authority of Congress. It is not necessary that there should be a law prohibiting it. It is necessary that there should be a law authorizing it, for the Constitution of the United States prohibits it when it denies to the President of the United States the power to make war.[80]

But Republicans disagreed, arguing that the president had discretionary authority to protect Americans and that, as commander in chief, he had the sympathies of the public on his side. Republican senator Elihu Root, a Roosevelt ally, argued that Congress *could* restrict the deployment of troops into foreign countries, but if it did so, the public might turn on Congress for putting American lives abroad in danger. In the absence of such congressional restriction, as long as he was not "making war," the commander in chief could deploy troops into foreign lands to protect the interests of Americans in other countries. In response to accusations that the president lacked independent authority to send troops abroad, Root invoked the commander in chief's *duty* to assertively promote his interpretation of American national security interests, an argument that would become dominant in the twentieth century. He said:

In my judgment, there is no law which forbids the President to send troops of the United States out of this country into any country where he considers it to be his duty as Commander in Chief of the Army to send them, unless it be for the purpose of making war, which, of course, he cannot do. Doubtless Congress could by law forbid the troops being sent out of the country; doubtless Congress has not done it; and I apprehend that any Congress that undertook to do it would find that there would be a general protest from the people of the United States against depriving the Commander in Chief of the Army of the power to protect our citizens under those circumstances which exist widely throughout the world in countries whose governments have not the power to maintain order within their jurisdiction.[81]

Bacon, the Democrat, argued that intervening between parties in a civil war in Nicaragua, China, or anywhere else constituted a use of force that needed to be authorized by Congress. Root, the Republican, argued that such interventions did not constitute making war but was merely foreign policy. The amendment was defeated without recorded vote in the Senate (which had a 52 to 44 Republican majority at the time), implying congressional consent to President Taft's interventions.[82]

The Tampico Incident and the Bombardment of Veracruz

During unrest in Mexico in April 1914, US admiral Henry Mayo stationed a number of navy warships off the coast of Tampico, to protect the US citizens who lived there. One of the ships sent a whaleboat to the city to fetch supplies, at which time the sailors were arrested, to be subsequently released after a few hours. As reported by President Wilson to Congress,

the release was followed by apologies from the commander and later by an expression of regret by Gen. Huerta himself. . . . Admiral Mayo regarded the arrest as so serious an affront that he was not satisfied with the apologies offered, but demanded that the flag of the United States be saluted with special ceremony by the commander of the port.[83]

Wilson supported Mayo's insistence on a twenty-one-gun salute and went to Congress to ask for support for military action in retaliation for the arrests. Before Congress ratified its approval for the use of force to solicit an apology,

Wilson ordered the navy to bombard a different city, Veracruz. His aim in the bombardment was to keep a shipment of arms from reaching the Huerta government in Mexico, of whom Wilson disapproved. Congress's discussions and authorization of force, however, focused on the original incident two hundred miles away in Tampico.

Congress was mostly swept up in bipartisan nationalistic pride as members made speeches supporting taking military action against the forces in Tampico that had offended American sailors. However, in the course of debating the authorization to use force, several legislators referred to the commander in chief's authority to start a war. Rather than vehemently declaring Congress's right to authorize the action, even Wilson's opponents argued that the commander in chief clause enabled him to act without prior congressional authority.

Progressive representative Henry Temple of Pennsylvania made an argument that would seem familiar today. Temple argued that the retaliation against Mexico was not an act of war, and as such, the president did not need permission from Congress to take it. He said,

> If we do not intend war—and I, for one, do not want war—this resolution is
> unnecessary. The President is Commander in Chief of the Army and Navy. He has
> all military powers short of the power to declare war, and the Congress will hardly
> delegate to him that authority. It is Congress, and only Congress, that can declare
> war. Why ask Congress to share the responsibilities of the Executive?[84]

Wilson and the Democrats applied nationalist pressure to members of both parties to support the resolution on patriotic grounds. For example, Senator James Reed, Democrat, said

> Let us at least certify . . . that the Congress of the United States is with the
> Commander in Chief of the Army and Navy of the United States; that it is
> not splitting hairs; that it is not caviling about the form of sentences or the
> construction of preambles, but that as one man, with one heart, one soul, and one
> purpose, the American people stand with President Wilson in his demand that
> the flag of the Republic shall be respected in Mexico as it is by the other nations
> of the earth.[85]

Democrats generally defined their own commander in chief's power in extremely broad terms. Democratic senator Hernando Money argued that "there are emergencies that invest men with extraordinary power, and it is not unconstitutional that they should so act, because the grant goes with them to do what is necessary to be done."[86] Rep. James Heflin invoked national pride, and received applause, when he argued that "the Commander in Chief of our Army and Navy has found conditions serious enough to send battleships to Mexican waters, it is the duty of every Member of Congress and of every patriotic American citizen to stand faithfully by him as he goes to uphold the dignity and the honor of this, the greatest Government on the globe."[87]

Republican senator George Norris noted and objected to the nationalist pressure Wilson put on the Congress, but even he defined Congress's role as secondary to presidential initiative. He asked,

> What would you think of a general—and the President is the Commander in Chief of the Army and the Navy—if, on the eve of battle, he called his subordinates about him in council of war and said, "I want to advise with you as to what we shall do on the morrow; I want your advice and cooperation; but I will tell you in advance what advice I want you to give me; and if you do not give the advice that I want, then you are discourteous to me; you are not treating me with respect?" So, taking the President at his word, we ought to be allowed, if we are taken into consideration at all, to give our honest judgment without being accused of doing anything that is discourteous, and without being accused of trying to get some party advantage.[88]

Republican senator Henry Cabot Lodge, who had been a robust defender of presidential unilateralism when Roosevelt was president, offered a tepid argument that the new commander in chief (a Democrat) did not have authority to proceed with a retaliation or invasion on his own.

> I am aware that the President, as he said in his message, could have gone on and taken more steps than he has taken under his constitutional authority as Executive and as Commander in Chief of the Army and Navy of the United States. But he has come to us. He has come to the body which, in foreign relations, exercises the power of declaring war. I think that he was right to do so. With Congress in session I think it would have been unwise for him to have proceeded further without the action of the Houses. I am sure that he would not desire to expose himself to the words of indictment uttered by Webster when he said, "No one declared the Mexican War; Mr. Polk made it."[89]

Lodge thought it would have been "unwise" but not "illegal" for the president to use force without congressional approval. Norris and Lodge were among the few who raised questions about the scope of the commander in chief's authority or the deference Congress should show to it. Many more members of the Republican party expressed a willingness to put aside their concerns about the resolution itself and support the (Democratic) commander in chief. For example, Republican John Langley said, "This resolution is not in the form that I would like to have it, and I reserve the right to vote for amendments to perfect it; but upon the main proposition, Mr. Speaker, I feel it my patriotic duty, under my oath of office, to follow the Commander in Chief of our Army and Navy and to give him the support he says he needs to preserve the honor of our flag."[90] Republican senator William Bradley noted his support for the president's actions in Mexico but argued that simply sending off a twenty-one-gun salute was not enough, and further actions against Mexico were necessary. In those remarks he said, "There is no Senator on this floor who will go further than I to uphold and sustain the President of the United States, the Commander in Chief of our Army and Navy, in this present difficulty. There is no Senator who has more love for the American flag than I have."[91] Republican Melville Kelly noted that "there is but one feeling and that a desire to stand behind him, as he represents the Nation and the flag. Now that the die is cast, Pennsylvania stands at attention and asks the desire of the Commander in Chief of the Army and Navy of the United States."[92]

Republican John Rogers agreed that Wilson might very well have the power to retaliate against Mexico without additional authority but also pointed out that if he needed Congress's permission, Congress had a duty to give it to him.

> He wants to be able to say to the world that, although in fact he probably has
> the right under the Constitution—by virtue of the clause which makes him
> Commander in Chief of the Army and Navy—yet in a potentially great question
> of this kind he also has every shadow of justification and of authority with which
> the Congress can clothe him. Can we, as patriotic men, rightfully or properly
> refuse him this thing which he has just come in person to ask us to give him?[93]

Republican representative Charles A. Lindburgh seemed a little more ambivalent but conceded the right of the president to dispatch the ships. At the same time, he invoked the president's electoral mandate as a justification for his actions:

According to the policy of the President, there is no lawfully constituted
governmental authority in Mexico, and yet the President has gone so far as
to practically declare war on a mob for the stated reason that it did not give a
21-gun salute, a frivolous demand sometimes practiced by civilized nations . . .
The President at the time, of course, did what he then believed to be right. He
dispatched a great fleet from our Navy to the Mexican waters as a result of his
belief. Now he asks Congress to back him. If the President had come to Congress
in advance for advice in regard to backing Admiral Mayo in the latter's demand
for a more formal salute, as an apology, which had substantially been given by the
arresting officer as well as by President Victoriano Huerta, I doubt that Congress
would have backed the admiral's frivolous demand. But the President has acted.
He has done what he had a constitutional power to do. He was elected President
by the people. By virtue of his high office he is Commander in Chief of all the
United States military forces. He sent a fleet to the Mexican waters.[94]

The House quickly voted 337 to 37 to say that the "president of the
United States is justified in the employment of armed forces of the United
States to enforce the demands made upon Victoriano Huerta for unequiv-
ocable amends" for the indignities suffered by the sailors.[95] Before the Senate passed the resolution, Wilson went ahead and ordered landing operations by the Marines in Veracruz to intercept a German vessel containing
American-made arms to be sold to the Huerta government. The Senate ratified the resolution approving retribution for Tampico a day later. Wilson
proceeded to bombard Veracruz, which the US Army would subsequently
occupy for seven months.

The Pancho Villa Expedition

In spring 1916 Pancho Villa found himself on the losing side of the violent
conflicts that followed the Mexican Revolution of 1910. In an apparent attempt to draw the United States into a war to his own political benefit, he
and a band of several hundred loyalists crossed the US border to attack a US
cavalry post and the town of Columbus, New Mexico. More than two dozen
Americans died in the attack. The Mexican government under Venustiano
Carranza sent President Woodrow Wilson some mixed messages, suggesting
that perhaps both countries could have the right to chase criminals into each
other's territory. But Carranza also expressed remorse over the attack and a

willingness to pursue and punish Villa. At the same time, he clearly stated that a US Army intervention would be considered "an invasion of national territory."[96]

Undeterred by the Mexican president's message, President Woodrow Wilson decided that he had the right to respond to Villa's raid and announced he was sending fifteen thousand soldiers into Mexico to "capture Villa and disperse his forces."[97] He did not seek congressional permission. When border raids by Villistas and other groups continued, Wilson mobilized and sent 150,000 militia men to the border. He considered asking Congress for a declaration of war against Mexico, but as the Carranza government consolidated power, it established control over the border and ended the raids, and the situation diffused. After it had spent ten months in Mexico, Wilson withdrew the army in January 1917.

After the troops had entered Mexico, Congress passed, without debate, a resolution that assumed that "the President has obtained the consent of the de facto government of Mexico for this punitive expedition," a questionable assumption given Carranza's mixed messages. Nevertheless, Congress stated that "the use of the armed forces of the United States for the sole purpose of apprehending and punishing the lawless band of armed men who entered the United States from Mexico on the 9th day of March, 1916, committed outrages on American soil, and fled into Mexico, is hereby approved."[98] Though Congress retroactively asserted its own authority to legalize the operation, the conversation members had about their right to do so reflected the new constitutional script as well as echoes of the older ones.

During spring and summer 1916 members of Congress debated whether the commander in chief had the authority to send fifteen thousand troops across the border without prior authorization. In these debates, they generally assumed that as members of Congress, their main role in regulating the intervention was to pass an official declaration of war if and when Wilson asked for one. They did not assert the need to regulate an undeclared war. Some members of Congress declared that public support for the Punitive Expedition was sufficient to justify the intervention and their deference to the president.

Members of Congress in both parties were deferential to the president in this case and conflated support with the flag with support for Wilson. Colorado senator Charles Thomas, a Democrat like President Wilson, merely noted that "we have an Army today, a gallant Army, in Mexico at the order of the

Commander in Chief and doing service to their country."[99] In the opinion of Sen. Thomas Walsh, Congress should not try to deliberate about going to war. Instead, it should wait for the president to tell them if war is appropriate. He said,

> it is better to leave it to the Chief Executive of this Nation, the Commander in Chief of our military and naval forces, to exercise his discretion, and let him come before the Congress if a situation arises which further complicates matters and ask us to place on the record specifically and expressly a declaration of war.[100]

The president's partisan opponents sounded many of the same themes. Republican senator Lawrence Sherman, argued that "these are soldiers, dispatched under an order of the Commander in Chief to pursue an ordinary land robber, murderer, and thief into a country that has no adequate government for the protection of life and property."[101] Republican Joseph Cannon opined that public approval, not congressional authorization, was required to justify the incursions: "The Commander in Chief of the Army and Navy-the President-ordered Gen. Pershing to cross the border and catch that bandit. . . . Public sentiment, I think, justified him in going."[102]

Some Republicans did object to Wilson's actions but did not assert Congress's right to regulate hostilities generally or to initiate an undeclared war. Rather, they would only frame Wilson's actions as illegal once the Pershing expedition was defined as amounting to a declaration of war. Republican Joseph Moore said, "He is undoubtedly the Commander in Chief of the Army and the Navy of the United States and he has power to call out the militia, but the President has no right to declare war without the consent of Congress."[103] Republican Halvor Steenerson stated that "he is not authorized to commit acts of offensive war or to begin a war of aggression without a previous declaration of war by Congress."[104] Republican senator Moses Clapp noted the dynamic that would come to dominate war powers in the late twentieth century when he observed that

> Congress has been placed in a position where it was no longer free to act upon its judgment with reference to the original merits of a question involving war, because, under our Constitution, while the function of declaring war is vested solely in the Congress, yet a President, as Commander in Chief of the Army and Navy, may take such action and may in effect bring on war, and then Congress, in order to avoid

the effect of a divided sentiment in this country as to the country or the people involved in that war, must vote aye and approve the course already adopted."[105]

Though a century old, this story should seem familiar to modern observers.

THE RISE OF CONGRESSIONAL DEFERENCE
TO THE COMMANDER IN CHIEF

The original story about the commander in chief clause held that it was a narrow title that conferred command authority, but no policymaking authority, on the president. When nineteenth-century members of Congress confronted ambiguous situations about how to interpret the constitutional distribution of war powers, they referred often to the general-in-chief script and to the precedents and texts that were associated with it. Even when they favored broad presidential wartime authority, they still defended their position in reference to the dominant constitutional script. Consistent with its rhetoric, lawmakers asserted their right to participate in war policy, especially around the initiation of the use of force.

Around the turn of the twentieth century, a new constitutional script emerged. It said that the commander in chief clause gave the president special patriotic military status, and it was accompanied by nationalistic and patriotic rhetoric that demanded that Congress defer to the commander in chief in policymaking decisions. The new rhetoric was bipartisan and widespread, and at least for a time, it almost completely replaced the general-in-chief script. In their words and actions, members of Congress also began to minimize Congress's war powers. In some of these instances, Congress did authorize the president's actions. But members did not deliberate explicitly over whether presidents were taking offensive or defensive actions under the commander in chief clause, at a time when such conversation might have illuminated that presidents were stretching those boundaries and when the United States was also imposing its will on its neighbors. Instead, the new script about the commander in chief helped to quiet congressional objections about both the constitutional balance of powers and the quasi-imperial turn in foreign policy. Many of the arguments that accompany this new script foreshadowed those that would be made later in the twentieth century.

CHAPTER 5

Scripts and Precedents

In chapter 3, I described how nineteenth-century members of Congress commonly used a particular logical-historical argument when discussing the commander in chief clause: that the president's constitutional war authority was analogous to that of any high ranking military officer, and that his title conferred some command authority, but no policymaking authority. Members used the script to explain to each other why narrow definitions of the commander in chief's authority were appropriate in some cases (like in initiating hostilities) and broad definitions of the commander in chief's authority were appropriate in others (like in giving commands to officers). However, that script was also interwoven with competing sets of ideas and commitments in congressional debates that brought about political constructions of broader presidential authority.

In this chapter, I describe how Congress applied the "general in chief" script when members strongly disagreed about wartime policy prior to 1898. Congressional speeches defining the commander in chief clause show that there was not just one version of the "general in chief" metaphor, but rather two competing ones. Both were narrow in scope, compared to arguments made by modern presidents. But one version was broader than the other, and the competition between these two scripts was prominent in congressional debates that at times created broad wartime authority for the president. More specifically, this chapter discusses the way that both proponents and opponents of the Mexican War referred to the general in chief script as they debated the commander in chief's authority to govern conquered territory. The scripted logic of that construction of authority then became embedded in the precedents set during those debates that would affect later debates. In the conclusion to the chapter, I discuss the ways in which these observations inform debates over the role of precedent in constitutional interpretation.

THE DUELING INTERPRETATIONS OF
THE "LIKE A GENERAL" SCRIPT

Members of Congress did not all agree about war policy, and they did not agree about whether the occupant of the White House could be trusted to make any good decisions about war policy on his own. So when legislators disagreed about war policy and the president's role in constructing that policy, they invoked two slight variations of the main constitutional script. To recall, the dominant narrative during the nineteenth century was that the commander in chief, by virtue of his title, was akin to "a general." But he could be a general "like George Washington" who took direct orders from Congress. Or he could be a general under "the laws of nations" and be supreme on the battlefield, taking no direction from uninformed legislators.[1] These two subscripts agreed that "a general" could not start a war. But they disagreed about how much wartime authority "a general" could have, and whether wartime enhanced the president's commander in chief battlefield authority relative to Congress.

Many speeches throughout the pre-WWI era refer to the authority of the commander in chief in relation to what were called the "laws of nations."[2] These "laws" were not codified in a body of international treaties, laws, or international organizations as we know them today. Rather, they were a set of theories, rules, and precedents set forth in treatises like the Swiss philosopher Emmerich de Vattel's *The Law of Nations* (1758), earlier writings by Hugo Grotius, and in American textbooks like James Kent's *Commentaries on American Law* (1826).[3] These texts laid out guidelines for how nation-states were to treat each other in commercial relations, treaties, and most importantly on the battlefield in the conduct of honorable war. Nineteenth-century courts also at times based their decisions on the laws of nations, a practice that continues in some circumstances and whose legitimacy is debated by legal scholars.[4] The very content of the "laws of nations" shaped, and was also shaped by, American politics and the American wars of the eighteenth and nineteenth centuries.[5]

In congressional disagreements, the "Washington as general" script tended to be invoked by those who were in the party that opposed the president. When members of Congress disagreed about foreign and military policy, those who preferred policy that could be accomplished through robust congressional powers often based their arguments on Washington's example. They often said that the commander in chief could take very few actions on his own authority because he possessed no policymaking powers. They also said that during war and peace alike, he was obligated to execute every command Congress gave him.

In the nineteenth century, members who preferred unilateral presidential action often invoked the competing narrative of the "general under the laws of nations."[6] They argued that based on loosely defined international historical precedents, during declared wars, generals had authority deriving from the nature of command that the Congress could not interfere with. Like the Washington-based model, "the general" in the laws of nations model also could not start a conflict. But in the "laws of nations" model, the commander in chief had the authority to execute a declared war without legislative oversight or approval.

For example, one debate over the implied authority of the commander in chief took place in January 1862 as the Senate was considering passing a bill to empower the president to take over rail and telegraph lines as part of the war effort. Two speakers exemplified the positions at each end of the spectrum. Republican senator Edgar Cowan relied on the "laws of nations" model to argue the (pro-presidential) case that Lincoln did not need congressional authority to take over the rail lines because the commander in chief clause gave him sufficient inherent authority to fight to win the war. Sen. Lyman Trumbull (a Democrat), relied on the "Washington as general" model to argue (the pro-Congress position) that Lincoln needed explicit authority from Congress to take over the rail lines (or do nearly anything).[7]

Cowan, the Republican, argued that Congress's power was only to declare war. He made the "laws of nations" argument that the legislature did not have power to regulate the prosecution of the war. Congress, he argued, could not tell the commander in chief of the army when that army "shall fight, where it shall fight, how it shall fight, and how it shall get to the place of action."[8] Furthermore, in his view, Congress did not have the power to tell the president to march, to go on horseback, or to ride on the rails because giving the army those kinds of directions was "the very essence" of the president's power.[9] He relied on a broad interpretation of the powers of military command, rooted in the uncodified

> laws of nations. They are established by the common consent of nations, regulated by the progressive humanity of civilization; and the President is the judge of them, and is responsible for his obedience to them; and if Congress were

to undertake to abridge, to alter, or diminish these laws of war as they are to be found in the laws of nations, the President would be bound to disregard them.[10]

Regarding the rail and telegraph bill, Senator Cowan concluded that it was unnecessary for Congress to grant Lincoln any additional domestic wartime authority.[11] It was better to leave Lincoln with total discretion and for Congress not to meddle in administration of the war.

Senator Trumbull took the opposite position. He argued, as the out-party Whigs had argued during the Mexican war, that "[t]he whole war power of this Government, by the Constitution, is expressly in Congress and nowhere else, with the simple exception that Congress cannot designate the Commander-in-Chief."[12] He echoed the familiar argument that if Congress did not write laws to manage the army, the commander in chief could give it orders, but if Congress chose to write such rules, the executive was bound to execute them. He made an analogy to the courts' authority to define the common law alongside Congress' lawmaking power:

> If Congress does not think proper to regulate the mode in which he shall manage
> that Army, he could manage it as armies are generally managed; just as if we
> were to create a court, and not pass any laws for the government of that court as
> to how it should administer justice, it would administer the law, perhaps, upon
> common-law principles, the Constitution guarantying a right of trial by jury
> and some common-law rights. But, sir, because we create a court, shall Congress,
> therefore, pass no law to regulate that court? The language of the Constitution is
> express. It says that Congress shall have power to raise and support armies, and to
> make rules for the government of those armies, and concerning captures on land
> and water."[13]

Trumbull (the Democrat) then suggested that Congress could go so far as to declare that the armies be armed with wooden swords, and Cowan (the Republican) questioned whether the president would be bound to command such a doomed army. Senator Trumbull replied that the president would be bound to command whatever army Congress supplied him. Then he backed away from his suggestion about the wooden swords, saying:

> I am not advocating it; but I am speaking of the power of Congress, and I am
> answering this monstrous assumption that the President of the United States,

the Executive of this country, is vested with the war power. Sir, the people of the United States have placed this power in their own representatives, in the Congress of the United States, simply providing that the President shall be Commander-in-Chief of the Army; and there is not one of the rules that the gentleman talks about that this Congress may not by a law change, and compel the President to execute.[14]

Even Republican supporters of Lincoln tended to agree with Trumbull that Congress had the right to regulate the conduct of the war. Republican Elbridge Spaulding of New York noted that "more than one hundred articles of war have been adopted by Congress for the government of our Army." Government of the army, he argued, included everything that might transpire in wartime. He continued, "Nothing in the range of civilized warfare is withheld from you in this crisis. Congress may, in the language of the Constitution, pass 'all the laws which may be necessary and proper' to suppress the 'insurrection.' If the laws now on the statute- book are not sufficient, it is our duty to pass other and more stringent laws, confer more power on the President, give him ample power to make our success complete and certain."[15]

While both the "Washington as general" and the "general under the laws of nations" models found adherents, the "Washington as general" model was more common prior to 1900. During the Civil War, a mixture of Democrats, Unionists, and Republicans concluded that the commander in chief's authority mostly derived from American law, not the "laws of nations," and voted for bills to authorize, define, and limit the wartime authority of the commander in chief. Unlike today's Congresses, they did not believe their own authority revolved entirely around spending money. At various points in the war, members of each party saw political and policy advantage in deferring to the president. Layered on top of those partisan tendencies, however, was a bipartisan support for the pro-Congress argument, exemplified by the laws Congress wrote to regulate the war and the Reconstruction, including enacting the Railroad and Telegraph bill being debated in the speeches described here.[16]

To illustrate the ways that the competition between two constitutional scripts and their attached precedents contributed to debates over the construction of nineteenth century constitutional war powers, I next discuss the evolution of the authority to "govern conquered territory" and the ways that constitutional scripts interacted with that authority across more than half a century. During the Mexican War, for the first time, Congress and the president had to establish the boundaries between their joint authorities to govern conquered territory. The dominant constitutional script regarding the commander in chief clause, and its two variants, combined with partisan politics, were integral to the logic by which Congress constructed this new presidential constitutional authority.

CONGRESS VS. THE LAWS OF NATIONS IN GOVERNING CONQUERED TERRITORY

Between the Founding and World War I, the United States grew from a cluster of states on the Eastern Seaboard to a continental power with territories stretching into the Caribbean and across the Pacific Ocean. Although the United States gained some of that territory through treaty negotiations, much of it was taken by military force. In the wake of these conquests, Congress engaged in recurring debates about the commander in chief's statutory and implied authority to govern conquered territory.

Governance is different than using military force merely to subdue an enemy. Governance begins when fighting ends. Governance of conquered territory included decisions about modifying or implementing preexisting local laws, devising mechanisms for keeping the peace, treatment of local property, and collection of taxes in conquered lands. Everyone agreed that the conquering power could make these decisions. The question was whether the commander in chief could make decisions in the name of the conquering power, or whether such decisions amounted to lawmaking that required Congress's input. There is certainly a structural dilemma here—it is much easier for commanders on the ground, under the authority of the commander in chief, to make rules for the territory they conquer than it is for legislators in a far-off capital to do so. But the easiest answer—that the president should govern as the conqueror—was not necessarily consistent with how Congress understood its war powers at the time. And of course, members of Congress often disagreed about the merits and purposes of war itself.

In the end, members of Congress, presidents, and courts developed a durable agreement that if Congress wanted to dictate to the commander in chief how to govern conquered lands, it had the constitutional right to do so; at the same time, presidents could govern temporarily in the absence of such guidance. The logic that supported that position was a middle ground between

the two competing narratives about the commander in chief's authority—
the "Washington as general" and "laws of nations general." The precedents
that were set collectively by President James Polk, Congress, and the Supreme
Court in the 1840s and 1850s, supported by familiar scripted logic, were repeated in members' reasoning and decisions during and after the Civil and the
Spanish-American Wars.

Making Law in Conquered Mexican Lands

The skirmish that led to the congressional declaration of war against Mexico took place in May 1846, and by the end of the war two years later, US
armed forces would control California, New Mexico, and parts of northern
and central Mexico all the way to Mexico City. The questions raised by this
conquest were introduced at a time when there was widespread recognition
of Congress's wartime authority and respect for the deferential precedents set
by George Washington. But previous territorial acquisitions in the Louisiana
Purchase and the Florida cession from Spain had not required Congress to
consider how the constitutional system would implement the rights of a conquering power. Of course, the United States was indeed a conquering power,
as it fought to dispossess Native Americans of their lands. But inside the members' of Congress frame of reference at the time, those lands had been acquired
by settlements with the European powers they understood to "own" them and
by treaties with individual tribes. Thus, debates about the specific authority
of a conquering general had not taken place in conversations about Native
American lands.

At the time of the Mexican War, these were new questions in the American context, but ones which were defined in well-known books about international norms. They were also introduced into a political environment in which
Democrats controlled the presidency, the Senate, and the House (at least initially), and in which many of the minority party Whigs opposed both the war
and president.[17]

The first discussion of the commander in chief's implied authority over
conquered territory took place as Congress was considering a resolution to
ask President Polk (a Democrat) for information about the orders he had
given to his generals regarding civil administration in Mexico. On August 15,
1846, three months into the conflict, US Army colonel Stephen Kearny announced to the people of New Mexico that his army was in control of their

territory: "I absolve you from all allegiance to the Mexican government, and from all obedience to General Armijo. He is no longer your governor; I am your governor."[18] As news of such actions arrived in Washington, members of Congress began to grapple with the specter of generals declaring themselves territorial governors and with the boundaries of the military authority of such governors. In December 1846, the first congressional debates about the disposition of conquered territory that invoked the commander in chief clause took place. They centered on whether the president, as commander in chief, could make any administrative rules that amounted to lawmaking in conquered lands, or whether he could merely hold territory, keep peace, and leave the rulemaking to Congress.

The resolution demanding copies of the president's orders regarding civil administration in Mexico was proposed by Whig representative Garrett Davis of Kentucky.[19] Davis and other Whigs argued that Polk had started the war illegally and was engaging in a war of conquest without legal authority.[20] Regarding the governance of conquered territory specifically, Davis articulated the "Washington as general" narrative to support his argument that the commander in chief had no authority to make law of any kind. He asked of the

> commander-in-chief—What character of office does he fill, and what character of functions is he to exercise? Exclusively military. And the power of sovereignty which is to be exercised by the victorious nation over conquered territory is not to be exercised by the conqueror who gains the victory at all, but by the Legislature-the representatives of the sovereignty of the people-and which is authorized by the Constitution to wage war and make conquests, and to be exercised by nobody else.[21]

Fellow Whigs joined Davis in criticizing Polk, agreeing that the commander in chief's power was purely military and did not extend to the creation of civil government. Ohio Whig Joseph Root argued that "neither the commander-in-chief, nor general, nor commodore, nor captain under his command, had power to do a single act that looked to the establishment of a civil government in a province under military possession. Their authority was purely military. They were bound to respect the rights of private citizens, and to leave the laws just as they found them."[22] Solomon Foot of Vermont pulled no punches, arguing that by setting up civil administration, Polk proved he was illegally waging a war of conquest:

Like the maniac, who, in the wildness of his delirium, imagines himself the commander-in-chief of all creation . . . So our commander-in-chief, bedizzened by his sudden elevation, struts forth upon a somewhat less magnificent theatre, but with hardly less magniloquent tones of command, and sends abroad his generals and his commodores, his Satraps and his Tetrarchs, not to meet and vanquish the enemy in battle, but to conquer whole states and provinces by proclamation! "The war is not waged with any view to conquest;" oh, no! and yet new territorial governments are organized, new laws are ordained, and new magistrates are appointed over these new and extensive acquisitions; and appropriations of the public money are called for to erect fortifications, in order to secure the permanent possession of the conquered regions.[23]

The Whigs thoroughly rejected arguments grounded in the laws of nations and traditions of command. Rep. Edward McGaughey argued that

no principle of that vague and uncertain code, called the laws of nations, inconsistent with our Constitution and laws, can be in force in this country. The powers and duties of the President, as the commander-in-chief of the army and navy, are defined by the Constitution and laws of the States, and not by the laws of nations. These commodores and generals, in the establishment of these civil governments, have acted under the orders of their commander-in-chief, the President, and therefore it becomes a subject of legitimate inquiry, had he the constitutional power to give them any such authority? The answer is a short one. The people of this country, and not their President, possess the sovereign power. He can wield no power beyond that with which the Constitution has clothed his office. If he does, he becomes a usurper and a tyrant.[24]

Perhaps surprisingly, the Democrats, who supported the war and the president, did not argue for a wide-ranging power for their own commander in chief. Instead, their arguments in favor of Polk's actions were narrowly tailored and respected a robust role for Congress in making law to regulate conquered territory. Rep. Joseph Woodward, Democrat from South Carolina, laid out the logic of the Democrats' argument. He argued vociferously for a robust congressional role in managing the war (consistent with the Revolutionary-era model) but simultaneously argued that the laws of nations also imposed some mandates on conquerors. He posited that the president's power to govern conquered territory came directly from the laws of nations regarding the responsibilities of a conquering army and flowed directly to the commander in chief of that army. While the war was Congress's to direct, the commander in chief had the implied authority to maintain peace in conquered lands. Because Woodward introduces and elaborates on several common strains of argument and integrates support for the Revolutionary model and the law of nations model for the commander in chief in a way that becomes enshrined in the eventual precedent, his remarks are worth quoting at length:

> Mr. Speaker, the war is our war, and not the President's; its ends and purposes are our ends and purposes; the army engaged in it is our army; and the generalissimo of that army, though designated by the Constitution, is our generalissimo; and in that capacity, like every other military officer, wholly subordinate to Congress, and to the civil authority of the land. Sir, the President, who is commander-in-chief of the army and navy of the United States, is not that political President who approves or vetoes your bills; who receives foreign Ministers, and sends corresponding ones abroad; who nominates federal judges and other high officers of state, and, by and with the advice and consent of the Senate, makes treaties. He is commander-in-chief of your armies, and only that; and, as such, is, under the Constitution, divested of his political coordinate relation to Congress. No military authority in this land is coordinate with the civil, but is everywhere, and to all intents and purposes it is subordinate. Sir, the Constitution might have designated you, the Speaker of this House, or the President of the Senate, as commander-in-chief of the army, just as well as the President; and, in that case, either of you, though without any political authority whatever, would yet have possessed all the military power the President has. So that the civil and political functions, in which he cooperates with the other branches of the Government, add nothing at all to his authority as a military officer. What, then, are the powers and duties of the commander-in-chief of the army? In the first part of my remarks, I have already stated, to execute the war; to fight the enemy; invade his territory, and reduce him to submission. But who is the enemy? The hostile sovereign, his army, and the people who give him succor; and not peaceable inhabitants, who have made no resistance, but submitted themselves, and taken protection. Such inhabitants, in case of a permanent conquest, might, under some circumstances, be required to receive law from the conquering sovereign, but the military commander has no civil authority over them. . . . The armies of the United States, having invaded and occupied a peaceful province of a hostile sovereign, and ejected him therefrom, and substituted our authority in lieu

of his, the laws of nations impose it upon us to take the place of the expelled sovereign to the extent that the process and administration of government make it necessary. Having driven away the natural political parent, we stand to them in loco parentis. The President is bound, in short, to see that the laws are faithfully executed, so far as such supervision was made indispensable by the new state of affairs. That was the duty of the natural sovereign; and the President, standing in the place of that sovereign, is, on our behalf, bound to do the same. He has no authority to make laws; to establish new political relations among the people; to disturb vested rights, or any other rights. He is to see that existing laws are executed. He is to have executed those same laws which the President of Mexico would have had executed, had he not been displaced and superseded. And as this is matter of duty, rather than right, it is, of course, meant that he go no further than has been made necessary by the deficient state of executive authority in the country.[25]

Other Democrats echoed all or part of Woodward's argument. In response to Whig objections, they grounded their definition of the commander in chief's discretionary authority in conquered territory in both the "laws of nations" and other American law and precedents. Thomas Bayly, Democrat of Virginia, echoing Woodward, further grounded the Democrats' position in American historical precedent from the War of 1812, when he said President Madison, "who was so profoundly versed in international law" supported General Harrison's orders in Canada "in which he continued all civil officers in the exercise of their functions, but required of them an oath of fidelity to the United States."[26] Bayly agreed that Congress could dictate to the president how to govern the conquered territories but claimed that until it legislated, there was an affirmative legal obligation on the commander in chief to govern them.[27] Rep. James Seddon, Democrat of Virginia, said that while as commander in chief, the president's authority was subordinate to Congress, until Congress acted, the laws of nations governed the behavior of the commander in chief. Even there, he argued, the president's powers were not implied constitutional powers but were governed by laws Congress had written requiring the president to uphold the laws of nations during wartime.[28]

This debate began with Davis's Resolution, asking for information from Polk about civil administration, which passed the House of Representatives on December 15, 1846, without a recorded vote. Polk quickly responded to the House on December 22 by transmitting to it the orders regarding martial government he had transmitted to his generals. He replied that "the orders and instructions were given to regulate the exercise of the rights of a belligerent over such portions of the territory of our enemy . . . occupied by our armed forces—rights . . . clearly recognized *by the laws of nations*" [my italics].[29] Polk's words and actions were echoed in his partisans' logic. He was careful to announce that he did not authorize the creation of civil government and that some actions taken by his generals did not meet with his official approval. He noted that

> among the documents accompanying the report of the Secretary of War will be found a "form of government" "established and organized" by the military commander who conquered and occupied with his forces the Territory of New Mexico . . . These have not been "approved and recognized" by me. Such organized regulations as have been established in any of the conquered territories for the security of our conquest, for the preservation of order, for the protection of the rights of the inhabitants, and for depriving the enemy of the advantages of these territories while the military possession of them by the forces of the United States continues will be recognized and approved.[30]

Polk's statement invoked logical and rhetorical arguments present in both subscripts. He asserted temporary authority to make rules to preserve order while recognizing the legitimacy of Congress's power to act and create governments in conquered lands. He achieved the outcome he and his party preferred, and the one that was most practical. But the logic by which that outcome was defended by members of Congress, by Polk, and by the courts recognized and reflected the arguments about narrow traditional definitions of command authority that were made by members of Congress across party lines.

As the war went on, members of both parties conceded some practical authority to the commander in chief, particularly on the issue of collecting taxes in conquered Mexican lands. Whig senator Daniel Webster of Massachusetts argued that it was appropriate for Polk to order his generals to collect taxes in Mexico. He stipulated that "Congress, the legislative agents of our sovereign, may at any time establish an entire code for the conduct of our armies in hostile countries, and may restrict their powers within the narrowest limits." But he went on to argue that Polk could collect taxes for the practical reasons that "the extension of our constitutional guarantees over countries occupied by our armies would be utterly subversive of all the rights of war. We could not march a step without finding impediments that could not be overcome."[31]

Democrats, too, edged toward a compromise between the obligations of conquering nations and the powers of Congress. Sen. Andrew Butler, Democrat of South Carolina, argued that "this being the first war of invasion, it is full of startling suggestions." He worried aloud that if the commander in chief could collect taxes from conquered territory and spend it to sustain the army, "what a commentary would it be on the futility of the supposed controlling power of Congress over the military responsibility of the Executive as the commander-in-chief of the armies of the republic!"[32] He was joined in these concerns by fellow South Carolina Democrat John C. Calhoun. Calhoun, who opposed the war, conceded that conquerors have a right to collect taxes but argued that the people of the United States, not the army, had conquered Mexico and therefore that the Congress, not the president, held that right.[33] One related question was whether it was appropriate for the president to collect duties from ships at occupied ports. Democrat Frederick Stanton defended the President Polk's discretion in such collections: "As it is the duty of the President to seize upon the revenue of the conquered port, he might, in the discharge of this duty, determine that he would not exact a duty so heavy as that imposed by the Mexican laws."[34]

Congress during this period was controlled by the Democrats at the outset of the war and was under divided control (Whigs in the House, Democrats in the Senate) for its last year. The legislature deferred practically to the president and did not act to regulate the taxing, tariff collection, and other governance activities before the war ended in February of 1848 with the Mexican cession of a large swath of what became the Southwest of the United States.[35] In practice, this left such actions in the discretionary authority of the commander in chief, a situation that seemed to have some bipartisan legitimacy in Congress. When Congress did not act, Polk did administer the conquered lands, though with public acknowledgement of Congress's eventual role in doing so.

After the war, the Supreme Court decided two cases that seemed to ratify this compromise. In *Fleming v. Page* (1850), the court said that Mexican territory did not become American territory subject to American law until Congress acted. Similarly, in *Cross v. Harrison* (1853), the Supreme Court ratified the compromise that had been articulated by the political branches. In its opinion, the military government of California authorized by the president during the war had been legally in charge of the Port of San Francisco and able to collect duties there, even after peace was reached, until the time that administrators were appointed under domestic law. It ruled that

> the formation of the civil government in California, when it was done, was the lawful exercise of a belligerent right over a conquered territory. It was the existing government when the territory was ceded to the United States as a conquest, and did not cease as a matter of course or as a consequence of the restoration of peace, and it was rightfully continued after peace was made with Mexico until Congress legislated otherwise, under its constitutional power, to dispose of and make all needful rules and regulations respecting the territory or other property belonging to the United States.[36]

That unanimous decision recognized and ratified the practical compromise that Congress and the president had come to and reflected the majority opinion in Congress. On the one hand, it recognized the historical responsibility of an army to govern conquered lands in wartime and therefore settled some of these questions in favor of Polk's and the Democrats' arguments. It also explicitly recognized that Congress had the power to legislate for conquered territory and end the temporary authority of the commander in chief. Going forward, members of both parties would refer to *Cross v. Harrison* as an authority to support the rights and responsibilities of the commander in chief to administer conquered territory.[37]

When questions about conquered territory first arose, the answers were unclear. The revolutionary model seemed to say that the commander in chief could take no actions whatsoever without Congress's permission. On the other hand, governing conquered territory according to "the law of nations" imposed on the conquering general the responsibilities to keep peace and order in occupied lands, regardless of the conqueror's domestic constitution or laws. The commander in chief also had the benefit (through his subordinate officers) of actually being present on the ground, while Congress was not. The resolution of the first congressional debates over these responsibilities of a conquering power was influenced by partisan politics as well as practicalities in the 1840s. Congress, controlled by the president's party, did not immediately step up to take on the role of governing conquered territory, allowing the commander in chief space to govern independently, at least temporarily. Even while he governed conquered territory, Polk recognized Congress's concurrent authority. Everyone recognized that military rule would eventually come to an

end and that when it did, Congress' authority would again dominate. Afterward, the courts recognized the validity of the compromise and its limitations.
This precedent, and the logic supporting it, was referenced in later congressional debates over the administration of conquered territory. Both scripts reap-
peared in those debates, although the new precedent was now prominent in
congressional reasoning. However, applying those precedents in the aftermath
of the Civil War was not straightforward.

Governance of Conquered Territory during and
after the Civil War

The Mexican War established that the commander in chief could make and
administer law in conquered territory, at least until Congress told him how to
dispose of it. The arguments advanced by both sides during that conflict, less
than two decades before the Civil War, were familiar to at least some members
of Congress who served during both conflicts. However, those precedents regarded military governors governing conquered *foreign* territory, not governing the American *states* under occupation by the Union army.

The Civil War raised the thorny question of whether the commander in
chief had implied authority to appoint military governors in certain border
and Confederate states. In both parties, members of Congress referred to Mexican War precedent when they argued that the commander in chief had the
right to govern conquered territory and to keep the peace until Congress established rules for the governance of the Southern states, although both of the
original scripts were articulated. At the same time, members of both parties
were skeptical of the commander in chief's ability to "establish civil governments," given Congress's constitutional authority to ensure Republican government in the states, but the lines between presidentially appointed military
and civil governors were often in the eyes of the beholder.

Could the commander in chief unilaterally appoint military governors in
conquered American states? Could he establish civil government there? Could
the commander in chief determine the conditions under which states would be
readmitted to the Union? Or did that authority belong to Congress? Abraham
Lincoln first elevated Andrew Johnson from loyalist Democratic senator from
Tennessee to provisional military governor of Tennessee in 1862; at the time,
there were not extensive congressional discussions about the implications of
this appointment for the authority of the commander in chief or Congress.[38]

Most congressional discussions of the legal authority of military governors took place from 1864 through 1867, when members of Congress regularly debated the authority of the commander in chief over the conquered states of the South once Union victory was assured. During that period, often referred to as "presidential reconstruction," first President Lincoln then President Andrew Johnson prescribed the conditions for Southern reconstruction, on terms that gave Southern states fairly wide leeway in managing their own affairs.

Members of both parties said that it was appropriate for the commander in chief to appoint provisional governors, as long as they were explicitly military. However, most legislators agreed that civilian authorities could not be appointed by the president. Andrew Thayer, Democrat of Oregon, made a common argument referring to Lincoln's 1864 state of the union address when he said,

> So far as we have the right by the laws of war to dictate terms to the conquered;
> and grant amnesty to domestic enemies, the proclamation of the President,
> accompanying his last annual message to Congress, was not only competent,
> right, and proper, but was clearly within the scope of his war powers as
> Commander-in-Chief of the military and naval forces of the nation. But when
> these people, or any portion of them, wish to organize a State government, and be
> admitted as one of the States of the Union, the consent of Congress is necessary,
> and upon this point there seems to be no difference of opinion.[39]

Democrat Thomas Eldredge was more critical of the provisional governors and admonished that civil government will "never commence until you have declared in the language of the Supreme Court, that the Executive, as Commander-in-Chief of the Army and Navy, cannot exercise a civil function. It will never commence until you have declared . . . [that the president], in the creation or organization of these pretended State governments, has invaded the prerogative of this body."[40]

Perhaps because Lincoln and Johnson promised to readmit the Southern states on more charitable terms than other Republicans did, Democrats and Unionists in Congress were predisposed to prefer that the commander in chief make the rules for reconstruction. Unionist Garrett Davis, who in other debates argued for congressional supremacy, specifically referred to *Cross v. Harrison* and the law of nations model as relevant precedents for presidentially led governance of conquered territory. He said:

[By *Cross v. Harrison*] when a foreign country is conquered by the arms of the United States, immediately upon the conquest and the acquisition of the possession by our Army the President, as Commander-in- Chief, may order, *under the rights of conquest*, the organization of such a military government, with civil powers, as may be necessary for the country and its inhabitants.[41] [My italics.]

When Andrew Johnson became president, Democrats also threw their support behind the military governance of the states. Democrat James Nesmith of Oregon agreed that it was appropriate for the president to require "several things of the southern people," in his capacity "as Commander-in-Chief of the Army and Navy of the United States."[42] Andrew Rogers, Democrat of New Jersey, argued that the commander in chief could appoint provisional governors and institute martial law, which was "the only rule of action for the special purpose of changing the existing state of things and restoring the civil government over the people."[43] Francis Thomas, Unionist from Maryland, was convinced that the commander in chief had "the power to erect military provisional governments as temporary expedients for peace and quiet." Thomas reflected the Mexican War compromise when he argued that "the power of Congress commenced where that of the President ceased. His power ceased when he withdrew his provisional governors."[44]

Many Republicans agreed, at least initially, with this robust construction of the commander in chief's authority to govern conquered territory. Joseph Defrees, Republican of Indiana, said that the people of the South had been "left without any government, either civil or military" and that the commander in chief should "organize some kind of government that would restore tranquility."[45] John Bingham remarked that in governing conquered Southern states, Congress could not interfere with the commander in chief.[46] Republican senator James Doolittle of Wisconsin opined that the president had broad authority to rule through military governors precisely because it was temporary. In his opinion, presidents were only holding territory until its people could assure him they were law abiding. Doolittle was confident that the presidential appointments "are not civil governors; but provisional governors."[47]

With the war over and Johnson in the White House, Republicans, far more than Democrats, became increasingly willing to call attention to the limits to the commander in chief's authority to govern Southern territory. Sen. William Fessenden, Republican of Maine invoked the "Washington as general" model when argued in 1866 that it could *not* be true that when Congress has raised an Army and get it into the field, we have no further power over it, cannot direct its operations in any way, cannot direct against whom its operations shall be carried, and cannot make any rules which regulate it in actual service. Why, sir, if that doctrine be true, we are at the pleasure of a military despot at any time who may happen to be Commander-in-Chief of the Army of the United States.[48]

Others made similar arguments.[49]

As time went on, however, Republicans recalled the precedents set during the Mexican War and more frequently recalled Congress's role in ending military governance. In 1865 Republican senator Jacob Howard of Michigan said that the commander in chief could govern the southern states through the military because "the will of the conqueror is the law . . . in the absence of acts of Congress," but only until Congress acted.[50] Burton Cook, Republican of Illinois, claimed that it was "the duty of the President, as Commander-in-Chief of the Army, to control the rebellious States thus reduced to subjection, to keep order to prevent anarchy and if, in his judgment, the best way to do this is to appoint provisional governors," but such authority was always subject to the will of Congress.[51] Thaddeus Stevens, Republican of Pennsylvania, felt that "the Commander-in-Chief of the armies . . . can only hold them under military rule until the sovereign legislative power of the conqueror shall give them law."[52] Other Republicans made similar arguments.[53]

The reality of Reconstruction was too messy and important to be decided solely by reflecting upon competing interpretations of precedents regarding conquered territory.[54] Both Presidents Lincoln and Johnson governed conquered territory initially and started the process of establishing civilian governments. Later, Congress took over both the governance and the reestablishment of recognized civil governments in the South. Arguments about the commander in chief clause were ultimately only a small part of the politics or law of the rebellious states' readmission to the Union. But these scripts did serve as familiar and accessible logic for members of Congress as they constructed their interpretations of the constitutional powers of the Congress and the president at that critical time.

Governance of Conquered Territory during and
after the Spanish American War

During the brief (April 21 to December 10, 1898) Spanish-American war, the
United States defeated Spain and through the Treaty of Paris in 1898 acquired
her territories in the Caribbean, the South Pacific, and the Philippines. The
prewar prospect of acquiring Spanish territory and the postwar reality of acquiring lands halfway around the world posed new questions for Congress
and the president. On the one hand, the precedents for the governance of conquered territory were more thoroughly fleshed out than they had been fifty
years earlier in the Mexican War. Both Congress and the president agreed that
Congress had the power to dictate how conquered lands would be governed,
but that in the absence of such laws, the commander in chief had the power
to govern conquered territory. Congress and the American people had been
entirely focused on Cuba in the lead-up to the war and were less prepared to
acquire the Philippines in the process of winning it. The people of the Philippines had also been fighting against Spanish rule, and when the Americans
acquired their territory, they continued the insurrection against rule by the
United States. Though some members of Congress did object to the annexation, the administration and the Republican majority defeated those objections.[55] Republican presidents McKinley and Roosevelt then used the logic of
the commander in chief's responsibility to ensure law and order in conquered
territory to fight a war against Philippine nationalists, to the dismay of at least
some Americans who did not want to replace the Spanish Crown in gunning
down local revolutionaries fighting for their own self-determination.[56]

Suppressing Insurrection in Conquered Philippine Lands

Aware of its prerogatives and historical precedents, Congress took a number
of actions to specify how the commander in chief was supposed to govern
conquered territory after the Spanish-American War. Reflecting the public
purposes of the war to aid the Cuban revolutionaries in throwing off Spanish rule (and not to establish an American empire in its stead), before war
was declared, on April 19, 1898, Congress passed the Teller Amendment. That
law stated that the purpose of war with Spain was to help bring about self-
government for the Cuban people. It empowered the commander in chief to
occupy Cuba for the purposes of "pacification" but disclaimed "any disposition

of intention to exercise sovereignty, jurisdiction, or control over said island except for pacification thereof, and asserts its determination, when that is accomplished, to leave the government and control of the island to its people." In so doing, it attempted to legislate early, rather than after the war, for the governance of conquered territories. (Congress would later substantially dial back that promise, by passing the Platt Amendment in 1901, which kept Cuba as a US protectorate for several decades.)

But Congress did not anticipate conquering the Philippines and so did not legislate for its governance at the outset of the war. Some members of Congress and other prominent anti-imperialists like former president Grover Cleveland opposed both the Treaty of Paris and the occupation of the Philippines. Opponents of the occupation at times linked their criticism to McKinley's use of force there. Rep. Henry Johnson, Republican of Indiana, disputed the commander in chief's authority to govern the Philippines on the grounds that the land was taken under false pretenses. In his view, "the Chief Executive of this nation had scarcely hidden himself behind the plea of a simple holding of the Philippines as the Commander in Chief of the Army and Navy," whereas his real goal was territorial expansion.[57]

However, across party lines there was general agreement that both the law of nations and American law and precedent demanded that McKinley govern the newly conquered territory by force. Seth Brown, Republican of Ohio, asked rhetorically, "What has he done as our Commander in Chief? . . . Has he not done what the recognized law of civilized nations authorizes? Is it not in accordance with that law that the conquering nation, having waged a just war, may take the property of the defeated nation as a compensation for expenses and losses? Is not that the accepted law of civilized nations?"[58] Republican Knute Nelson of Minnesota noted that until Congress legislated, the occupied territory was legally held and administered by the commander in chief:

> The Supreme Court has settled it in the case of *Cross vs. Harrison*. I claim that
> we hold the Philippine Islands to-day practically as we held New Mexico and
> Upper California after the war with Mexico—we hold them by conquest; and the
> government there is lawfully in the hands of the executive department, under the
> President as the Commander in Chief.[59]

Charles Grosvenor, Republican of Ohio, said the president was *compelled* to pacify the Philippines until Congress acted: "He could send that treaty to the

Senate of the United States and await their action, and even if the delay in that body shall fill a hundred thousand graves and make widows and orphans in this country, he is powerless to turn another wheel, except to exercise his right as Commander in Chief of the Army and hold these possessions until the treaty is acted upon.[60]

The now-well established precedent also told Congress that if it wanted to end the president's control over the Philippines, it had the right to do so. Thetus Sims, Democrat of Tennessee, said that the commander in chief could govern the Philippines "by means of our military and naval forces until Congress provides some other form of government or we dispose of them."[61] Rep. William Hepburn, Republican of Iowa, said that Congress could invest "the independence of that territory of ours with just such political rights as we choose. It is for us to determine-the Congress-and not the President of the United States. He simply, in his connection with them, is the Commander in Chief."[62]

Members of both parties recognized Congress's role in legislating for the governance of the Philippines, but for a variety of reasons, some of them anti-imperialist, some of them racist, they were collectively reticent to act on their responsibility. In June 1898, Democratic senator John Morgan of Alabama proposed measures to empower and constrain the governance of other conquered territories, especially Pacific islands. Referring to *Cross v. Harrison* and other precedents, he said,

> The state of the law in this country on the subject of the powers of the President of the United States when he, as Commander in Chief of the Army and Navy, occupies a foreign country under a declaration of war, is ascertained and settled by the Supreme Court of the United States in such a way that, in my opinion, it is necessary for us to prescribe to the President certain regulations and to give to him certain powers which he may exercise in those Spanish countries which he is now occupying as Commander in Chief of the Army and Navy, so that the relations between the Government of the United States and the military governments, or whatever they are, which he may establish in those places shall be somewhat defined.

In 1901 Congress finally acted to impose a transitional civilian government in the Philippines, which would be headed by future president William Howard Taft.[63] But in the course of putting down the insurrection there, thousands of Americans and hundreds of thousands of Filipinos died. Congress was ambivalent about the United States becoming an imperial power. In their ambivalence, members relied on precedent and repeated narratives about the scope of the commander in chief's authority to make it easier for the president to conquer a foreign nation half a world away.

CONGRESSIONAL REASONING ABOUT
THE COMMANDER IN CHIEF

In the time period I studied, members of Congress overwhelmingly looked to the past for how to answer questions about constitutional interpretation. They occasionally talked about how their decision in that moment would reverberate years, decades, or centuries down the road. But far more often, they talked about history—primarily American history, but also a vaguely defined history of war in the world—as sources of authority for how to interpret the Constitution. George Washington, by many accounts, did think that his actions as commander in chief would be seen as precedent for the future and limited himself accordingly. He was right. Generations of legislators did, in fact, rely on his example when constructing the military and political authority of the commander in chief. But his was not the only historical precedent from which members of Congress drew their conclusions. As time went along, Congress's own laws, court decisions, and written histories themselves also guided them. And not all presidents would be so deferential to Congress, creating structural dilemmas in which Congress would face collective action problems in responding to presidential initiative.

It is clear from the many references to *Cross v. Harrison* that a Supreme Court decision provided helpful evidence to legislators about how to interpret the uncertain boundary between presidential and congressional powers. It should be noted, however, that in the most often-cited cases during this period, the courts had simply ratified an interpretation of the commander in chief clause that had been reached more or less as a political consensus by the other branches. And the court decision came several years after the political branches themselves had to resolve the matter in question. Moreover, even with a court precedent on the books, members of Congress felt free to cite other sources to argue against its relevance to new situations.

So history mattered. Perhaps surprisingly, books also mattered to Congress.

Widely read textbooks like Kent's account of the law of nations and Story's description of Congress's war powers gave its members authoritative sources from which to reason and argue. Their arguments were discussed nearly as often as precedents set by Washington. Of course, the most salient books also changed over time. International historical norms also provided examples for congressional debates—particularly in defining the unenumerated powers of the president in the absence of congressional legislation.

The constitutional scripts invoked by members of Congress defined boundaries between the authority of the branches of government and highlighted relevant books and historical precedents to support those boundaries. But just because members of Congress could cite these variously authoritative sources when making their arguments about the meaning of the commander in chief clause does not mean that their sources were actually relevant or appropriate to the debate at hand.[64] When Washington was in command of the Revolutionary Army, he was not president, and in fact there *was no* president. So that example was not precisely applicable to later controversies under the Constitution of 1787. Similarly, Kent's description of a nation's obligations at war referred explicitly to "nations," "belligerents," and "governments." The writers on the laws of nations were addressing what nations could do to each other, not speaking directly to questions about whether one part of a government—the legislative branch—could direct another part of government, the commander in chief, in particular ways. Logically, it seems odd that members of Congress would invoke these works to claim inherent right of the commander in chief over the rights of Congress itself.

The application of historical precedent to definitions of war powers, whether initially or later, was a fairly superficial form of congressional reasoning. Members did not all dig back into the original examples and question the applicability of those precedents to the current environment. This pattern has implications for similar arguments about the relevance of historical precedents to the construction of presidential war powers authority in the modern period.

Moreover, partisanship and the policy preferences of the congressional majority were integral to the precedents that were actually set because the preferences of individual members are aggregated by partisan majorities' control over the legislative agenda.[65] The evidence presented here has shown that members of Congress often referred to precedents and constitutional scripts as sources of authority when they confronted new questions about the boundaries to the commander in chief's powers. But the historical precedents to which they referred were not set in a vacuum. Majoritarian rules and party politics had shaped the historical and legal precedents upon which later members of Congress relied.[66]

Consider, for example, the discussion of the governance of conquered territory above. There, the most important precedent, set during the Mexican War, held that the commander in chief had broad implied authority to govern conquered territory in the absence of congressional dictates. That Mexican War precedent, set by a partisan Congress and ratified by the Supreme Court, was an important precedent that was widely cited as justification for a war fifty years later against the Philippine people that Congress did not declare. The initial, enabling precedent was set because the Democratic majority in Congress in 1847 supported President Polk's war and trusted him to execute it without their direction. That precedent was interwoven with received narratives and easily passed down to the next generation of lawmakers. It broadened the implied authority of the commander in chief, with consequences for another war decades in the future. Thus, that initial partisan majority had implications for later events in the Pacific, though no one at the time intended it.

These considerations are relevant to discussions among legal scholars about how to weigh historical practices when interpreting the constitution. The political circumstances and imperatives at any given moment, combined with political actors' own constitutional theories, combine to create historical events that might be seen to set constitutional precedents. And the dominance of one party in Congress at a particular moment in time profoundly shapes the actions that Congress takes or does not take. The precedents that are set, at least by Congress, while justified by meaningful understanding of constitutional authority, are also crafted to solve particular short term policy problems. So when presidents, courts, or others rely on simple lists of congressional actions and inactions to justify the broad use of presidential war powers, that practice is almost certainly not capturing the substance of Congress's constitutional interpretation.[67]

Scholars debate the normative worth of invoking precedents to justify uses of constitutional war powers. Some have argued that historical precedents have definitively legitimated presidential war-making today.[68] Others dispute that claim and the role that precedent has played in such presidentialist arguments.[69] Bradley and Morrison argue that constitutional reasoning through historical precedent always tells a story about one branch acquiescing to the other, but often with inaccurate understanding of why that acquiescence took place and what acquiescence might look like from within each branch.[70] Zeisberg also cautions that precedent may contribute to poor decision making if precedents from a very different historical security context are invoked in a new one.[71] The case studies presented here offer more examples of why we ought to be skeptical of the ways that political actors use historical precedents in their constitutional reasoning.

In this project, I describe the reasoning used by members of Congress during moments of deliberative constitutional construction. Members of Congress referred to logical scripts that incorporated historical and legal precedents and well-regarded academic books. However, just because members used accessible scripts to define their positions on constitutional meaning does not mean that the historical precedents embedded in those scripts were logically coherently relevant to the decision at hand. Presidents and their advocates today may be engaging in politically motivated, methodologically sloppy application of historical precedents, rooted in the constitutional narrative they want to support. That is, more or less, how members of Congress invoked precedents about war powers in the nineteenth century as well.

But members of Congress were not engaging in legal or academic debates over the definitions of the commander in chief clause. They were engaged in an iterative project of defining his authority *politically*. As such, members cited sources that could justify their other arguments about what the president should be able to do in a particular moment. They did not systematically litigate the relevance of the precedents they used in their arguments. Simple, repeated stories about constitutional meaning and relevant precedents were easy for legislators to understand and apply in new and ambiguous situations. Their debates, however, involved more than just theoretical constitutional interpretation and also reflected members' partisan and policy preferences.

In the main policy projects that required the use of the military during the nineteenth century, these constructions of the commander in chief clause were sufficient to the task. Defending the borders from Native Americans, putting down internal insurrections, fighting wars with major global powers like England, France, and Spain, could all be accomplished with a Congress-centric division of authority. The president had both statutory and collectively defined implied authority to defend the borders and put down insurrections. Congress was willing to authorize wars with major powers. Neither presidents nor congressional partisans pushed for a different construction because their goals were able to be accomplished within the bounds of the dominant norms.

Except when they weren't. There were moments when the policy preferences of the president, or the policy preferences of the Congress, or the practicalities of war-making made the widely accepted interpretations of the commander in chief clause inconvenient. During the Mexican War, when the norms around the superiority of the Congress came into conflict with the prowar policy wishes of the congressional majority and the practical dilemma of governing conquered territory, norms were not determinative. In fact, both policy and partisan political preferences were more prominent in members' interpretations of the commander in chief clause than has so far been suggested. We turn to those preferences next.

CHAPTER 6

Scripts, Congressional Preferences, and Battlefield Emancipation

This chapter describes the interactions between constitutional scripts about the commander in chief clause, partisanship, and congressional beliefs about slavery during debates over emancipation. As with many questions about the scope of the commander in chief's authority, the constitutional legitimacy of battlefield emancipation was unclear when the question was first raised. President Abraham Lincoln himself acted as if the commander in chief clause did not grant him the authority to free enslaved people in conquered territory. As members of Congress debated the authority of the commander in chief, they used familiar constitutional scripts as evidence for and against the legitimacy of battlefield emancipation. The congressional debates that predated the Emancipation Proclamation show how legislators' beliefs about slavery and trust in President Lincoln interacted with their interpretation of the Constitution and their willingness to define the legitimacy of otherwise questionable wartime commands.

There are shelves of books devoted to Emancipation, and I do not pretend to add much to those accounts.[1] That scholarly literature highlights the interactions between self-emancipation and congressional and presidential actions, which is not my focus here.[2] Scholars who have written about the proclamation have often noted the role of the "laws of nations" argument in antebellum political discourse and in congressional debates about whether and how to legally free enslaved people.[3] However, previous work has not traced the specific connections between prior congressional interpretations of the commander in chief clause and the way the clause arose in congressional debates over emancipation. By analyzing the emancipation debates with a focus on the commander in chief clause, my analysis suggests that not just the "laws of nations" script but also the "Washington as general" script were used to justify particular political positions in the debate about emancipation. Hopefully this perspective helps illuminate aspects of the process of battlefield emancipation that have not been highlighted before.

The debates analyzed here suggest that members of Congress across party lines arrived at an unlegislated consensus in the spring of 1862 that battlefield emancipation was at least a politically legitimate application of the "battlefield command" authority of the commander in chief, consistent with the "laws of nations" interpretation of the president's command authority. The congressional majority wrote one bill about how to deal with enslaved people during the Civil War, but in their deliberations, a different majority also expressed support for battlefield emancipation under the authority of the commander in chief. Lincoln's proclamation was a logical product of the partisan and policy mix in Congress and the constitutional narratives that members relied upon. This debate suggests that both congressional action and inaction might help construct politically legitimate interpretations of the Constitution.

PARTISANSHIP AND CONSTITUTIONAL SCRIPTS

Constitutional scripts supply a logic and a set of precedents that can rhetorically ground lawmakers' decisions when they are confronted with constitutionally ambiguous policy questions. But even those who argue that words and ideas are crucial elements in sustaining political orders do not suggest that they are the only factors to do so. Though previous chapters suggest that members of Congress are capable of deliberating meaningfully about constitutional text and applying law and historical precedent to novel situations in intelligible ways, we should be under no illusion that even in the nineteenth century, when they did so often, faithful constitutional construction was their primary motivation. Members of Congress were then, as they are now, nominated by party coalitions and elected by their constituents to address pressing policy questions. They also had strong personal beliefs, particularly about such major issues as war, peace, race, and the moral abomination of slavery. So when they deliberated about constitutional meaning and applied constitutional scripts to novel questions, they did so while also reflecting upon their own strongly held political, partisan, moral, and policy considerations.

As we incorporate policy preferences and partisan politics into our understanding of Congress's use of constitutional scripts and construction of constitutional order, we must recall that the branches of government are not nearly as separated as the framers of the constitution might have imagined them to be. Partisanship and ideology connect the three branches and at times affect each branch's willingness to curtail the others' authority. All evidence suggests that members of Congress in the nineteenth century believed the commander in chief clause conferred some limited authority on the president, consistent with narratives that equated it to the authority conferred upon any typical "general." However, within this framework, the president's supporters tended to construe his implied authority broadly while his opponents tended to interpret his authority narrowly. At any given moment, a member of Congress's partisanship was a pretty good guide to how much discretionary power he thought the president should have.

Though I have not highlighted this, partisanship has been evident in many of the congressional conversations discussed in previous chapters. Federalists thought that John Adams could be trusted to use the navy to protect merchant ships without starting a broader war with France, while Democratic-Republicans were skeptical. Democrats thought Polk could be trusted to govern conquered lands without direction from Congress, while Whigs wanted to tie his hands. Some Republicans thought Lincoln could be trusted to suspend habeas corpus with little regulation from Congress, while Democrats and Unionists thought strict regulation was required. In each case, members of the opposite party were less trusting, less willing to grant broad discretionary authority to the commander in chief, and preferred to tightly regulate his behavior in law. In this chapter, I argue that we can better understand important historical applications of constitutional war powers if we recognize that these interrelated factors—members' received constitutional understanding, their partisan relationship to the president, and their policy preferences—are intertwined in Congress's actions and members' justifications for those actions.

As they do today, at the individual level, nineteenth-century members of Congress reacted to novel questions about the authority of the commander in chief at least in part based on their own partisan relationship to the president at that moment. Lawmakers were confronted with genuinely debatable questions about the commander in chief's authority. In talking through what the Constitution meant, they used received constitutional scripts and related historical and academic citations to talk about the constitutional balance of powers and to explain their decision on the question at hand. However, and not coincidentally, they also managed to adopt the interpretation that was most consistent with their other political views. It is easy to notice the close resemblance between what members of Congress said the commander in chief clause meant, based on their reading of history and the law, and what it was most convenient for the clause to mean, given their partisan political incentives and policy preferences. Their arguments provide evidence that when confronted with constitutional ambiguity, they often responded to that ambiguity with motivated reasoning.[4] Congressional speeches show that legislators who shared the president's party affiliation and policy views usually (but not always) supported broader discretionary authority for him. That preference is evident even when the member was simultaneously subscribing to norms that constrained unilateral presidential authority. As noted in other scholarship, routine partisan support for broader authority for a copartisan president is a powerful resource for presidents who want to increase their constitutional power at the expense of Congress.[5]

PARTISANSHIP, TRUST, AND POLICY PREFERENCES

Why might members of the president's party and members of the out-party define the Constitution differently? There are two overlapping pathways that lead members to such definitions. The first is that members of Congress are more willing to trust the president in their own party. In the speeches about the commander in chief clause collected for this project, members of the president's party were frequently heard to make statements such as "he is trustworthy" and that he "can be trusted" with discretion, and that he therefore does not need to be directed by Congress. Research has shown that the partisan social identity that might give rise to such trust was present both among both congressional lawmakers and the mass public even when the Republican party was less than a decade old, during the Civil War.[6] That trust is probably partly a guess about shared social identity, shared values, shared political fates and partly an evaluation of the president's professional reputation.[7] The discussion that follows will show that it is possible for presidents to build trust among out-partisans as well and that such trust can translate into real authority.

Second, partisan interpretations of executive authority are also clearly related to members' policy positions.[8] Some scholars have credited shared policy preferences for Congress's modern deference to the president's definition of war powers.[9] Members of Congress considering questions about the scope of the commander in chief's constitutional authority might not have had strong opinions about the balance of powers but probably did have strong opinions about slavery, expansionism, civil rights, race, imperialism, federalism, and the other political questions that are wrapped up in decisions about war powers. Those policy positions are formed by long-standing, electorally relevant public debates, whereas interpretations of the commander in chief clause arise only occasionally. Their agreement with the president on policy seems to affect their support for the powers of his office. We can see the effect of policy positions in cases where members of the president's party disagree with him about policy and find ways to narrowly interpret his powers, as well as in cases where members of opposition parties agree with him about policy and find ways to broadly interpret his powers.

Most of the time, partisans of the president both share the president's policy preferences and trust him as a member of their in-group. When his party controls Congress, then, Congress as a body is more likely to grant the president discretionary authority beyond the bounds of what they would accept for a president of the opposing party. It is important that the majority party controls the congressional agenda. That majority determines whether bills or resolutions that either authorize and empower or constrain presidential actions even come up for a vote. To the degree that the majority party has incentives to empower or constrain a particular president because of partisan and policy alliances, its agenda control decides whether a particular vote or debate will take place.[10]

As one of the most heated and consequential nineteenth-century debates over the authority of the commander in chief, the debate over battlefield emancipation does an especially good job of illustrating how these varying aspects of partisanship and trust interact with constitutional scripts to support broad but carefully defined authority for the commander in chief. Battlefield emancipation was not a solely presidential construction of the commander in chief clause. Congress debated legal and battlefield emancipation for months before Lincoln's orders. The Second Confiscation Act at least tentatively legally authorized his action. But debates in Congress before his order also politically legitimated it by defining battlefield emancipation to be within the commander in chief's constitutional authority. Constitutional scripts, debates between the "Washington" and "law of nations" versions of the dominant constitutional script, trust and distrust of Abraham Lincoln, members' moral and policy preferences about slavery, and partisan majorities in Congress all affected the political legitimacy of the justifications offered for Lincoln's proclamation.

THE EMANCIPATION PROCLAMATION

When President Lincoln issued the Emancipation Proclamation on January 1, 1863, he did so without reference to any authorizing legislation. This was unusual for several reasons. First, it was an unusual action because the proclamation was a major change in US policy on the issue that had defined the most contentious debates of the prior half century. Indeed, the "federal consensus" that had served as the basis for many of the signature laws of the antebellum period held that slavery was legal within states that wanted to authorize it and that the federal government could not say otherwise.[11] The proclamation was also unusual because in the nineteenth century, presidents mostly acted based on statutory, not constitutional, power. It was further unusual because it did not reference Congress's Second Confiscation Act, which had plausibly authorized the order and which Lincoln had referred to in his September 1862 "warning" proclamation. Finally, it was an unexpected order because in issuing it, Lincoln reversed the position he had publicly articulated during 1861 and early 1862. To this day, Civil War historians do not agree about why Lincoln changed his mind.[12] So how he, and the political system more generally, came to view the order as a constitutionally legitimate, politically tenable action invites additional investigation.

Overall, the congressional debate over battlefield emancipation of enslaved people shows how the authority associated with the commander in chief clause was politically constructed, with members' moral preferences, partisanship, trust in the president, and received constitutional narratives each playing a role. The "Washington as general" and "laws of nations" arguments about the commander in chief clause were referred to often in these congressional debates. The debates about the relevance of the commander in chief's authority to battlefield emancipation illustrated that trust is a component of partisanship but is also separate from it. There were Republicans who mistrusted Lincoln and preferred not to let him act on his own. There were Unionists who trusted Lincoln and preferred to empower him over the Republicans in Congress. There were also Republicans who trusted Lincoln to the extreme of rejecting Congress's authority entirely.

Debates over battlefield emancipation also show how members' moral beliefs about slavery itself affected their interpretations of the Constitution. This is displayed most clearly among the Republicans who opposed battlefield emancipation in theory but supported it in practice. They made vociferous arguments that the commander in chief lacked the authority to free enslaved people on the battlefield. However, when Lincoln issued the proclamation, their strong preference to end slavery, perhaps combined with a preference to support their own party's president, overrode those objections.

Background

The Emancipation Proclamation of January 1, 1863, said (emphasis mine):

> Now, therefore I, Abraham Lincoln, President of the United States, by virtue of the power in me *vested as Commander-in-Chief, of the Army and Navy of the United States in time of actual armed rebellion against the authority and government of the United States, and as a fit and necessary war measure for suppressing said rebellion,* do . . . order and designate as the States and parts of States wherein the people thereof respectively, are this day in rebellion against the United States . . . And by virtue of the power, and for the purpose aforesaid, I do order and declare that all persons held as slaves within said designated States, and parts of States, are, and henceforward shall be free; and that the Executive government of the United States, including the military and naval authorities thereof, will recognize and maintain the freedom of said persons.

Lincoln based this proclamation not on congressional law but on the undefined power of the commander in chief to issue military orders about battlefield tactics during wartime. He argued that by freeing the people enslaved by the Confederacy, he denied a battlefield advantage to the enemy and that by encouraging their defections and using their labor to support the Union army, he gained a significant tactical advantage. In later defenses of the proclamation, he specifically defended it based on military necessity. In his Conkling letter of August 1863, he defended the right of a commander in chief to take property in wartime.[13] In Lincoln's April 1864 letter to Albert G. Hodges, he said there was

> indispensable necessity for military emancipation . . . I was, in my best judgment, driven to the alternative of either surrendering the Union, and with it, the Constitution, or of laying strong hand upon the colored element. I chose the latter. In choosing it, I hoped for greater gain than loss; but of this, I was not entirely confident. More than a year of trial now shows no loss by it in our foreign

relations, none in our home popular sentiment, none in our white military force,—no loss by it any how or any where [*sic*]. On the contrary, it shows a gain of quite a hundred and thirty thousand soldiers, seamen, and laborers. These are palpable facts, about which, as facts, there can be no cavilling [*sic*]. We have the men; and we could not have had them without the measure.[14]

Lincoln correctly anticipated little loss in "home popular sentiment," perhaps in part because members of Congress across party lines had tacitly agreed beforehand that an order like the Emancipation Proclamation fell within the bounds of the narrow authority conferred by the commander in chief clause and because Northern public opinion supported its overall goal. In his support in Congress, Lincoln benefited from policy agreement with his own partisans and from the trust he had earned among some out-partisans.

The authority to issue battlefield commands had always been central to how members of Congress construed the commander in chief clause. As noted in chapter 1, members of Congress throughout the nineteenth century spoke matter-of-factly about the president's constitutional authority to move troops from one place to another during peacetime within US territory and in both American and enemy territory during wartime.[15] Legislators referred to the commander in chief's authority to "direct campaigns" and to "urge" and "recommend" military advances and retreats.[16] His will, "in conducting a war, carrying on its field operations, was to be paramount."[17] It was his responsibility to "undertake expeditions" and to adopt "active and speedy measures . . . to weaken the enemy, and cut off his supplies."[18] They sometimes used more violent language to describe his military authority. He was "to draw the sword," to "open fire," to "strike a blow" at the enemy, "to attack the enemy where he could hit and hurt."[19] The commander in chief's authority was to "take life."[20]

Yet, the commander in chief's authority on the "battlefield" was a contested question during the Civil War. From the start of the war, there were debates about whether the Confederate states were American territory in the throes of an insurrection or whether they were an enemy nation to be subdued. The definition of the conflict affected how members of Congress thought about and rhetorically constructed the authority of the commander in chief. From the very beginning of the war, Congress was actively part of discussions about what to do with rebels, their property, and the enslaved people that they considered to be their property. The questions they confronted lacked clear precedents. Were people in the Confederate states to be considered traitors and subject to legal proceedings to convict them of treason? Were they to be considered lawbreaking American citizens, whose property rights were protected by the Fifth Amendment to the Constitution? Were they to be considered foreign adversaries, subject to the laws of war? What about Southerners who were not active participants in the rebellion? Congressional lawmakers had to figure out what authority Congress had, and what authority the commander in chief had, to deal with rebel fighters, the citizens of the Confederate states, and the people they enslaved. As they did so, they had to contend with the Union's changing fortunes on the battlefield, the rising antislavery sentiment among Northern Republicans, the threat that the border states would secede, and the cautious decision making of President Lincoln.[21]

After a month of consideration but little recorded congressional debate, in August 1861 Congress passed the First Confiscation Act. The act had been proposed by Sen. Lyman Trumbull of Illinois, who in his long career affiliated with both the Democratic and Republican parties and was a leading proponent of legislation to "confiscate" rebel property, including enslaved people. The First Confiscation Act permitted courts to condemn the property, including enslaved people, of rebels as they were captured and convicted of treason. That law began the process of emancipation but was narrow and neither dealt with people who had escaped slavery nor with the larger question of whether the war would ultimately end slavery itself.[22]

President Lincoln opposed slavery. But he was also convinced that slavery was legal under American law and that his task in prosecuting the Civil War was to restore the rule of law. He also believed, at least at the outset, that the only way to win the war was to keep the border states in the Union by leaving the slavery question out of the conflict. Thus, though he signed the bill, Lincoln and his administration did not vigorously enforce the First Confiscation Act.[23] Lincoln also resisted other efforts to turn the war into a war to end slavery. When his first secretary of war, Simon Cameron, tried to argue publicly that enslaved people should be freed and armed, Lincoln soon thereafter appointed him to be minister to Russia.[24] When Gen. John C. Fremont declared martial law in Missouri and freed all enslaved people there, Lincoln reversed his order and said that generals could only free people through the courts, as mandated in the weakly framed First Confiscation Act. He also revoked Maj. Gen. David Hunter's May 1862 order freeing enslaved people in the area of his command.[25] He argued in a letter to Senator Browning in 1861 that battlefield emancipation was a war measure and could never be permanent.[26]

In December 1861 Trumbull proposed a potentially more sweeping bill, the Second Confiscation Act. As proposed, it would have "declared and made free all the slaves of persons in arms against the government."[27] When passed the following summer, after a series of congressional debates and moderating amendments, the law would free the slaves of those who "commit the crime of treason against the United States . . . [or who] incite, set on foot, assist, or engage in any rebellion."[28] The final bill was narrower in scope than had been initially proposed and again relied on court proceedings to free enslaved people who escaped or were confiscated by the military. Even so, some worried that it went too far to overturn the states' traditional rights to legislate regarding slavery.[29]

During the course of the debates over the Second Confiscation Act, Congress talked a great deal about the relative wartime powers of Congress and the commander in chief.[30] Opponents of battlefield emancipation, who often referred to the "Washington as general" model of limited presidential authority, were located at the extremes of both the Republican and Democratic parties. The strongest abolitionist Republicans opposed battlefield emancipation, arguing that the authority of the commander in chief was extremely limited and that Lincoln needed congressional authority to emancipate people in rebel territory. These abolitionists had watched Lincoln slow-walk the enforcement of the First Confiscation Act and wanted to take discretion out of his hands, as well as to ensure emancipation would have the permanence of law. At the opposite end of the political spectrum, some Democrats, supporters of slavery, also opposed the idea of battlefield emancipation, arguing that the commander in chief had no power to affect property in the United States because to do so required him to illegally declare martial law. They also disputed Congress's power to end slavery.

But in the middle, many Republicans, Democrats, and Unionists agreed that the commander in chief had some unilateral military authority to emancipate enslaved people in rebel territory, based on the president's battlefield command authority. This line of reasoning had been articulated in speeches and writing by John Quincy Adams several decades earlier and was promoted by some abolitionists.[31] Adams's arguments for the legitimacy of battlefield emancipation were reprinted by abolitionist editor William Lloyd Garrison in 1861. There was precedent for such an order in American history, as both the royal governor of colonial Virginia, Lord Dunmore, and British General Henry Clinton had freed enslaved people in the "rebellious colonies" during the American Revolution, although, notably, this British precedent was rarely cited by members of Congress seeking to argue for such an action.[32] In 1838 Gen. Thomas Jesup had offered emancipation to black Seminoles who surrendered to the army during the second Seminole War.[33] Sen. Orville Browning wrote Lincoln early in the war, urging military emancipation, and Sen. Charles Sumner made both private and public arguments for it as well.[34] Military emancipation was also supported by Lincoln's own solicitor general, who publicly advocated for such an order during the spring of 1862.[35] It was also consistent with the "laws of nations" model for the authority of the commander in chief. That middle ground reasoning, that by the traditions and necessities of war a commander in chief had authority to free an enemy's slaves, would eventually be adopted rhetorically by a broad spectrum of members of Congress and later by Lincoln himself in the Emancipation Proclamation.[36]

In the following sections, I briefly describe the arguments about the commander in chief's authority made by at least five distinct groups of members of Congress during the debate over the Second Confiscation Act. Partisan supporters and opponents expressed a range of opinions about the legitimacy of battlefield emancipation. Only partisan opponents of the president would stay committed to their opposition. Though the debates were politically complicated, and members' beliefs about slavery and their partisanship affected the precise authority they believed the commander in chief should have in this situation, all who commented on the commander in chief clause relied on one or another familiar form of the "general in chief" model for understanding the commander in chief's authority.[37]

Opponents of Battlefield Emancipation:
Democrats and Unionists

Predictably, Democratic and third-party supporters of slavery argued that the commander in chief lacked authority to free people enslaved by Southerners. Some slaveholding Democrats and Unionists railed against the possibility of military emancipation as an illegal act of martial law. Democrat Lazarus Powell, senator from Kentucky, criticized those who claimed that the right to emancipate people and confiscate property derived from unilateral executive power:[38] "I deny that the President of the United States, that any general commanding our forces, ay, that the Government by virtue of any or all of its departments, can declare martial law."[39] Charles Wickliffe, Kentucky Unionist, conceded that under the laws of nations, a battlefield commander might have some rights of capture, but that did not include any right to seize private property on land, because "the rules of civilized war forbid it."[40] Garrett Davis, who had been a Whig opponent of the Mexican War and who owned slaves, remained an outspoken adherent to an argument he had made during two decades earlier—namely that the commander in chief had the powers of a general but served the will of Congress.[41] Relying on constitutional text and precedents from American history, he reminded his colleagues that

> the whole war power of the Government is vested by the Constitution exclusively in Congress. It alone can declare war and may authorize general hostilities, as against Great Britain in 1812, or may limit them, as against France in 1798. The President cannot raise and support armies, or impose taxes, or borrow money, or make appropriations to support them, or to conduct any operation of Government. He cannot call out the militia to execute "the laws of the Union, suppress insurrections, or repel invasions," except so far as he is authorized by the laws of Congress. He is simply the Commander-in-Chief of the Army and Navy, and of the militia when in the service of the United States; and as such, he is clothed with no more authority, nor can he do any other acts, than the senior general in the service of the United States or any other citizen might, whom the Constitution had designated as such commander-in-chief.[42]

Opponents of Battlefield Emancipation: Republicans

Some of the strongest Republican advocates of emancipation agreed with slaveholding Democrats that the president lacked authority to enact battlefield emancipation as commander in chief.[43] They argued that Congress needed to legislate under its constitutional war powers to resolve the issue of enslaved people in conquered territory. Proponents of this position and the broad scope of Illinois senator Trumbull's original Second Confiscation bill would have preferred to use congressional power to force Lincoln to take more dramatic and permanent steps to emancipate enslaved people. Their reasoning reveals reliance on the "Washington as general" model of limited presidential power and also shows a rejection of the federal consensus, mistrust of Lincoln, and a desire to force his hand on the slavery question.

Antislavery Republican senator Jacob Howard of Michigan declared that the president's "mere capacity as Commander-in-Chief renders him in no respect independent of the authority of Congress. It does not place him above the law. He is still our general and bound to execute our behests."[44] He asked, with irony that repudiated arguments made by his fellow Republicans, "Is nothing left to [the people's] representatives but to furnish the men, the materials and the money; and are their orders as to the mode in which, and the purposes for which, these shall be used, totally powerless and void?"[45] A few months later, in extensive remarks, Howard gave a history of the colonies, the Revolution, and the Founding, which, he said, refuted the notion that the commander in chief had any power at all over the army that could not be regulated by Congress. Echoing the "Washington as general" narrative, he declared that the commander in chief "is but the general employed by the State to command that army; that is, to order and direct its operations as an instrument of making war for the defense and protection of the State. His functions are but those of an agent of the State to promote her interests by fighting her enemies."[46] Antislavery Republican senator Benjamin Wade proclaimed that "it depends upon Congress, not upon him, to say whether that war shall continue, and to prescribe precisely upon what principles it shall be governed."[47] Similarly, Republican senator John Sherman opined that "the President can conduct this war only in the manner and in the mode we may prescribe by law. Therefore it is that Congress ought to regulate the mode in which the President may seize this property."[48]

These Republicans couched their support for legislative emancipation in constitutional language that favored Congress. Republican senator and antislavery activist Charles Sumner, who had earlier argued in favor of battlefield emancipation, argued in Congress in the spring of 1862 that "there is nothing which may be done anywhere under the rights of war, which may not be done by Congress."[49] In his view, Congress could at any time "limit or enlarge" the powers of the commander in chief. [50] Further, "because the property in question is in the boundaries of the United States, it is Congress that has power over punishments and confiscations, not the president as commanding general."[51] Senator John Hale, who had been the Free Soil candidate for president in 1852, said that although the president was commander in chief, "Congress, the legislative power sitting superior to him or any other magistrate in the nation, may regulate, modify, and direct whatever principles they please their chief commander shall act upon and execute."[52] Rep. Elijiah Babbitt, Republican of Pennsylvania, argued that "the powers of Congress seem express, while those of the President are only implied, from his being Commander-in-Chief."[53]

Antislavery Republican representative John Bingham of Ohio argued that the power of confiscation and emancipation "is a war power; but . . . the Constitution has invested the war power in Congress, and the power to pass all laws needful to its execution."[54] He argued that President Lincoln himself doubted that his commander in chief powers extended so far as to emancipate enslaved people in conquered Confederate territory but noted that Lincoln said that as president he would certainly have to enforce laws passed by Congress. Republican senator David Wilmot, who was a former free-soiler but not an antislavery activist, argued that the commander in chief had "no power to emancipate slaves, except as actually connected with his military operations, and here he is limited to the actual power of the force under his command."[55]

Some other Republicans expressed concerns about ending slavery, and conceded there might be a military prerogative to emancipate, but explicitly worried that battlefield emancipation would not be permanent. They argued that the commander in chief could free enslaved people as a military necessity but that it would be better if Congress legislated to ensure emancipation's legality and permanence once peace returned. Rep. John Killinger, a Pennsylvania Republican, argued that "as the Commander-in-Chief of the Army and Navy, [Lincoln] is invested with large discretion in this direction," but that he still believed emancipation "requires the safeguards of legislation." Republican representative John Wallace of Pennsylvania argued that Lincoln's "power as Commander-in-Chief in time of war is omnipotent, as against the enemy, but when peace is restored and the military authority is withdrawn, his military power ceases, and the civil law resumes her peaceful sway. No proclamation of his has any legal effect or force beyond his military lines. Whatever property he seizes and appropriates is taken by the law of capture."[56]

Ambivalent Support for Battlefield Emancipation: Republicans

Other Republicans didn't seem to care at all about the constitutional roots of the authority to emancipate Confederate slaves, but as advocates for the policy, they were sure that authority existed somewhere. Their support for battlefield emancipation seemed to derive entirely from their support for the outcome itself. Charles Sedgwick, Republican of New York, declared that it "remains a mere question of legislative or of military discretion, according as you hold that the power resides in Congress, or, absolute and independent of Congress, in the Commander-in Chief of the Army, or the commander or a military district."[57] Antislavery advocate Republican William Fessenden of Maine couldn't find "prohibitions as must inhibit either the Commander-in-Chief of the Army or the Congress of the United States from employing confiscation or emancipation, if in their wisdom necessary, in prosecuting this war."[58] Republican John Gurley of Ohio argued that the Constitution meant whatever it needs to mean in order to preserve the union. In his view, the Constitution's "authors never intended to tie the hands of legislators, judges, nor the Commander-in-Chief, that traitors might run riot over a country; they gave us, sir, a Constitution that has within it the element of perpetuity, and which undoubtedly permits confiscation, and even emancipation, when they become absolutely essential to national salvation."[59] Massachusetts Republican Thomas Eliot said that Congress had every right to pass such an emancipation law, but that even without such a law, the president could take that step based on his military rights.

Strong Supporters of Battlefield Emancipation: Republicans

As might be expected, some conservative Republicans adopted a sweeping and broad definition of the implied powers of the commander in chief. [60] Their arguments referred to familiar narratives but also explicitly acknowledged their trust in President Lincoln. Senator Orville Browning, for example, argued that the Congress's power in executing a war was limited to voting for the war, for the size of the army itself, and for supplies; at the same time, Congress could not micromanage the commander in chief. As for the matter of the confiscation of property, he said, "Of his power to act in the premises I have not the slightest doubt. . . . the Constitution vests in him powers in time of war which do not exist, or, if they exist, are dormant, in time of peace." Wartime confiscation of people enslaved by the enemy and other property, he argued, was an inherently executive act, and since authority to emancipate slaves flowed from international historical traditions, congressional legislation was unnecessary.[61] He also argued against the Second Confiscation Act by arguing that the federal courts would find it unconstitutional.[62] As the bill was being finally debated in July, he supported the congressionally granted discretion the bill left to the commander in chief, saying that "I have confidence in the judgment, patriotism, and discretion of the President."[63] Edgar Cowan, Republican of Pennsylvania, also questioned the necessity of the Second Confiscation Act, arguing that the implied constitutional authority of the commander in chief was sufficient to free slaves in land occupied by the military. In his opinion, the president had "absolute authority to do a thing by the laws of war, under which the commander-in-chief of an army always acts as against his enemy, under no restraints whatever."[64]

Republican Support for Emancipation, by Whatever Means Necessary

Note that wherever the constitutional authority came from, there was policy agreement among many Republicans that the people enslaved by the Confederates *should* be freed. But the messy compromises that led to the ineffectual drafting of the Confiscation Acts reflected conflicting arguments about how to bring that policy goal about. Some preferred to etch emancipation concretely into law, limiting Lincoln's discretion. They made their argument in constitutional language that favored Congress. Others saw battlefield emancipation as consistent with the commander in chief's command authority and trusted Lincoln to act properly with broad wartime powers. A politically astute observer would suspect that none of these Republicans would vote to punish President Lincoln if he relied on the commander in chief clause to free the people enslaved by the Confederacy. And with Republicans in charge of Congress, there was no effort to do so after the order was issued.

Support for Battlefield Emancipation: Democrats and Unionists

Crucially, it was not only Republican members of Congress who supported a definition of the commander in chief's authority that encompassed battlefield emancipation of the people enslaved by the enemy. Some Democrats and Unionists agreed with the Republicans who said emancipation was justifiable as a military necessity. They also may have felt that, since President Lincoln had used such authority cautiously in the past, it was better to have him act alone than to leave decisions over emancipation in the hands of congressional Republicans. Democrat Hendrick Wright of Pennsylvania argued that while it was unwise to emancipate all enslaved people, if it was done on the battlefield, "it is a matter that must depend upon the emergencies of the occasion."[65]

Several Unionists spoke in favor of that middle ground, arguing that the

Constitution did not allow Congress to emancipate people in the states but that the "laws of nations" and traditions of war allowed the commander in chief to do so on the battlefield and in conquered territory. Rep. Horace Maynard, a slaveholding Unionist from Tennessee, claimed that Congress could not emancipate enslaved people because during wartime the legislature's powers were severely curtailed by international laws of war.[66] However, he acknowledged that if war created such a power, it already belonged to the president. He said that Congress "may declare war and make peace; we may create and supply armies and navies, or we may refuse to do both; but the war power belongs to the President, as the Commander-in-Chief of the Army and Navy, and is defined by the code of international law."[67] Rep. William Sheffield, a Rhode Island Unionist, argued that the Constitution was silent on most of the commander in chief's specific powers. He asked:

> Where is your constitutional power to say that your enemies are to be killed in battle, or to be made prisoners of war? How are you to annoy and subdue the enemy? The Executive, or the war executing power, is to do this. The people have committed this power to him. In executing this duty he may visit on those who oppose its execution any measure of justice which is warranted by the laws of war. The powers of Congress end when the Army is in the field in battle army. The Executive is at its head as Commander-in- Chief.[68]

Moderate West Virginia Unionist senator Waitman Willey was skeptical that the president could emancipate slaves "by a mere proclamation on paper, [but] when he can seize upon the slave-owner and upon the slave himself and set him free, I imagine he has the power to do it as the Commander-in-Chief of the Army."[69] Unionist representative Benjamin Thomas of Massachusetts, in a long monologue about the history of slavery, argued that the commander in chief had implied constitutional authority to free the people enslaved by his enemies:

> If the commander of a military district shall find that the slaves within it, by the strength they give to their rebellious masters—by bearing arms, or doing other military service, or acting as the servants of those who do—obstruct his efforts to subdue the rebellion, he may deprive the enemy of this force, and may remove the obstruction by giving freedom to the slaves. This, it is apparent, is not a civil or legislative, but a strictly military right and power, springing from the exigency,

and measured and limited by it, to be used for the subduing of the enemy, and for no ulterior purpose.[70]

Congressional Resolution

After long debate, Congress passed the Second Confiscation Act, which freed enslaved people who came behind Union lines and established a range of punishments for convicted traitors. The act was full of self-contradictory compromises and did not resolve many key questions about the future of slavery.[71] In partial enforcement of that law, on September 22, Abraham Lincoln issued the first of two Emancipation Proclamations. In the first proclamation, as required by the law, he warned the South that on January 1, 1863, all slaves in states still in rebellion would be freed.[72] This preliminary proclamation was criticized by some congressional Unionists. One such critic complained that the proclamation was too broad a reading of the act, appeared to make law, and being "legislative in character" was not within Lincoln's authority. Unionist representative John Crisfield argued that military authority extended to whatever "retards or embarrasses the march of his army, he may abate or remove; whatever is necessary to its subsistence and protection, he may take; whatever enables the force in front to keep up the resistance, he may destroy. But his authority is limited to these objects. He is not a law maker; he can make no rule but for the government of his army, nor for a wider space than the extent of his own lines."[73] Such criticism seemed to imply that the compromises within the Second Confiscation Act might not be legitimately broadly construed. At the same time, these Unionist comments also seem to imply that in conquered enemy territory, there might be authority for battlefield emancipation.

The Proclamation and Congressional Reaction

On January 1, 1863, when Lincoln issued the second (and better-known) Emancipation Proclamation, he did not ground his authority in the Second Confiscation Act. Instead, he claimed that his authority derived from military necessity and in implied military power in the commander in chief clause. Historians note that Lincoln may have actually come to favor military emancipation during the spring or early summer of 1862 (during and after Congress's debates, as well as during other wartime developments).[74]

In Congress, responses to the proclamation were predictable, but there was no great bipartisan objection to the order, or at least to grounding it in the commander in chief clause.[75] Certainly, some representatives from slaveholding border states criticized the order after it was issued. Slaveholding senator Lazarus Powell, Democrat of Kentucky, who had argued against military emancipation before the proclamation was issued, reiterated his objections afterwards.[76] Emancipation, he argued, amounted to unconstitutional and illegal theft. William Allen, Democrat of Ohio, complained six weeks after the proclamation was issued that while the proclamation had been billed as a war measure, "yet nothing has transpired . . . and our prospects for a suppression of the rebellion far from brilliant."[77]

On the other side of the aisle, Republicans defended Lincoln's authority to issue the proclamation, often relying on "laws of nations" rhetoric. Charles Sedgwick, Republican of New York, who hadn't had a strong opinion about whether commander in chief clause conferred the authority on the president to emancipate enslaved people, approved of it afterward. He confirmed that "the law of nations clearly sanctions the emancipation of the enemy's slaves by military force and authority."[78] James Ashley of Ohio said that "in time of war, by the laws of war, as Commander-in-Chief he may confiscate enemy's property and emancipate all slaves."[79]

As the end of the war came into view, members of Congress again debated whether Lincoln's emancipation of Southern slaves "henceforward" could be maintained after the hostilities ended.[80] Republican Thomas Eliot of Massachusetts argued the order was permanent and "irrevocable" because while he had power "as Commander-in-Chief, [to] strike off the chain . . . he cannot in any capacity, as chieftain or as President, make of a freedman a slave." Unionist senator Garrett Davis, an enslaver, argued that while emancipation may have been a military necessity, it required compensation, a position shared by Lincoln himself.[81] Senator John Sherman, Republican of Ohio, argued that the president's order would not be legal when the war ended and that therefore Congress had better act to ensure emancipation survived the end of the war:

> In time of war [the president] is Commander-in-Chief of our Army and Navy;
> but is this power sufficient to change the laws of States and communities, or
> do they extend beyond the lines of our armies, and especially will they extend
> into the future peaceful times which we hope may soon come upon us? I shall
> hereafter endeavor to show that Congress is invested with clear power to guaranty
> emancipation to slaves who enter our armies; but where can such a power be

found for the President? Even if, in the opinion of Senators, the proclamation is effective, if it has the power and efficacy of law, it is our duty to give to that proclamation the sanction of the legislative authority.[82]

In agreement that at some point the president's military authority, and the legality of enforcing a military order, would end, Republicans in Congress worked with Lincoln in the effort throughout 1864 to pass the Thirteenth Amendment.[83] That amendment abolished slavery under the authority of the Constitution, which would have to be enforced in and by the former states of the Confederacy in order to be readmitted to the Union.

Highlighting the rhetorical history of the commander in chief clause sheds new light on these well-analyzed debates. Kleinerman, for example, notes some of the same dynamics I describe here in his discussion of the Confiscation Acts. But he is puzzled by the "extravagant theories about the supremacy of Congress" that were articulated by some members of Congress. Such theories make much more sense in the longer historical timeline of the "general in chief" narrative.[84] Similarly, Civil War historian Mark Neely is puzzled by the many references during these debates to the president as a "glorified colonel" and to members' references to *Cross v. Harrison*. The consistent historical narrative surrounding the commander in chief clause helps make sense both of references to that court case (about tariffs at the Port of San Francisco at the end of the Mexican War) and of repeated references to the president as "general."[85] This analysis suggests that those concepts and precedents were raised in debates over emancipation because they were interwoven with the dominant constitutional narratives that helped to define the nature of the president's wartime authority.

My findings also support scholars like Mariah Zeisberg who argue that explicit congressional action may not be necessary to politically legitimate presidential uses of war powers. While ending slavery involved several overlapping constitutional questions, especially about federal power, the debates described here suggest that a cross-partisan consensus existed in the Thirty-Seventh Congress that battlefield emancipation required no prior congressional authorization. Although the Emancipation Proclamation is sometimes seen as a questionable or even extralegal use of presidential authority, Congress did not act to either empower or punish the president because a congressional majority believed a combination of two arguments. Moderates across party lines believed that battlefield emancipation was consistent with the commander in chief's authority under the "laws of nations" and that Lincoln could be trusted to use that power narrowly. Liberals believed that emancipation of enslaved people was a good outcome, overriding their misgivings about whether the president had constitutional authority under the "Washington as general" model to order battlefield emancipation. Together those two groups comprised a congressional majority that would tolerate Lincoln's order and his constitutional justification for it. Certainly, congressional conservatives (some Democrats and Unionists) thought emancipation was bad policy, opposed the president, and argued he had insufficient power to issue the order. But the conservatives were outnumbered. Lincoln may well have known after the congressional debates concluded in the summer of 1862 that battlefield emancipation had sufficient political legitimacy to be a viable option.

Coda: Scripts Also Support Novel (and Narrow)
Constructions of the Commander in Chief

Chapter 1 showed that it was widely agreed in the nineteenth century that, while Congress had the authority to write laws governing military discipline and dismissals, the president had substantial discretionary authority to execute those laws and unquestioned superiority over all other military officers. But Congress in at least one instance curtailed even that long-standing interpretation of the commander in chief clause.

In 1864 and 1865 Republicans tended to support broad discretionary authority power for (Republican) President Lincoln. In one such debate, Republicans posited that the commander in chief had authority to dismiss officers, including generals, from service, arguing that "there must be an arbitrary power residing somewhere in the Government having in its control the organization of the Army" and that it was the president who monopolized that arbitrary power.[86] Democrats, on the other hand, argued dismissal power was not arbitrary and could be regulated by Congress. They wanted to constrain the commander in chief's dismissal power by requiring that he consult a nonpartisan board before dismissing officers.[87]

Just a few short years later, the parties switched sides in this argument. When Democrat Andrew Johnson became president, Republicans wrote laws limiting the president's authority over his cabinet and his own generals. They wrote bills to specifically empower General Grant at the expense of President

Johnson, even though some of these members of Congress had been vociferous supporters of presidential authority in the chain of command when Lincoln had been president. They passed the Reconstruction Acts over the howling opposition of the Democrats, who cried loudly about the acts' theft of the commander in chief's authority over his subordinates.

As these members of Congress understood them, three provisions of the Reconstruction Acts seemed to interfere directly in the chain of command by giving authority to military officers that was explicitly denied to the president. One part of the First Reconstruction Act empowered the generals governing Southern military districts to remove civilian state officials from office "subject to the disapproval of the General of the Army" (not the president). In another provision, the Army Appropriations Act of 1867 said that all presidential orders to the army should be issued through the general in chief (Grant), who could only be removed from office with the assent of the Senate. Additionally, section 10 of the Third Reconstruction Act said that "no district commander ... shall be bound in his action by any opinion of any civil officer of the United States." The president, in that language, was assumed by members of Congress to be the relevant civil officer.

Unsurprisingly, congressional arguments about these bills were heated, polarized around racial and Reconstruction policy, and partisan. Democrats, who opposed strict Reconstruction of the South, obviously opposed the bill on its policy merits. But they also argued against it by invoking the constitutional script that said that it violated the widely agreed upon norms of the president's supremacy in the chain of command.[88] Democratic senator Charles Buckalew of Pennsylvania echoed common themes when he argued that Congress could not "intervene between" the commander in chief and "his subordinate" because of the implied authority granted by the commander in chief clause. In his understanding, the commander in chief had

> one power under this head which no man can deny or doubt; and that is the power of giving orders to his inferiors in military rank. The most especial characteristic of a commander-in-chief is that he shall issue his orders to his subordinates and that they shall be bound to obey them. To be sure our President must issue his orders according to law; he cannot command his inferior officers to do acts which are illegal; but so long as he complies with the laws his orders are to be obeyed, being given in his capacity as Commander-in-Chief, charged with the execution of the law.[89]

Rep. Edwin Wright, Democrat of New Jersey, argued that the Appropriations Act in particular tore "away from him by a single act of this Congress his powers under the Constitution of the United States, which makes him Commander-in-Chief of the Army and Navy of the United States."[90] Kentucky Democrat representative Elijah Hise said that the appropriations bill stripped "the Executive, as Commander-in-Chief of the Army and Navy of the United States, of all power to issue the necessary orders for the government and action of the military forces of the United States, except through the General of the Army . . . regardless of the will of the President and his paramount authority over him."[91] Senator Hendricks objected to the provision excusing generals from being bound by the opinions of the president because "he is the Commander-in-Chief of the Army. We cannot say that he is less, nor take from him any power which he possesses rightfully as such commander."[92]

Even some Republicans were uncomfortable with the reach of the bills. For example, Sen. James Dixon, Republican of Connecticut, argued that "Congress has power to make rules for the government of the Army; . . . those rules must be consistent with the Commander-in-Chiefship of the President of the United States. He has a right to act as commander."[93]

But the majority of Republicans stood by the bills' language and justified their actions under the Washington-as-general script. A few Republicans argued the president had no authority to remove officers at all.[94] Republican senator Timothy Howe of Wisconsin said that Congress's enumerated powers were plenty robust to justify the bills in question and argued the president had no power of removal at all that would apply to General Grant.[95] Most Republicans argued that the commander-in-chief's powers could be legitimately restricted because they were subordinate to Congress's authority to regulate the armed forces. Republican Thomas Jenckes said that the Appropriations Act's purpose "was to use the Army to keep the peace, repress violence and secure freedom of action for all," and in that, the commander in chief was powerless "against the power of Congress."[96]

Despite vociferous objections from Democrats, the Republican Congress passed the Reconstruction Acts over President Johnson's vetoes. Johnson signed the 1867 appropriations bill despite voicing strong objections. As expected, the majority party's interpretation of the Constitution is the one that became law, at least temporarily extending Congress's authority and overriding the otherwise consensus-based superintendence authority of the commander in chief.

The Reconstruction Acts of 1867 are a straightforward case of an opposition party legislating to limit the authority of a president attempting to subvert the will of the majority party in Congress. They are also an extraordinary case of Congress temporarily attempting to reconstruct the nation and the Constitution as a multiracial democracy. What makes this example interesting to the history of the commander in chief clause is that Republicans, who only a few years earlier had supported broad authority for their own Republican president, acted to limit his successor's authority over senior military officers. In doing so, they overturned precedents and widely accepted norms that the commander in chief clause conferred a type of command authority that was often interpreted to be outside the scope of congressional review. Certainly, they relied on widely accepted alternative constitutional reasoning—that Congress always had the power to issue directives to the president. The episode shows quite clearly that congressional members and the parties were less committed to specific textual interpretations than to their broader policy goals. This was an extreme example of the proposition that partisanship can cut both ways—in unified government it can expand presidential power, but in divided government, it can help to curtail it.

But such actions do not always determine long-term changes in the construction of presidential authority. When Reconstruction-era Republicans legislated congressional intervention in the chain of command, this did not leave a lasting precedent. As white supremacists regained power in the South and began to argue that Reconstruction itself was illegitimate, the constitutional arguments made by the Radical Republicans were also repudiated. The command provisions of the Reconstruction Acts were eventually overturned and moreover were used by both parties as an example of congressional overreach in the ensuing decades. Democrats continued to bring up the constitutional arguments against the bills for decades.[97] Even when Congress debated creating a general staff in 1903, Republicans argued for the bill by reassuring each other and the Democrats that it was not in any way a repeat of the 1867 bill. Notably, the Reconstruction Acts stood out as an example of an illegitimate congressional overreach *in both parties* for a generation.

THE ROLE OF CONSTITUTIONAL SCRIPTS IN
CONGRESSIONAL DEBATES

The debates discussed in this chapter show that while members of Congress were clearly aware of relevant constitutional scripts, their interpretations of the Constitution were not entirely determined by those scripts. Congressional legislators had, as they have now, strongly held moral and political preferences that guided their actions. But when justifying those actions, the nineteenth-century congressmen did seem to draw upon well-known constitutional interpretations that were consistent with those preferences.

Partisan ideology played a role in the development of members' choice of constitutional scripts. The Whigs, in particular, played a special role in nineteenth-century ideas about the separation of powers. Emerging out of a political coalition opposed to the populist, reconstructive president Andrew Jackson, the Whigs, unlike most political parties, had firm positions about the subservient role that the president should play in the political system. Their ideas fit neatly with the "Washington as general" version of the commander in chief script. When they most used that argument, during the Mexican War, they were also the out-party and opposed to expansion through wars of aggression as a policy. As the Whigs dissolved and reformed as the Republican party, some of their preference for the "Washington as general" version of the script continued among Republicans and can be heard in Republican arguments for strong congressional war powers during the Civil War. But the Republicans were less committed to congressional power than the Whigs had been, and when narrow construction of the commander in chief clause came into conflict with other strongly held beliefs like moral opposition to slavery, Republicans were willing to define presidential power more expansively to achieve those policy goals.

Members of Congress have always been able and willing to adopt what looks like a partisan interpretation of the commander in chief clause. That apparent partisanship is composed of either trust in the president or shared policy preferences, or both combined. Members of Congress don't seem to need presidents to pressure them for them to adopt partisan reasoning about the commander in chief's constitutional powers. Certainly, when presidents actively or publicly pressured members of Congress to support a broad reading of presidential power, such pressure seems to affect some legislators in the president's party.[98] However, nineteenth-century presidents did not have the staff to lobby Congress on every question. Nor did presidents in this period have a record of campaign statements to put themselves at the center of public policymaking on every question. Lincoln himself did not make a strong case for either legislative or battlefield emancipation and acted during the beginning of the war as if both were illegitimate. Though his allies made the case for battlefield emancipation, Lincoln stayed out of the fray for a long time. However, once he took the step of issuing the order, his partisans fell in line.

With their copartisans willing to trust them with more discretion, early twentieth-century (and later) presidents who were willing to exploit that support were able to stretch those boundaries in ways that would have been unrecognizable in the early nineteenth century. Lincoln's Emancipation Proclamation didn't redefine the authority of the commander in chief, at least not at the time. It was a use of authority that was consistent with at least one version of the dominant constitutional script and didn't immediately seem to create new powers or lasting precedents. It wasn't until the twentieth century that presidents extracted Lincoln's action from its historical context and tried to use it as an example of prerogative power to justify broad presidential authority.[99]

The Emancipation Proclamation has at times been described as a use of extralegal prerogative power. In contrast, the analysis presented here shows that battlefield emancipation was at the time understood across party lines to be an acceptable application of narrowly defined authority derived from the commander in chief clause and was comprehensible according to the narratives commonly used to understand that clause. Congress played a central and active role in defining the boundaries of that authority—even in defining authority that they did not in fact write into law. This situation parallels Zeisberg's arguments about John Kennedy and Franklin Roosevelt, who used presidential war powers in questionable ways but within the congressionally defined national security order of the time period. Similarly, Lincoln adeptly reacted to fill the space that Congress—through its talk, not through its law—had defined as politically legitimate for him to occupy.[100]

Conclusion

This book has been a study of Congress's interpretations of the commander in chief clause prior to World War I. When members of Congress talked about the clause during this time period, they did not do so in an offhand way. Rather, they talked about the authority it conferred or did not confer upon the president. They repeatedly expressed the belief that the title granted some traditional military authority that was disassociated from policymaking authority, and they almost universally denied that the title conferred any authority to initiate hostilities. But that language, and its implications for the separation of powers, changed over time. Around the year 1900, members began to use the term commander in chief as a synonym for the president himself and began to conflate the title with his political role. That rhetorical and narrative shift accompanied Congress's willingness to grant the president more discretionary authority to define and use war powers.

This account should be useful to scholars and others who study constitutional war powers and their evolution over time. I show that around the year 1900, members of Congress adopted a new constitutional script about the commander in chief clause that reflected a new understanding of the relative war powers authority of the Congress and the president. The timing of that rhetorical shift and the patterns of behavior that accompanied it challenge dominant ideas about when the president began to accumulate new war powers authority. The evidence suggests that many characteristics of the modern constitutional order for war powers, including deference to the president, were present by the turn of the twentieth century. It also suggests that many characteristics of the modern constitutional order were present within the original order as well. Members of Congress relied on historical precedents as justifications for their actions, as presidents do today. Legislators responded to constitutional questions with a mix of political beliefs, partisan support for their own party's president, and constitutional logics, as they do today. This research illuminates new questions about the development of war powers, and it also speaks to scholarly debates about the role of congressional deliberation and authorization in legitimizing the use of force.

Becoming aware of constitutional scripts helps us better understand the overall worldview that supported the original constitutional order for war powers. Fisher, Griffin, and others characterize the original constitutional order as one in which Congress asserted and defended its rights to declare wars, authorize undeclared wars, and to regulate the use of force.[1] Existing work describes the patterns in Congress's behavior. The analysis in the preceding chapters adds to this body of research by supplying descriptive evidence regarding Congress's reasoning as it engaged in those constitutionally assertive behaviors. Members of Congress relied on a limited range of logic and reasoning as they talked about the commander in chief clause. Following Farrar-Myers, I have described this repeated reasoning as constitutional scripts.

Constitutional scripts seem to help conceptually organize a constitutional order. They supply a logic and a set of precedents that can rhetorically ground lawmakers' arguments when they are confronted with constitutionally ambiguous policy questions. The scripts I identified in previous chapters were not rigid—members of Congress used them to justify and ground the creation of novel constitutional authority. Nor were they entirely prescriptive—members used the same scripts to argue for opposite policy actions. The scripts themselves did not seem to originate in Congress, as they seemed to be familiar to many lawmakers from different places and parties and referred to texts and precedents as external sources of interpretive authority. A different research project, like Dearborn's study of the narrative of the president as national representative, might shed more light on these scripts' origins.[2] But they did seem to serve as meaningful frameworks through which members of Congress understood the Constitution and how to apply it.

Examining constitutional scripts helps to illuminate some important elements of what changed between the "original" and "modern" constitutional orders. It is not the case that in the original order, Congress always construed presidential war powers extremely narrowly. Members of Congress in the early republic did argue that the commander in chief clause conferred some implied authority upon the president, authority that under certain circumstances, such as battlefield emancipation, was quite broad. Nor is it the case that Congress maintained its control over war powers in the nineteenth century by always carefully deliberating about constitutional meaning. Its members took some meaning for granted and deliberated on the issues that fell outside that consensus. Instead, this analysis suggests that Congress constructed constitutional war powers authority in line with one of a few coherent theories. Those constitutional theories, embedded in repeated scripts, defined a range of legitimate actions and told members of Congress when to act and when not to act. When they chose not to act, they justified their reticence within the received framework of the constitutional script. When they chose to act, they debated what to do within the same framework. When the script changed, they were willing to legitimate a different and broader set of presidential actions, and Congress's role in deliberation over the use of force became less prominent.

Although I did not examine the interplay between presidential and congressional interpretations of constitutional scripts, the signals that scripts sent up and down Pennsylvania Avenue about the range of potentially legitimate uses of war powers might have affected these dynamics as well. Farrar-Myers, in particular, thought of constitutional scripts as conversations between the branches of government. Members of Congress listen to presidents, and especially to messages from presidents in their own party. Presidents also listen to members of Congress. Research shows that presidents today craft their war policy in response not only to bills and resolutions that Congress passes but also to the preferences about potential uses of force that members of Congress express in floor speeches and committee hearings. Presidents know that lawmakers can affect the media, public opinion, and their own political fortunes and anticipate congressional reactions even before they make decisions about how to interpret and apply their war powers in particular situations. This means they consider how much partisan support they have in Congress as they make decisions about the use of force.[3] Upon closer inspection, constitutional scripts might be evident in the decisions made in both branches and in the construction of legitimacy today as well. Future research may want to look more deeply into this signaling and presidents' awareness of it, as well as into the origins of different constitutional scripts at different points in time.

Though this analysis focuses on politics and political development that took place more than a century ago, it suggests that we should be attentive to the ways that similar processes may be taking place in Congress's construction of constitutional authority today. It implies we should interrogate the interests and values that have shaped the constitutional discourse around war powers in the modern era and pay special attention to the stories that current and future members of Congress tell about how the constitutional system works.

The scripts to which members of Congress referred in previous chapters were deeply intertwined with historical precedents. Members justified their actions by referring to the set of precedents implied by their script and then by their actions set precedents that were available to be incorporated into future scripts. The precedents that Congress set in any given moment, and the logic with which a congressional majority set those precedents, were not entirely predetermined by their received understandings. Members of Congress actively participated in reasoning about constitutional scripts and their applicability to a particular situation.

The preceding chapters illuminate debates about the relevance of precedent to the evolution of constitutional war powers.[4] Courts, of course, have established practices around relying on legal precedent. But presidents in the modern period have also used historical precedents, especially lists of haphazardly collected and dissimilar historical examples of military deployments, to justify presidentially initiated uses of force.[5] Similarly, I find that using constitutional scripts and political reasoning, members of Congress extracted historical precedents from their original circumstances when they constructed constitutional war powers in the early republic. The account presented in previous chapters shows that if modern presidents have developed constitutional scripts that are based in loose application of historical precedent, this is not a modern innovation or unique to the executive branch.

This thick description of congressional constitutional interpretation may be relevant to other scholarly research agendas as well. One debate among critics of the modern constitutional order focuses on whether Congress must legislate in order to legitimize the use of force. Some insist that congressional action is required to legitimize the use of force and believe that if Congress engaged in a more routine practice of legislatively authorizing the use of force, this might cause presidents to retract their arguments that they alone possess the right to do so.[6] Mariah Zeisberg and others, on the other hand, argue there can never be one perfectly balanced point in the system of shared war powers, and even additional congressional authorizations could never reach such a balance. Zeisberg in particular argues that formal congressional authorization is not the only way to legitimize the use of force and that Congress can participate meaningfully in constructing legitimate authority to use force even without expressly authorizing it. A "better" balance of war powers, according to her argument, could be achieved if each branch uses its own strengths to construct legitimate policy at any given moment.[7]

Like Zeisberg, I find evidence that in practice, Congress in the early republic seemed able to confer politically legitimate war powers authority on the president not just by authorizing his actions but also by agreeing to a definition of the commander in chief clause that included his right to take certain actions. During the "original constitutional order for war powers," Congress actively defined the boundaries between the separation of powers both by legislating and by *not* legislating. Members of Congress helped create legitimacy for presidential use of commander in chief authority even without legislating in extraordinary cases like the Emancipation Proclamation or the use of the navy as a protective convoy, and in routine cases like troop movements within the country's borders. They helped to define unlegislated presidential authority by actively discussing the commander in chief's independent power and especially by connecting his actions to the constitutional scripts that acted as shorthand summaries of their understanding of the distribution of powers. When members legislated, it was because congressional majorities believed that to accomplish policy ends they preferred, they had an obligation to act because the president lacked authority to act on his own. When members did not legislate, it was usually because majorities consciously agreed that the president already had sufficient constitutional or statutory authority to take the actions they preferred (though there were some temporary stalemates that also prevented congressional action). My systematic examination of the commander in chief clause supports the contention that Congress can confer political authority and acquiesce to presidential claims of authority through a variety of actions and inactions.

In the conversations I examined, members of Congress seemed to confer practical legitimacy on certain types of commander in chief authority with minimal amounts of deliberation. By reading the commander in chief clause to include the ability to remove generals from command, or to move troops and ships from place to place, they created space for the president to use constitutional authority completely uncontested. The fact that over time that uncontested space grew underscores the importance of Congress's participation in its legitimation. Congress participated in construction of the boundaries between congressional and presidential war powers both by legislating and by not legislating, and both by deliberating and by not deliberating.

The conclusion that Congress seems able to construct legitimate constitutional authority through inaction might seem to suggest that Congress's modern inaction and its acquiescence to presidential assertions of authority today is unproblematic. That is definitely not my intent. My investigation also finds evidence to support the arguments made by Fisher and others that in the original constitutional order, Congress insisted that the use of force was only legitimate when it derived from congressional action. I merely note that if it appears that today's Congress helps construct legitimate presidential war powers authority through actions it takes and does not take, that situation is not a modern innovation. It also accurately describes the practice by which Congress participated in the construction of constitutional meaning in the original constitutional order.

As analysis of the evolution of war powers continues, my work suggests scholars should consider more nuanced accounts of the political development of constitutional war powers. It casts a bit of doubt on rigid periodizations between the "original" and "modern" orders for war powers, demarcated by the initiation of the Korean War or the initiation of the Cold War. It supports a more contingent, "intercurrent" understanding of political development, with multiple streams of political pressure culminating in precedents that become important through a historically and institutionally contingent process.[8] The development of constitutional scripts themselves may be a stream in this intercurrent process.[9] The scripts I examine, though important logical and rhetorical arguments themselves, were also interwoven with competing sets of ideas and commitments in congressional debates that brought about political constructions of broader types of presidential authority.

The idea that Congress should patriotically defer to a president who oversteps his war powers authority was not new in 1950. Nor was red-scare type flag waving to rally wavering members of Congress to a deferential constitutional position. Nor was the idea that Congress owed deference to the foreign policy management by the executive branch. There really were differences between the ways that Congress and the president approached the division of war powers between the early republic and the modern period. But some of the key features of ideas in modern constitutional order developed around the year 1900. And the process by which those features evolved may have been more layered and interwoven with seemingly disparate political ideas, racial orders, and other political developments than is often acknowledged.[10]

The case studies in previous chapters show that members of Congress used scripts to frame the constitutionally legitimate range of outcomes, but their desired outcomes were also fundamentally shaped by their own policy goals, personal beliefs, and by their partisan orientation to the presidency. Individual members of Congress who took leading roles in these debates, and partisan congressional majorities that legitimized their arguments, helped shape the evolving logic of the constitutional scripts over time. Just as presidents and courts can shape constitutional meaning based on a mixture of received ideas and their own partisan and policy goals, such was the case with Congress in the nineteenth century. Just as modern Congresses are thought to make constitutional and war powers judgments that are shaped by partisan relations to the presidency and foreign policy goals, so did Congress in that period.[11]

Because members of Congress clearly identify with political parties, and because they organize their institutional rules around partisanship, it is easy to dismiss congressional constitutional construction as rooted in partisanship and parochial policy interests, and therefore less authoritative than the interpretations of the other branches. But presidents' and courts' interpretations of the constitutional text are similarly encumbered by partisanship as well as by views about policy, security, and racial worldviews related to policy. Those who think about the separation of powers and Congress's constitutional construction of meaning should never ignore the role that partisan interest plays in that construction. But highlighting the role it plays in congressional interpretation should also prompt a deeper consideration of the ways that politics and ideas affect presidents, lawyers, and judges at different points in time. And Congress's ability to articulate a definition of the boundaries between congressional and presidential war powers, and to police that boundary for more than a century, indicates that Congress can make the kind of consistent constitutional judgements that are often associated with the other branches.

Congress's actions in the case studies described here were affected by structural issues, just as they are in modern Congresses. Presidents and subordinate military officers can create crises, or even start wars, by their actions while armed and outside the territory of the United States, regardless of whether those actions are preauthorized by Congress. The case studies show that Congress has always struggled to assert itself once a president (like Polk) or a general (like Jackson) has unilaterally initiated military force. Even during the original constitutional order for war powers, members' preferences about the war itself and their partisan relationship to the president affected their perception of the action's legitimacy alongside their interpretations of the Constitution. Their responses to presidential overreach, when they did occur, as with the passage of the Habeas Corpus Act, often took considerable time because of Congress's collective action problems. Congress's Cold War deference to presidential unilateralism, including its silence about Truman's intervention in Korea, may not have been so unique to the modern period.

Were those earlier structural dilemmas any different from the ones that arise today? Perhaps the dominant constitutional scripts help distinguish them. During the original constitutional order for war powers, the "general in chief" script told members of Congress that presidents could not initiate the use of offensive force. So members of the opposition party and others who opposed questionable presidential actions had solid rhetorical arguments, complete with well-known precedents, to rely upon as they criticized the commander in chief and attempted to overturn his actions. Members who supported the president's actions defended him within the bounds of accepted logic and reasoning. In cases like the Mexican War, this led to Democrats who supported the war arguing (ironically) that presidents could not start wars on their own (and that Polk's actions were legitimate because he had not done so).

These examples suggest that the character of the deliberative process is interwoven with culturally dominant theories about the Constitution.[12] Identifying constitutional scripts helps us better understand the overall worldview that supported the original constitutional order for war powers, in which Congress accepted more responsibility for making decisions about the use of force. The scripts and precedents they invoked defined when and why Congress should act. During the original constitutional order, it was not just that Congress *had* debates about uses of war powers. It was important that *in* those debates, they articulated to themselves, to the president, the courts, and the public that presidential authority was narrow and congressional authority was broad. Both variants of the original "general in chief" script told members themselves that the president's war powers authority was limited and that they needed to be particularly attentive to authorizing any offensive uses of war powers. The script used before 1900 fostered repeated congressional deliberation about the use of force. It encouraged members of Congress to consider both whether the American people would support a use of offensive force, and to also consider whether an adversary would perceive a particular action to be an act of offense. Congress was not always good at this—it often considered those issues according to racial worldviews that led to inadequate consideration of the effects US actions would have on others. Members of Congress had a hard time classifying the use of gunboat diplomacy as a use of force in cases like the annexation of Hawaii and did not discuss the commander in chief clause at all in some cases that seemed to involve cases of "defense" and "protection" of white civilians.[13] But that original constitutional worldview facilitated both branches participating in decisions about the use of state violence.

The script that emerged in the early twentieth century did not nurture that deliberation. Instead, it encouraged members to defer to the president as commander in chief and as a nationally elected official. There were a variety of partisan and policy reasons that Congress was deferential to early twentieth-century executive uses of force. And it is not clear exactly why lawmakers latched onto this new script at the time that they did, or exactly what role it played in their understanding of war powers. But after the emergence of the "national representative" script, when members of Congress deferred to the president, they did so by citing a new constitutional interpretation of the commander in chief clause that said that Congress's role in war powers was to defer to the president. The debates that feature those scripts were not as focused on defining the distribution of powers at the line between offense and defense. Instead they hinged the commander in chief's authority on whether an action was "popular" and whether it amounted a "war." "War" is a much higher standard for congressional authority than an "act of offense." By defining congressional authority as only necessary for "war," presidents can take a far larger range of military actions without the need for congressional authorization or even deliberation. In addition, by connecting the commander in chief's authority to use force to his popularity, and the popularity of the action, the newer script also encourages the legitimization of conflict through propaganda and dehumanization of the adversary that help generate "popularity."

This analysis has implications for those who argue about what might be done to restore some of Congress's prominence in war powers decision making today. Constitutionally legitimate, democratic interbranch deliberation may be easier or harder to produce, depending on how members of Congress understand the Constitution's text. The actual content of their constitutional theories might affect Congress's choices to take on those debates and legislative actions that signal shared government to the executive branch. If Congress is to reassert itself in war powers in the future, it may need to justify a shift away from the current presidentially dominated balance of powers based on a coherent and popular theory of governance that legitimates its right to do so.

The evidence here implies that the congressional deliberation about constitutional authority that scholars are looking for in the modern period may be hard to find not because Congress is incapable of deliberating about the

Constitution, but because members do not currently believe they have a role in doing so. Lawmakers in the nineteenth century believed themselves competent constitutional interpreters. Then, as now, members of Congress represent the people and most probably understand the Constitution the way that ordinary Americans do. As George Lovell finds, ordinary Americans seem perfectly capable of interpreting the Constitution and reasoning about how it applies to new situations.[14] But today, as Peabody and others note, members of Congress have probably been taught that it is the court's job, not the Congress's job, to interpret the Constitution, and that their role in foreign affairs is to declare major wars, not to define, debate, and legitimate all uses of hostile force.[15] There are no quick fixes to that problem. Even with modified institutional structures or more legal staff to advise them, if members of Congress step up to construct constitutional authority, especially in novel ways, they must speak the language of nonspecialists and talk to other members and to the public that have been taught deference to the courts in constitutional interpretation and deference to presidents in war powers.[16] In order for members of Congress to participate in the construction of authority, they have to believe they have a role as representatives in doing so, as do members of members of the press who report on their words and voters who listen to them.[17] Members of Congress may help to construct constitutional scripts, but they also receive them from the public's understanding of the constitutional system. Textbooks, civics classes, media coverage, and legal training all have a role to play in creating members of Congress who shy away from robust congressional war powers authority, or who use it actively.

The constitutional scripts identified here evolved alongside ideas about constitutional representation and the democratic legitimacy of the president and Congress. Members' decisions about how to apply those received understandings were also wrapped up in socially, racially, and politically constructed ideas about what actions constituted offense and defense, which Americans deserved military protection, and which international norms deserved respect.[18] If we imagine a future in which the constitutional system continues to exist and evolve, we should expect that changes in those broader ideas and values about nationhood and security, citizenship and representation, will also affect how the political system constructs the balance of war powers.

Notes

INTRODUCTION

1. As James Madison and Elbridge Gerry put it when they proposed to amend an early draft of the Constitution to specify Congress's authority to declare war. Max Farrand, ed., *The Records of the Federal Convention* (New Haven: Yale University Press, 1911), 319. For elaboration on the broad original meaning of "defense," see Michael D. Ramsey, *The Constitution's Text in Foreign Affairs* (Cambridge, MA: Harvard University Press, 2007). For elaboration on the early agreement that Congress had a dominant role in decisions about war, see especially Louis Fisher, *Presidential War Power*, 3rd edition (Lawrence: University Press of Kansas, 2013) as well as his entire body of scholarly work, and Stephen M. Griffin, *Long Wars and the Constitution* (Cambridge, MA: Harvard University Press 2013). See also William Conrad Gibbons, "The Origins of the War Power of the Constitution," in *Congress and United States Foreign Policy: Controlling the Use of Force in the Nuclear Age*, ed. Michael Barnhart (Albany: State University of New York Press, 1987, 9–38); Ann Van Wynen Thomas and A. J. Thomas Jr., *The War Making Powers of the President* (Dallas: Southern Methodist University Press, 1982); and Francis D. Wormuth and Edwin B. Firmage, *To Chain the Dog of War* (Dallas: Southern Methodist University Press, 1986). But of course, there are some dissenting voices, most prominently John Yoo, "War and the Constitutional Text," *University of Chicago Law Review* 69, no. 4 (2002): 1639–1684.

2. Ramsey, *Constitution's Text in Foreign Affairs*, 240.

3. Modern presidents and their advisors argue that the commander in chief clause gives them the authority to define the national security interests of the United States and then to use the military to defend those interests as he sees them. For example, presidents decades apart in two different parties have ordered airstrikes against the nation of Libya without seeking or receiving congressional authority to initiate those attacks. In 1986 President Reagan justified his airstrikes against Libya under his "authority under the Constitution, including my authority as Commander in Chief of United States Armed Forces." (Ronald Reagan, "Letter to the Speaker of the House of Representatives and the President Pro Tempore of the Senate on the United States Air Strike against Libya," April 16, 1986, available at the American Presidency Project, http://www.presidency.ucsb.edu/ws/?pid=37143.) President Barack Obama used similar language when he justified his own initiation of air strikes against Libya in 2011, saying that he authorized the airstrikes pursuant to his "constitutional authority to conduct U.S. foreign relations and as Commander in Chief and Chief Executive." "For these purposes, I have directed these actions, which are in the national security and foreign policy interests of the United States, pursuant to my constitutional authority to conduct U.S. foreign relations and as Commander in Chief and Chief Executive." (Barack Obama, "Letter to Congressional Leaders Reporting on the Commencement of Military Operations against Libya," March 21, 2011, available at the American Presidency Project, http://www.presidency.ucsb.edu/ws/?pid=90174.) In addition, John Yoo, deputy White

House counsel to President George W. Bush, articulated this argument in a memo supporting broad unilateral executive action in the days after September 11, 2001. He argued that the president has "broad constitutional authority to use military force in response to threats to the national security and foreign policy of the United States." (John C. Yoo, Memorandum Opinion for the Deputy Counsel to the President, "The President's Constitutional Authority to Conduct Military Operations against Terrorists and Nations Supporting Them," U.S. Department of Justice, September 25, 2001, https://www.justice.gov/file/19151/download.) President Donald Trump, employing the same logic, in ordering an airstrike against Syria in 2017, said that he "acted in the vital national security and foreign policy interests of the United States, pursuant to my constitutional authority to conduct foreign relations and as Commander in Chief and Chief Executive" (Donald J. Trump, "Letter to Congressional Leaders on United States Military Operations in Syria," April 8, 2017, available at the American Presidency Project, http://www.presidency.ucsb.edu/ws/?pid=123728).

4. Such a shift certainly constitutes a "durable shift in governing authority," and one that the field of American political development should seriously try to explain. (Karen Orren and Stephen Skowronek, *Search for American Political Development* [West Nyack, NY: Cambridge University Press, 2004], 139.) The authority to initiate the use of hostile force is not the only congressional power that might someday be ceded to the executive branch (think, for example, of the authority to "make rules concerning captures" or the appropriation or confirmation powers), highlighting the importance of understanding such changes.

5. For a comprehensive examination of the president's preclusive powers as commander in chief, considered from the vantage point of presidential claims under the commander in chief clause, see David J. Barron and Martin S. Lederman, "The Commander in Chief at the Lowest Ebb: A Constitutional History," *Harvard Law Review* 121, no. 4 (2008): 941–1112.

6. Though they disagree about whether this situation is normatively desirable. On the argument that the modern order is unacceptable, see Fisher, *Presidential War Power*; also idem., "The Korean War: On What Legal Basis Did Truman Act?" *American Journal of International Law* 89, no. 1 (January 1995): 21–39; idem., *Military Tribunals and Presidential Power: American Revolution to the War on Terrorism* (Lawrence: University Press of Kansas, 2005); idem., *Congressional Abdication on War and Spending* (College Station: Texas A&M University Press, 2000). On the argument that the modern order is constitutionally legitimate, see most prominently Yoo, "War and the Constitutional Text"; also idem., "The Continuation of Politics by Other Means: The Original Understanding of War Powers," *California Law Review* 84, no. 167 (1996): 174.

7. Griffin, *Long Wars*; Fisher, "Korean War."

8. For example, Fisher, *Congressional Abdication*; Stephen R. Weissman, *A Culture of Deference: Congress' Failure of Leadership in Foreign Policy* (New York: Basic Books, 1995.)

9. Even during a period of supposed deference, Congress was involved in the Cold War in multifaceted ways. Robert David Johnson, *Congress and the Cold War* (New York: Cambridge University Press, 2006).

10. Though many believe the War Powers Resolution might have done more harm to congressional authority than good. See Louis Fisher and David Gray Adler, "The War Powers Resolution: Time to Say Goodbye," *Political Science Quarterly* 13, no. 1 (Spring 2008):

1–20; John Hart Ely, *War and Responsibility: Constitutional Lessons of Vietnam* (Princeton: Princeton University Press, 1993).

11. See, for example, William G. Howell and Jon C. Pevehouse, *While Dangers Gather: Congressional Checks on Presidential War Powers* (Princeton: Princeton University Press, 2007); Douglas L. Kriner, *After the Rubicon* (Chicago: University of Chicago Press, 2010); James Meernik, "Congress, the President, and the Commitment of the U. S. Military," *Legislative Studies Quarterly* 20, no. 3 (August 1995): 377–392; Jong Hee Park, "Structural Change in U.S. Presidents' Use of Force," *American Journal of Political Science* 54, no. 3 (July 2010): 766–782.

12. Mariah Zeisberg, *War Powers: The Politics of Constitutional Authority* (Princeton: Princeton University Press, 2013).

13. The 2021–2023 debate about the repeal of the twenty-year-old, post-9/11 Authorization to Use Military Force is an example of Congress's intermittent attention to its own war powers authority in the initiation and legitimation of the use of force.

14. Griffin, *Long Wars*, 14.

15. Rogers Smith, "Which Comes First, the Ideas or the Institutions?" in *Rethinking Political Institutions: The Art of the State*, ed. Ian Shapiro, Stephen Skowronek, and Daniel Galvin (New York: New York University Press, 2006), 91–113; Karen Orren and Stephen Skowronek, "Institutions and Intercurrence: Theory Building in the Fullness of Time," *Nomos* 38 (1996): 111–146. Other scholars have developed similar frameworks to describe constitutional stability and change. Keith Whittington argues that constitutional evolution, which seems to encompass the idea of shifting orders, can take place through explicit interbranch negotiations and interactions that fall short of constitutional amendment (see his *Constitutional Construction: Divided Powers and Constitutional Meaning* [Cambridge, MA: Harvard University Press, 1999]). Though they refer more to policy commitments and institutional arrangements, not legal authority per se, Tushnet seems to agree that "new constitutional orders" can be brought about by consensus rather than constitutional amendment, and Skowronek argues that electorally derived reconstructive politics can remake long-standing commitments. See Mark Tushnet, *The New Constitutional Order* (Princeton: Princeton University Press, 2003) and Stephen Skowronek, *The Politics Presidents Make: Leadership from John Adams to Bill Clinton* (Cambridge, MA: Harvard University Press, 2017).

16. Gordon Silverstein, *Imbalance of Powers* (New York: Oxford University Press, 1997) and Louis Fisher, *Supreme Court Expansion of Presidential Power: Unconstitutional Leanings* (Lawrence: University Press of Kansas, 2017).

17. See Fisher, *Presidential War Power*, and his entire body of scholarly work; Griffin, *Long Wars*; Gibbons, "Origins of the War Power of the Constitution"; Van Wynen Thomas and Thomas, *War Making Powers of the President*; Wormuth and Firmage, *To Chain the Dog of War*.

18. On the shift over time, generally, see Silverstein, *Imbalance of Powers*; Fisher, *Supreme Court Expansion of Presidential Power*; and Louis Henkin, *Foreign Affairs and the Constitution* (Mineola, NY: Foundation Press, 1972.)

19. Of course, conceptions of security were multifaceted in that time period as well.

180 *Notes to Page 5*

See Daniel H. Deudney, "The Philadelphian System: Sovereignty, Arms Control, and Balance of Power in the American States-Union, circa 1787–1861," *International Organization* 49, no. 2 (1995): 191–228.

20. William D. Adler, *Engineering Expansion: The US Army and Economic Development, 1787–1860* (Philadelphia: University of Pennsylvania Press, 2021).

21. On the arguments relating to "protecting Americans abroad," see Victoria Farrar-Myers, *Scripted for Change: The Institutionalization of the American Presidency* (College Station: Texas A&M University Press, 2007); Peter Raven-Hansen, "Constitutional Constraints: The War Clause," in *The U.S. Constitution and the Power to Go to War: Historical and Current Perspectives*," ed. Gary M. Stern and Morton H. Halperin (Westport, CT: Greenwood Press 1994), 29–54; Arthur M. Schlesinger Jr., *The Imperial Presidency* (Boston: Houghton Mifflin, 1973). In contrast, according to my research, at least during the nineteenth century, members of Congress did not consider a broad right to "protect Americans" to be a power associated with the commander in chief clause, though some aspects of defensive power were part of a widely held understanding.

22. Fisher, *Supreme Court Expansion of Presidential Power*; Martin Sheffer; *Judicial Development of Presidential War Powers* (Westport, CT: Praeger, 1999); Gordon Silverstein, "Judicial Enhancement of Executive Power," in *The President, the Congress, and the Making of Foreign Policy*, ed. Paul E. Peterson (Norman: University of Oklahoma Press, 1994), 23–48; also Silverstein, *Imbalance of Powers*. Courts have also enabled expansion of executive war powers by relying on the political question doctrine, in which the Supreme Court refuses to intervene on behalf of Congress's potential interests. For example, see Oetjen v. Central Leather Co. 246 U.S. 297 (1918), Youngstown Sheet and Tube v. Sawyer, 343 US 579 (1952), or Goldwater v. Carter 444 US 996 (1979).

23. Griffin calls the initiation of the Korean War an "amendment level change" in the constitutional order (*Long Wars*, 30). See also Fisher, "Korean War"; Michael J. Glennon, *Constitutional Diplomacy* (Princeton: Princeton University Press 1990); and James L. Sundquist, *The Decline and Resurgence of Congress* (Washington, DC: Brookings Institution, 1981), 1. Some argue Cold War congressional deference itself may have developed as a policy-based rejection of the congressional isolationism that kept the United States out of the early years of World War II (Sundquist, *Decline and Resurgence*, 111.) Certainly, a broad culture of deference developed in Congress in the twentieth century: see Weissman, *Culture of Deference*.

24. Sarah Burns argues that the shift is due to modern legalism, especially the empowerment of the Office of Legal Counsel (OLC), and dates the modern growth of presidential war powers to Robert Jackson's argument for the lend-lease program. See Burns, *The Politics of War Powers: The Theory and History of Presidential Unilateralism* (Lawrence: University Press of Kansas, 2019), 140. On the importance of the OLC, see also Rebecca Ingber, "The Obama War Powers Legacy and the Internal Forces That Entrench Executive Power," *American Journal of International Law* 110, no. 4 (October 2016): 680–700; Charlie Savage, *Power Wars: Inside Obama's Post-9/11 Presidency* (New York: Little, Brown, 2015.)

25. Griffin, *Long Wars*. On the role of the vast national security bureaucracy in that shift, see Douglas T. Stuart, *Creating the National Security State: A History of the Law That*

Transformed America (Princeton: Princeton University Press, 2008). See also Silverstein, *Imbalance of Powers*, and Burns, *Politics of War Powers*.

26. Christopher J. Deering, "Congress, the President, and Military Policy," *Annals of the American Academy of Political and Social Science* 499 (September 1988): 136–147; Edward J. Laurance, "The Changing Role of Congress in Defense Policy-Making," *Journal of Conflict Resolution* 20, no. 2 (June 1976): 213–253; Park, "Structural Change."

27. David Rohde, "Presidential Support in the House of Representatives," in Peterson, *The President, the Congress and the Making of Foreign Policy*, 101–128; also James M. Lindsay, "Parochialism, Policy, and Constituency Constraints: Congressional Voting on Strategic Weapons Systems," *American Journal of Political Science* 34, no. 4 (November 1990): 936–960; also Stern and Halperin, *U.S. Constitution and the Power to Go to War*; Sundquist, *Decline and Resurgence*; Laurance, "Changing Role of Congress."

28. Ely, *War and Responsibility*.

29. Zeisberg, *War Powers*, 101.

30. For a thorough examination see Fisher and Adler, "War Powers Resolution;" Meernik, "Congress, the President, and the Commitment"; and Sundquist, *Decline and Resurgence*.

31. See, for example, Park, "Structural Change"; Rohde, "Presidential Support"; Sundquist, *Decline and Resurgence*.

32. See, especially, Orren and Skowronek, "Institutions and Intercurrence."

33. See Fisher's description of President Eisenhower, in *Presidential War Power*, 116–124.

34. Ryan C. Hendrickson, *The Clinton Wars: The Constitution, Congress, and War Powers* (Nashville: Vanderbilt University Press, 2002).

35. On the presidential construction of modern war powers, see Griffin, *Long Wars*; Stuart, *Creating the National Security State*; Ingber, "Obama War Powers Legacy"; and Savage, *Power Wars*.

36. See, for example, the separate categories of responses by the constitutional system to "reprisals against natives" and against "civilized" nations in such catalogues as Henry Bartholomew Cox, *War, Foreign Affairs, and Constitutional Power: 1829–1901* (Cambridge, MA: Ballinger, 1984).

37. John A. Dearborn, *Power Shifts: Congress and Presidential Representation* (Chicago: University of Chicago Press 2021).

38. Bailey, for example, shows that presidential claims to special democratic authority as "nationally elected representative" appeared repeatedly throughout the nineteenth and twentieth centuries. See Jeremy Bailey, *The Idea of Presidential Representation: An Intellectual and Political History* (Lawrence: University Press of Kansas, 2019).

39. For a summary, see Paul Pierson and Theda Skocpol, "Historical Institutionalism in Contemporary Political Science," in *Political Science: The State of the Discipline*, ed. Ira Katznelson and Helen V. Milner (New York: W. W. Norton, 2002), 693–721.

40. See, for example, Robert C. Lieberman, "Ideas, Institutions, and Political Order: Explaining Political Change," *American Political Science Review* 96, no. 4 (December 2002): 697–712.

41. George Thomas, "Political Thought and Development," *American Political Thought: A Journal of Ideas, Institutions, and Culture* 3, no. 1 (Spring 2014): 114–125.

42. Vivien Schmidt, "Reconciling Ideas and Institutions through Discursive Institutionalism," in *Ideas in Politics and Social Science Research*, ed. Daniel Beland and Robert Henry Cox (Oxford: Oxford University Press, 2011), 47.

43. Whittington, *Constitutional Construction*, 4. Susan Burgess also describes a range of engagement with constitutional text and meaning she labels "levels of constitutional consciousness." See Susan R. Burgess, *Contest for Constitutional Authority: The Abortion and War Powers Debates* (Topeka: University Press of Kansas 1992).

44. Court-focused accounts highlight the role that particular court cases like United States v. Curtiss-Wright Export Corporation (1936) played in fundamentally affecting the trajectory of both executive actions and cases thereafter. Fisher (*Supreme Court Expansion of Presidential Power*) shows that the *Curtiss-Wright* case in 1936 was wrongly decided and traces its influence through subsequent decisions made by courts. He also argues that presidential lawyers relied on the dicta both in that case and in other decisions to assert broader authority. Similarly, Schlesinger (*Imperial Presidency*) and others focus on executive precedents and arguments to explain change over time. See, for example, Jeffrey Tulis, *The Rhetorical Presidency* (Princeton: Princeton University Press 1987) and Sidney M. Milkis, "Ideas, Institutions, and the New Deal Constitutional Order," *American Political Thought* 3, no. 1 (2014): 167–176. In terms of war powers, Stephen Griffin argues that the ideas and actions that have produced the modern constitutional order were created in the executive branch, in response to the Cold War and a perceived need for international leadership (Griffin, *Long Wars*).

45. See, for example, Neal Devins and Keith E. Whittington, eds., *Congress and the Constitution* (Durham, NC: Duke University Press, 2005).

46. Tushnet has argued for reducing the court's role in constitutional lawmaking. See his *Taking the Constitution away from the Courts* (Princeton: Princeton University Press, 1999). For arguments favoring "departmentalism," or the right of each branch to participate in interpreting the Constitution, see Burgess, *Contest for Constitutional Authority*; Louis Fisher, *Constitutional Dialogues: Interpretation as Political Process* (Princeton: Princeton University Press, 1988); and Walter F. Murphy, "Who Shall Interpret? The Quest for the Ultimate Constitutional Interpreter," *Review of Politics* 48, no. 3 (Summer 1986): 401–423. Others, however, are skeptical that a body composed of hundreds of people can ever possess a coherent understanding of the Constitution. See Kenneth A. Shepsle, "Congress Is a 'They,' Not an 'It': Legislative Intent as Oxymoron," *International Review of Law and Economics* 12, no. 2 (June 1992): 239–256. Others ask whether a body composed of partisan politicians can possess an understanding of the Constitution that is stable over time. Of course, a similar question might be asked of courts or presidents. On judges' willingness to follow their own attitudes in decisions, see, for example, Jeffrey A. Segal, "Separation-of-Powers Games in the Positive Theory of Congress and Courts," *American Political Science Review* 91, no. 1 (March 1997): 28–44.

47. Barbara Sinclair, "Can Congress Be Trusted with the Constitution? The Effects of Incentives and Procedures," in Devins and Whittington, *Congress and the Constitution*, 307. See also Louis Fisher, "Constitutional Interpretation by Members of Congress," *North Carolina Law Review* 63 (1985): 707–747 and idem., *Constitutional Dialogues*.

48. Bruce Ackerman, *We the People: Foundations* (Cambridge, MA: Belknap Press, 1991).

49. Donald Morgan, *Congress and the Constitution: A Study of Responsibility* (Cambridge, MA: Belknap Press, 1966).

50. He observes that "when the constitutionality of early legislative acts finally reached the courts—often many years after their enactment—the judges tended at best to repeat arguments previously made by executive officers or in Congress. . . . even when the courts ultimately did pass on the constitutionality of federal legislation, congressional and legislative arguments were often more thorough and persuasive." See David P. Currie, "Prolegomena for a Sampler: Extrajudicial interpretation of the Constitution," in Devins and Whittington, *Congress and the Constitution*, 18–38.

51. Witko et al., for example, analyze congressional speeches to examine the influence of campaign contributions on congressional behavior. Christopher Witko et al., *Hijacking the Agenda: Economic Power and Political Influence* (New York: Russell Sage Foundation, 2021). Katznelson and Lapinski argue explicitly that studies of American political development should center Congress and its lawmaking processes and outcomes in order to fully understand institutional change over time. Ira Katznelson and John S. Lapinski, "At the Crossroads: Congress and American Political Development," *Perspectives on Politics* 4, no. 2 (June 2006): 243–260.

52. Mark Tushnet, "Evaluating Congressional Constitutional Interpretation: Some Criteria and Two Informal Case Studies," in Devins and Whittington, *Congress and the Constitution*, 269–292.

53. Weissman, *Culture of Deference*.

54. For example, Kriner, *After the Rubicon*.

55. Currie, "Prolegomena for a Sampler."

56. Fisher, *Presidential War Power*; Tushnet, "Evaluating Congressional Constitutional Interpretation"; Ely, *War and Responsibility*.

57. Zeisberg argues against the idea of settled procedures and divisions of labor in authorizing war powers. She posits that the branches of government should adapt their interpretations and constructions of war powers authority to the security context of their own time but should also have to justify their constitutional politics to each other. In her view, the branches should be responsive to each other's political authority and distinctive governing capacities. Zeisberg, *War Powers*.

58. Griffin, *Long Wars*.

59. Curtis A. Bradley and Trevor W. Morrison, "Historical Gloss and the Separation of Powers," *Harvard Law Review* 126, no. 2 (2012): 411–485.

60. Zeisberg, *War Powers*, 251.

61. Peter J. Spiro, "War Powers and the Sirens of Formalism," *New York University Law Review* 68 (1993): 1338.

62. As Levinson and Pildes argue, the Madisonian system of checks and balances, which prioritizes freedom from tyranny over responsive governmental efficiency, was quickly replaced by political parties that in unified government deliver efficient policy and in divided government deliver the prospect of executive accountability. See Daryl J. Levinson and Richard H. Pildes, "Separation of Parties, Not Powers," *Harvard Law Review* 119, no. 8 (2006): 2311–2386.

63. Americans in the nineteenth century believed a combination of legal principles applied to Native Americans. First, they believed that Native Americans had no right to own the territory on which their people had lived for millennia, because after European powers discovered and then sold or ceded western territory to the United States, which Congress subjected to territorial organization, their territory itself belonged to the United States (under the "doctrine of discovery"). Second, and simultaneously, they believed that relations with Native Americans were governed by treaties with the tribes themselves, and while presidents were responsible for enforcing those treaties under the treaties themselves and the Militia Acts, Congress also participated in overseeing enforcement of and reneging on those treaties through legislation like the Indian Removal Act. For a far more thorough discussion of these conflicting frameworks, and the ways they contributed to ideas about inherent powers and eventually executive control over foreign affairs, see Sarah H. Cleveland, "Powers Inherent in Sovereignty: Indians, Aliens, Territories, and the Nineteenth Century Origins of Plenary Power over Foreign Affairs," *Texas Law Review* 81, no. 1 (November 2002): 1–284. For a detailed discussion of how the United States saw its territories and the Native Americans who lived there, see, for example, Paul Frymer, *Building an American Empire: The Era of Territorial and Political Expansion* (Princeton: Princeton University Press, 2017). As Mary Dudziak notes, "The laws of war traditionally focused only on wars between states. The wars of empire fell outside the law; they were instead matters of imperial governance." See Mary L. Dudziak, *War Time: An Idea, Its History, Its Consequences* (New York: Oxford University Press, 2012), 31.

64. There are some who argue that presidential war powers derive from the executive vesting clause of the Constitution (for example, Ramsey, *Constitution's Text*, or Saikrishna B. Prakash and Michael D. Ramsey, "The Executive Power over Foreign Affairs," *Yale Law Journal* 111 [2001]: 231–356) or from his diplomatic powers (H. Jefferson Powell, *The President's Authority over Foreign Affairs* [Durham, NC: Carolina Academic Press, 2002]). I leave a systematic analysis of Congress's construction of those powers to others. Notably, they rarely appear in the speeches in which members talk about the commander in chief clause in the period I study. For the counterargument, that the vesting clause does not grant executive authority over foreign affairs, see Curtis A. Bradley and Martin S. Flaherty, "Executive Power Essentialism and Foreign Affairs," *Michigan Law Review* 102, no. 4 (February 2004): 545–688.

65. "congressional military spending": Fisher, *Congressional Abdication*, as well as Ralph G. Carter, "Defense Budgeting, 1981–1988: The Impacts of Ideology, Party, and Constituency Benefit on the Decision to Support the President," *American Politics Quarterly* 17, no. 3 (1989): 332–347; "Congress's regulation of ongoing conflicts": e.g., Kriner, *After the Rubicon*; "or civil-military relations": Mitchel A. Sollenberger, "Presidential and Congressional Relations: An Evolution of Military Appointments," in *Congress and Civil-Military Relations*, ed. Colton C. Campbell and David P. Auerswald (Washington, DC: Georgetown University Press, 2015), 17–35; "very few efforts have been made": One exception is when Wormuth and Firmage break down war powers into many interrelated powers and describe their historical uses separately. They do not, however, integrate them into a coherent, focused story. Wormuth and Firmage, *To Chain the Dog of War*. Another exception is David J. Barron and

Martin S. Lederman, "The Commander in Chief at the Lowest Ebb: Framing the Problem, Doctrine, and Original Understanding," *Harvard Law Review* 121, no. 3 (2008): 689–804, and idem., "Commander in Chief at the Lowest Ebb: A Constitutional History." See also R. Gordon Hoxie, "The Office of Commander in Chief: An Historical and Projective View," *Presidential Studies Quarterly* 6, no. 4 (1976): 10–36.

66. See Barron and Lederman, "Commander in Chief at the Lowest Ebb: A Constitutional History," and idem., "Commander in Chief at the Lowest Ebb: Framing the Problem, Doctrine, and Original Understanding."

67. See Griffin, *Long Wars*, 85; Bradley and Morrison, "Historical Gloss;" and Richard F. Grimmett, *Instances of Use of United States Armed Forces Abroad 1798–2008* (Washington, DC: Congressional Research Service, 2010).

68. One additional, practical reason that the analysis ends at the beginning of World War I was that when members of Congress began using the commander in chief title as a simple synonym for and a way to refer to the president, it stopped being as meaningful a way to track congressional understanding of war powers.

69. The approach here is similar to that used by Robert J. Spitzer in his authoritative description of the establishment and evolution of the veto power. See Spitzer, *The Presidential Veto: Touchstone of the American Presidency* (Albany: State University of New York Press, 1988).

70. To our knowledge, this task has never been attempted before, because the *Congressional Record* and its early predecessors are not keyword indexed. Until optical scanning and powerful search software recently became available, it would have been impossible to find every reference to any particular phrase among thousands upon thousands of congressional speeches. Fortunately, we had access to the Heinonline search system, which digitally matches search terms to optically scanned copies of the proceedings and debates of both houses of the United States Congress throughout American history. Early records of the proceedings of Congress are not as comprehensive or reliable as later verbatim records. Therefore there may be more reliability for later searches than later. The records available through the Heinonline search system we used were *The Annals of the Congress of the United States* (1789–1824), the *Register of Debates in Congress* (1824–1837), the *Congressional Globe* (1833–1873), and the *Congressional Record* (1873–1917). We did not extend this analysis to congressional committees, which might be a fruitful extension of this work, particularly after the Civil War as standing committees began to do more of Congress's work.

71. Did we miss a few? Unfortunately, we probably did. But we have no reason to believe we systematically missed any great or biased number of the references to the commander in chief in the available documentary record. The entire dataset will be made available to the public and I welcome additional mentions that we could not find.

72. For the purposes of the book's argument, I have collapsed some smaller categories that I developed early on—for example, early in my coding process, I found many speeches referring to the commander in chief's power to appoint officers, and many referring to his power to dismiss them. In the final version of the book, I grouped both sets of questions relating to the commander in chief's power to appoint and dismiss officers together as "chain of command." Other researchers might find more nuanced gradations to be useful,

and they are welcome to examine the speeches and look for ways to recode into categories more useful for their analytical purposes.

73. If it was truly ambiguous, I categorized such speeches as "miscellaneous." If one definition seemed clearer than the other, that was the category into which I placed it.

74. This pattern of speech is also noted in presidential remarks by Richard J. Ellis, *The Development of the American Presidency* (New York: Routledge, 2012), 522n114.

75. One might expect that the types of authority discussed might vary over time. Those issues are defined by the United States' position relative to its adversaries, technology, and the beliefs and actions of members of Congress and presidents. Today, a type of authority that might appear on a list like this might involve questions about the commander in chief's implied constitutional authority (or lack thereof) to order airstrikes under UN auspices. Obviously, that was not a type of authority they talked about in the nineteenth century. Rather, in the years prior to World War I, Congress talked about the commander in chief clause in relation to authority over subordinate officers, state militias, the governance of conquered territory, domestic troop movements, and the like. See figure 1.1.

76. 33 Annals of Cong. 773–774 (1818–1819), Proceedings and Debates of the House of Representatives of the United States, at the Second Session of the Fifteenth Congress, Begun at the City of Washington, Monday, November 16, 1818.

77. 33 Annals of Cong. 643–644 (1818–1819), Proceedings and Debates of the House of Representatives of the United States, at the Second Session of the Fifteenth Congress, Begun at the City of Washington, Monday, November 16, 1818.

78. In putting commander in chief references into categories, I coded according to the following criteria: Does the sentence in which the phrase "commander in chief" appears explicitly refer to a particular type of authority or power (regardless of whether the member argues whether or not such a power exists)? If the sentence itself is not explicit, does the speech's broader argument clearly and explicitly refer to a type of power or authority? If the answer to either question was yes, the speech got put into that category. If the answer to either question was no, the reference was categorized as "miscellaneous."

79. Victoria Farrar-Myers notes the prevalence of repeated public reasoning that takes place in the conversations that the members of Congress and presidents have about how to apply the provisions of the Constitution to particular policy debates. She argues that repeated reasoning, or constitutional "scripts," anchor future discussions and thereby affect institutional development. Farrar-Myers, *Scripted for Change*.

80. See chapter 5 for a discussion of this compromise and its ratification by the courts.

81. Bailey, in *The Idea of Presidential Representation*, explains that arguments about whether the president was a primarily a democratic national representative or a law enforcement officer were as old as Hamilton and Madison. He argues that the idea of the president as national representative was not a product of the progressive era but was a recurring claim made by Jefferson, Jackson, and Cleveland in the nineteenth century. I do not dispute his argument but merely point out that such claims had not been widely accepted as grounds for expanded presidential war powers until the early twentieth century.

82. My analysis does not divide war powers history into neat pre-1900 "traditional" and post-1900 "modern" categories. There are examples of similar behavior and similar

rhetoric both before and after the turn of the twentieth century. But I do identify a significant change in members' of Congress attitudes toward the president that occurred at the same time as other noteworthy changes in the presidency, like the institutionalization of the bureaucracy and an expanded public role for presidents. See Stephen Skowronek, *Building a New American State: The Expansion of National Administrative Capacities 1877–1920* (New York: Cambridge University Press 1982); Peri Arnold, *Remaking the Presidency: Roosevelt, Taft and Wilson, 1901–1916* (Lawrence: University Press of Kansas 2009); and Tulis, *Rhetorical Presidency.*

83. To readers who would prefer more historical detail, I apologize for keeping the context brief, and to readers who prefer more political science and legal analysis, I apologize for staying close to the descriptive nature of the project.

CHAPTER 1: STABLE INTERPRETATIONS OF THE COMMANDER IN CHIEF CLAUSE

1. See David J. Barron and Martin S. Lederman, "The Commander in Chief at the Lowest Ebb: Framing the Problem, Doctrine, and Original Understanding," *Harvard Law Review* 121, no. 3 (2008): 689–804, and idem., "The Commander in Chief at the Lowest Ebb: A Constitutional History," *Harvard Law Review* 121, no. 4 (2008): 941–1112.

2. Neal Devins and Keith E. Whittington, eds., *Congress and the Constitution* (Durham, NC: Duke University Press, 2005).

3. Though just because that is the case in the modern era does not mean that judicial supremacy was always the norm in constitutional understanding and practice. See, for example, Keith Whittington, *Political Foundations of Judicial Supremacy: The Presidency, the Supreme Court, and Constitutional Leadership in U.S. History* (Princeton: Princeton University Press, 2007).

4. For example, Abner Mikva, "How Well Does Congress Support and Defend the Constitution?" *North Carolina Law Review* 61 (1983): 587–611 and Larry Alexander and Frederick Schauer, "On Extrajudicial Interpretation," *Harvard Law Review* 110, no. 7 (May 1997): 1359–1387. Brien Hallett sees the merits in a deliberative approach to initiating war but thinks Congress as constructed by the Constitution has never been able to do the job properly. See Brien Hallett, *Declaring War: Congress, the President, and What the Constitution Does Not Say* (New York: Cambridge University Press, 2012).

5. In his discussion of the ways in which Congress built the institutions of the modern presidency on the idea of the chief executive as chief representative, John Dearborn argues that whether institutional arrangements and ideas are challenged or not by political actors is an important way to assess whether ideas are important to institutional development. See John A. Dearborn, *Power Shifts: Congress and Presidential Representation* (Chicago: University of Chicago Press, 2021), 24.

6. 1 Annals of Cong. 761–762 (1789–1790), Proceedings and Debates of the House of Representatives of the United States, at the First Session of the First Congress, begun at the City of New York, March 4, 1789.

7. Some examples: Mr. Howe, January 6, 1863, 37th Cong., 3rd Sess., 33 Cong. Globe 190; Mr. Trumbull, January 23, 1868, 40th Cong., 2nd Sess., 39 Cong. Globe 705; Mr. Grosvenor, April 7, 1898, 55th Cong., 2nd Sess., 31 Cong. Rec. 3686; Mr. Bartlett, June 26, 1902, 57th Congress, 1st Sess. and Special Session of the Senate, 35 Cong. Rec. 7468; Mr. Borah, February 17, 1909, 60th Cong., 2nd Sess., 43 Cong. Rec. 2540.

8. Mr. Howe, January 6, 1863, 37th Cong., 3rd Sess., 33 Cong. Globe 190.

9. Mr. Bartlett, June 26, 1902, 57th Congress, 1st Sess. and Special Session of the Senate, 35 Cong. Rec. 7468.

10. Sen. John Stockton (D), February 23, 1870, 41st Cong., 2nd Sess., 42 Cong. Globe 1507.

11. Sen. John Scott (PA), 41 Cong. Globe 2164 (1870).

12. Statutes at Large, 12th Cong., 1st Sess., June 18, 1812, 755.

13. Representative Carlile, February 6, 1863, 37th Cong., 3rd Sess., Cong. Globe 733.

14. Article I, section 8, clause 14.

15. Said Sen. John Dix (NY), "The title of lieutenant general . . . is descriptive of the relation in which the commander of the armies in Mexico will stand to the President as commander-in-chief of the armies of the United States under the Constitution. He cannot be in Mexico in person, and he must, therefore, command there by his lieutenant or deputy, by whatever name the latter may be called" (January 18, 1847, 29th Cong., 2nd Sess., Cong. Globe 184). There was agreement across party lines. Sen. George Badger (Whig-NC), argued that the president would remain the superior commanding officer and could choose whom to appoint to the position, and so creating another high rank in the army was no threat to his authority. He said that "by an express provision of the Constitution—by the inevitable necessity of the case—the major general or lieutenant general, or by whatever other title he may be called, is at last under the absolute control and direction of the President of the United States, who is the sole constitutional commander-in-chief" (January 18, 1847, 29th Cong., 2nd Sess., Cong. Globe 184).

16. Polk's opponents assured each other and the president's supporters that their opposition to the new rank was not based on a constitutional, but rather a policy question. That they agreed on the supremacy of the commander in chief in the chain of command did not mean they gave the president what he wanted. There was skepticism in the Senate that the position was really necessary for efficient command, and there were rumors that Polk was trying to elevate Sen. Thomas Hart Benton (D) to the rank of lieutenant general to diminish Scott's position and to "choose a successor." The bill was tabled on a vote of 28–21, with Democrats supporting their own president's position but both Democrats and Whigs voting against (January 18, 1847, 29th Cong., 2nd Sess., Cong. Globe 186). Congress instead agreed to allow the number of major general positions to be reduced by attrition until only one was left. After General Zachary Taylor was nominated by the Whigs and became president, Winfield Scott again became the sole major general in command of the army. See Archibald King, *The Command of the Army: A Legal and Historical Study of the Relations of the President, the Secretaries of War and the Army, the General of the Army, and the Chief of Staff, with One Another* (Charlottesville, VA: Judge Advocate General's School, 1960).

17. Representative Washburne (R-IL), February 2, 1864, 38th Cong., 1st Sess., Cong. Globe 430.

18. "distrusted Grant": During the second half of the Civil War, it had become clear to all that Lincoln was more moderate in his prosecution of the war than some Republicans in Congress preferred. Some Democrats argued against creating a new rank and argued instead for expansive discretionary powers for President Lincoln, whom they trusted more than they trusted congressional Republicans or Ulysses Grant. To that end, some Democrats argued against creating the lieutenant general position because it could tie the hands of the commander in chief. (For example, Senator Nesmith [D-OR], February 12, 1864, 38th Cong., 1st Sess., Cong. Globe 587). There was also some concern voiced that the president did not have effective mechanisms to remove such a high-ranking general if he got out of control. (Sen. Reverdy Johnson [Unionist], February 13, 1864, 38th Cong., 1st Sess., Cong. Globe 594; James Lane [R-IN], February 12, 1864, 38th Cong., 1st Sess., Cong. Globe 591). However, those constitutional concerns were not widespread, even among the president's opponents. "the majority agreed": As Sen. Andrew Johnson (a Democrat) dismissively put it, "The object is to appoint a lieutenant general. What for? To supersede the President of the United States? Certainly not; because the Constitution of the United States would render any act of that description upon our part wholly nugatory" (February 13, 1864, 38th Cong., 1st Sess., Cong. Globe 594 [1864]).

19. King, *Command of the Army*.

20. He said of the general of the army, "He is to-day called by law general of the Army, and yet every man on this floor knows that as a matter of fact he has no command, and has no right to issue commands to the Army except as directed by the President and Secretary of War" (January 5, 1903, 57th Cong., 2nd Sess., 36 Cong. Rec. 503).

21. January 5, 1903, 36 Cong. Rec. 505.

22. Republican George Prince cautioned that "in the days gone by there was considerable friction between the Commanding General of the Army, the Secretary of War, and the President; but, my judgment for it, those contentions in those days were as gentle zephyrs compared with what will come in the near future between the General Staff and the Secretary of War" (April 5, 1904, 38 Cong. Rec. 4304).

23. The exception was temporary and was thoroughly rejected by both parties as a precedent for future action. Democrats continued to bring up the constitutional arguments against the bills for decades. In 1871 Sen. Francis Blair (D-MO) recalled that "the command of the troops who were to put the acts into execution was taken away from the constitutional Commander in-Chief" (41st Cong., 3rd Sess., Cong. Globe 116 (1871), appendix). In 1879 Rep. Richard Townshend of Illinois was one of several Democrats arguing in favor of a bill to cut military appropriations for the army to explicitly refer to the controversial bill from a decade earlier (April 2, 1879, 46th Cong., 1st Sess., 9 Cong. Rec. 169). In 1908 Rep. Frank Clark (D-FL) raised the issue while arguing about a bill to fund street cars. In a wide ranging diatribe about the Reconstruction "laws—if such acts of a mutilated Congress, so palpably and avowedly in conflict with the Constitution can be called laws," he noted that "the President of the United States, who is the constitutional Commander in Chief of the Army, was deprived of all control over the Army" (February 22, 1908, 42 Cong. Rec. 43, appendix).

24. Jefferson Davis (D-MS), June 13, 1860, 36th Cong., 1st Sess., Cong. Globe 2869; Lazarus Powell (D-KY), June 13, 1860, 36th Cong., 1st Sess., Cong. Globe 2870.

25. Charles Ernest Chadsey, *The Struggle between President Johnson and Congress over Reconstruction* (New York: Columbia University, 1896).

26. Sen. Garrett Davis (KY-Unionist) argued that Congress could not usurp the president's authority to appoint military officers. He argued that the commander in chief "is the constitutional superior, head, and director of both the civil and military administration of the Government, and all persons employed in those services are bound to submit implicitly to his orders. Within those pales Congress cannot impinge upon him" (40th Cong., Special Session, Cong. Globe 63–65 (1867), appendix). Sen. Thomas Hendricks (D-IN) argued that "if the effect of this section is to take from the President his power which is conferred upon him as the Commander-in-Chief of the Army, then it is in plain and palpable' violation of the Constitution" (February 15, 1867, 39th Cong., 2nd Sess., Cong. Globe 1386).

27. For an elaborate description of the debate in the first Congress over the removal power, see James Hart, *The American Presidency in Action, 1789: A Study in Constitutional History* (New York: Macmillan, 1948), 155–214.

28. Representative Randolph had made some controversial comments about the Army on the floor of the House. Later that evening, an Army captain named McKnight came up to Randolph, "jerked his coat," and called him a "Virginia ragamuffin." Randolph felt his honor had been insulted, and that he had been threatened for actions performed as part of his official duties. Since his assailant was an army captain, he appealed to President John Adams for punishment of the officer in question. He argued, "The power of the Commander-in-chief of the Army, in his opinion, was sufficient to afford a remedy, and to restrain men under his command from giving personal abuse and insult" (10 Annals of Cong. 373–374 [1799–1801]). President Adams, however, returned Randolph's letter to the House and publicly criticized the appeal, arguing that only the Congress could protect the privileges of its members (John Adams, "Special Message," January 14, 1800, available at the American Presidency Project, http://www.presidency.ucsb.edu/ws/?pid=65687). The majority party Federalists in Congress agreed with Adams's interpretation and a House committee voted to censure Randolph for undermining the powers of Congress by appealing to the executive for redress of his grievances, saying that "the subject [is] exclusively cognizable in this House, and . . . Mr. Randolph's conduct was derogatory from the rights of the House" (10 Annals of Cong. 445–446 [1799–1801]).

29. For example, in 1856 the Congress was caught in a controversy about retirements from the navy. After the Mexican War, Congress had approved the creation of a naval retirement board composed of senior officers, to help with the military drawdown. However, members of Congress were unprepared for the public's objections when that board forced more than fifty high-ranking officers to retire from the service. Since the executive branch was responsible for executing the controversial retirements, the constitutional questions related to whether the president had a proper oversight role regarding the retirements and whether Congress had a right to question those decisions, order reinstatements, or legislate a new process. In the end, Congress replaced that system with a new law that allowed affected officers to appeal their forced retirements to a court of inquiry convened by the secretary of war. The court had the power make recommendations to the president to confirm the man's retirement or to restore him to the active or reserved list. The president was given

the statutory ability to renominate retired soldiers who had been approved by the board, and they would be returned to service after being confirmed by the Senate. See Public Acts of the Thirty-Fourth Cong. of the United States Laws of the United States. In a separate debate in 1865, Congress considered a bill that would have forced officers who had been on leave for more than three months out of the service. The bill was perceived to be a criticism of President Lincoln and did not pass the Republican-controlled Congress.

30. January 7, 1865, 38th Cong., 2nd Sess., Cong. Globe 135.

31. John Missall and Mary Lou Missall, *The Seminole Wars: America's Longest Indian Conflict* (Gainesville: University of Florida Press, 2004).

32. November 16, 1818, 15th Cong., 2nd Sess., 33 Annals of Cong. 643–644.

33. November 16, 1818, 15th Cong., 2nd Sess., 33 Annals of Cong. 817–818.

34. November 16, 1818, 15th Cong., 2nd Sess., 33 Annals of Cong. 773–774. Another Virginia Republican, George Strother, admonished that "if it is your right and your duty to stoop beneath the Commander-in-chief, to lay hold of a Major General, it is equally incumbent upon you to descend into the ranks; place a private soldier into legislative inquisition, and gravely discuss, and sagely decide, upon his demerits" (the implication being that that would be a foolish interpretation of Congress's powers) (November 16, 1818, 15th Cong., 2nd Sess., 33 Annals of Cong. 833–834).

35. Missall and Missall, *Seminole Wars.*

36. John D. Weaver, *The Brownsville Raid* (New York: W. W. Norton, 1970).

37. January 16, 1907, 59th Cong., 2nd Sess., 41 Cong. Rec. 1210.

38. 41 Cong. Rec. 685 (1907).

39. For example, note the assumption of the right to command in the following argument: "With a power, and as the case might lie, under a duty of calling out the militia of twenty-four States simultaneously, to say that the President can only command in person, and not by delegated authority, is to deny to him, in totidem verbis, the very power which the States gave him by the Constitution" (Mr. Dwight, 2 Part II Cong. Deb. 2103–2104 [1826], amendment of the Constitution; Mr. Cass, January 19, 1855, 33rd Cong., 2nd Sess., Cong. Globe 312; Mr. Bayard, February 6, 1863, 37th Cong., 3rd Sess., Cong. Globe 728–32; Mr. Davis, February 9, 1864, 38th Cong., 1st Sess., Cong. Globe 520; Mr. Hulings, 51 Cong. Rec. 150 [1914]; Mr. Dwight, 2 Part II Cong. Deb. 2103–2104 [1826], amendment of the Constitution).

40. The authority over state militias when called into federal service was divided fairly clearly by the Constitution, which grants Congress several powers: "To provide for *calling forth* the Militia to execute the Laws of the Union, suppress Insurrections and repel Invasions; To provide for *organizing, arming, and disciplining*, the Militia, and for *governing such Part of them* as may be employed in the Service of the United States reserving to the States respectively, the Appointment of the Officers, and the Authority of training the Militia according to the *discipline prescribed by Congress.*" It also designates to the president the power to "be commander in chief of the Army and Navy of the United States, and *of the militia of the several states, when called into the actual service* of the United States."

41. February 6, 1863, 37th Cong., 3rd Sess., Cong. Globe 728–732.

42. Sen. Lazarus Powell (D-KY) argued that the commander in chief could not call civilians into service because "a man is not in the actual service of the United States as a soldier,

and is not liable to the exclusive control of the President as Commander-in-Chief, until he has been mustered in" (March 2, 1863, 37th Cong., 3rd Sess., Cong. Globe 1383).

43. As shown by the final motion to recommit the bill, which failed 11–35. See Voteview .com, at https://voteview.com/rollcall/RS0370749.

44. "going through state governors": November 4, 1811, 12th Cong., 1st Sess., 23 Annals of Cong. 781–782; Sen. Christopher Gore (Federalist), September 19, 1814, 13th Cong., 1st Sess., 28 Annals of Cong. 97–100. "whether states should really . . .": Rep. Carter Harrison (R), 8 Annals of Cong. 1703–1704 (1798–1799), history of Congress. During the Civil War, the House debated whether to allow the president to appoint vacant officers' positions in volunteer regiments raised by the states. Some Republicans argued that the commander in chief had the responsibility to make sure that officers were competent, but the Democrats' definition won out and the offending provision was not included in the final bill. Chapter 200, 37th Cong., Sess. 2, An Act: To Define the Pay and Emoluments of Certain Officers of the Army, and for Other Purposes. See July 17, 1862, page 594; June 13, 1862, 37th Cong., 2nd Sess., Cong. Globe 2664.

45. "within US territory": Rep. Thomas Fitzsimons (Pro-Administration), 3 *Annals of Cong.* 1105–1106 (1791–1793), appendix to the History of the Second Congress; Mr. Hickman, February 5, 1862, 37th Cong., 2nd Sess., 32 Cong. Globe 611. "in both American and enemy territory . . .": Rep. Owen Lovejoy (R), February 5, 1862, 37th Cong., 2nd Sess., 32 Cong. Globe 613; Sen. James Grimes (R), June 21, 1862, 37th Cong., 2nd Sess., 32 Cong. Globe 2831; Representative Pomeroy (R), February 25, 1863, 37th Cong., 3rd Sess., 32 Cong. Globe 1242; Rep. Henry Dawes (R), February 2, 1863, 37th Cong., 3rd Sess., 33 Cong. Globe 653; Mr. Dawes, February 2, 1863, 37th Cong., 3rd Sess., 32 Cong. Globe 653; Rep. Michael Griffin (R), January 30, 1899, 32 Cong. Rec. 1255.

46. Sen. Orville Browning (R), June 26, 1862, 37th Cong., 2nd Sess., Cong. Globe 2919.

47. Sen. George Hoar (R), April 18, 1898, 55th Cong., 2nd Sess., 31 Cong. Rec. 4033.

48. Sen. Joseph B. Foraker (R), January 17, 1907, 59th Cong., 2nd Sess., 41 Cong. Rec. 1254.

49. "order a regiment forward": Sen. Stephen Douglas (D), February 2, 1847, 29th Cong., 2nd Sess., 16 Cong. Globe 304; Sen. James Grimes (R), January 15, 1862, 37th Cong., 2nd Sess., 32 Cong. Globe pt. 1:311; "send troops now in service": Rep. Thaddeus Stevens (R), December 18, 1861, 37th Cong., 2nd Sess., 32 Cong. Globe pt.1:103; "to conduct and control . . .": Sen. Orville Browning (R), June 28, 1862, 37th Cong., 2nd Sess., 32 Cong. Globe pt. 4:2969; Sen. John C. Calhoun (D), March 18, 1848, 30th Cong., 1st Sess., 17 Cong. Globe 479.

50. Sen. Edgar Cowan (R), January 29, 1862, 37th Cong., 2nd Sess., 32 Cong. Globe pt. 1:516; Rep. Thaddeus Stevens (R), February 25, 1863, 37th Cong., 3rd Sess., 33 Cong. Globe pt. 2:1263.

51. "direct campaigns:" Rep. William Davis (R), January 28, 1863, 37th Cong., 3rd Sess., Cong. Globe 531–534; Rep. James Johnson (D), January 27, 1868, 40th Cong., 2nd Sess., 39 Cong. Globe 769. "urge" and "recommend": Rep. John Lovett (Federalist), 26 Annals of Cong., 1180–1181; 1183–1184 (1813–1814): Proceedings and Debates of the House of Representatives of the United States, at the Second Sess. of the Thirteenth Congress, begun at the City of Washington, Monday, December 6, 1813.

52. 29th Cong., 2nd Sess., Cong. Globe 308 (1847), appendix.

53. This is consistent with Barron and Lederman's findings that there was no nine-teenth-century consensus that the commander in chief clause granted a preclusive or un-regulatable prerogative to direct military force and the conduct of campaigns. Barron and Lederman, "Commander in Chief at the Lowest Ebb: A Constitutional History."

54. "Pacificus no. I, [29 June 1793]," *Founders Online*, National Archives, https://found ers.archives.gov/documents/Hamilton/01-15-02-0038.

55. James Madison opened debate in 1790 by declaring that it is "necessary to pass a law authorizing the President of the United States to call out the militia," because "the Consti-tution only says that he shall be commander-in-chief of the militia when in the service of the United States, without giving him the power of ordering it out." December 6, 1790, 1st Cong., 3rd Sess., 2 Annals of Cong. 1817–1818.

56. Chapter 28, 2nd Con., 1st Sess., "An Act: To Provide for Calling Forth the Militia to Execute the Laws of the Union, Suppress Insurrections, and Repel Invasions," 1 Stat. 264, 265.

57. George Washington, "Proclamation—Cessation of Violence and Obstruction of Jus-tice in Protest of Liquor Laws in Pennsylvania," August 7, 1794, available at the American Presidency Project, http://www.presidency.ucsb.edu/ws/?pid=65477.

58. It was supplanted by an 1807 law that expired after two years and used much the same language: "An Act Authorizing a Detachment from the Militia of the United States," Acts of the Tenth Congress of the United States, Session I Ca. 40. 1808. References to the 1795 law were made by, among others, Rep. John Holmes of Massachusetts (no party), November 16, 1818, 15th Cong., 2nd Sess., 33 Annals of Cong. 601–602; Mr. Holmes, of Massachusetts, November 16, 1818, 15th Cong., 2nd Sess., 33 Annals of Cong. 601–602; Rep. Henry Dwight (Adams party), 2 Part II Cong. Deb. 2103–2104 (1826), amendment of the Constitution; Rep. Peleg Sprague of Maine, 2 Part II Cong. Deb. 2113–2114 (1826), amendment of the Constitu-tion; Rep. William Davis (R), January 16, 186, 37th Cong., 2nd Sess., Cong. Globe 342; Sen. Lazarus Powell, February 24, 1863, 37th Cong., 3rd Sess., Cong. Globe 1192.

59. Rep. Robert Wright (Democratic Republican), November 4, 1811, 12th Cong., 1st Sess., 23 Annals of Cong. 739–740. Wright argues that the president, in executing a declared war (in this case to invade Canada), and also as commander of the militia and of the army, may use them however he sees fit in order to execute the war. Also Representative Clay, November 4, 1811, 12th Cong., 1st Sess., 23 Annals of Cong. 743–744. Also Rep. Hugh Nelson, (R-VA), November 4, 1811, 12th Cong., 1st Sess., 23 Annals of Cong. 779–780.

60. Sen. David Daggett (Federalist), September 19, 1814, 13th Cong., 3rd Sess., 8 Annals of Cong. 71–72.

61. However, when the British repeatedly harassed coastal towns and threatened Bos-ton, the state's militia was called up to serve under federal command. *American State Pa-pers: Documents, Legislative and Executive, of the Congress of the United States*, part 5, vol. 3 (Washington, DC: Gales and Seaton, 1860).

62. Martin v. Mott (1827).

63. "The Constitution of the United States . . . vests in Congress the power to, provide for calling out the militia to suppress insurrections and repel invasions. The act of Congress of the 28th of February, 1795, provides that, whenever the United States shall be invaded,

or in imminent danger of invasion, the President may call out any portion of the militia to repel the meditated attack, and, to this end, may direct his orders to any officer of the militia without a requisition upon the Governors of the states" (November 16, 1818, 15th Cong., 2nd Sess., 33 Annals of Cong. 601–602).

64. 2 Part II Cong. Deb. 2113–2114 (1826), amendment of the Constitution.

65. 2 Part II Cong. Deb. 2103–2104 (1826), amendment of the Constitution.

66. However, Attorney General George Wickersham issued an opinion on February 19, 1912, that the 1908 law was unconstitutional because the militia could not be sent abroad as an army of occupation "under conditions short of actual warfare" (April 24, 1914, 63rd Cong., 2nd Sess., 51 Cong. Rec. 7210).

67. "Public Law 63–90 / chapter 71, 63rd Cong., Sess. 2, "An Act: To Provide for Raising the Volunteer Forces of the United States in Time of Actual or Threatened War." Statutes at Large 38. Main Section Stat. 347, 351.

68. Jerry Cooper, *The Rise of the National Guard: The Evolution of the American Militia 1865–1920* (Lincoln: University of Nebraska Press, 1997), 154.

69. As Representative Sewall put it, "Perhaps, if war was declared, the President might then, as Commander-in-Chief, exercise a military power over these people; but it would be best to settle these regulations by civil process. In this country, this power is not lodged wholly in the Executive; it is in Congress" (5th Cong., 8 Annals of Cong. 1789–1790).

70. Chapter 15, 37th Cong., 2nd Sess., "An Act: To Authorize the President of the United States in Certain Cases to Take Possess., of Railroad and Telegraph Lines, and for Other Purposes." See Public Acts of the 37th Congress, 37 Cong. Globe 37 (1862) Main Section Stat. 334, 335.

71. See Voteview.com, 37th Congress, House vote 100, Senate vote 159, at voteview.com /rollcall/RH0370100, voteview.com/rollcall/RS0370159.

72. Abraham Lincoln, "Executive Order—Authorizing General Winfield Scott to Suspend the Writ of Habeas Corpus," July 2, 1861, available at the American Presidency Project, http://www.presidency.ucsb.edu/ws/?pid=69791.

73. Abraham Lincoln, "Special Sess., Message," July 4, 1861, available at the American Presidency Project, http://www.presidency.ucsb.edu/ws/?pid=69802.

74. Said one Republican, "The whole country is at war; that the law of war is in operation in Wisconsin as well as in Kentucky, in New York as well as in Mississippi? . . . If a man is found actually engaged in furnishing means to the enemy, he is taken by the law of war, and held by the law of war, and by him who is Commander-in-Chief of our armies in time of war" (Sen. James Doolittle [R] December 10, 1862, 37th Cong., 3rd Sess., Cong. Globe, 37).

75. 38th Cong., Special Sess., Cong. Globe 46 (1863), appendix.

76. U.S. Statutes at Large, 37th Cong., 3rd Sess., chap. 81.

77. For a discussion of this issue, see Mariah Zeisberg, *War Powers: The Politics of Constitutional Authority* (Princeton: Princeton University Press 2013), chap. 1.

78. Alexander and Schauer, "On Extrajudicial Interpretation."

79. Though different authors argue for different political constructions of judicial supremacy. Knight and Epstein, for example, point to political construction during the Jefferson administration. Jack Knight and Lee Epstein, "On the Struggle for Judicial Supremacy,"

Law and Society Review 30, no. 1 (1986): 87–120. Whittington argues, instead, that judicial supremacy was not really established until the twentieth century (see his *Political Foundations of Judicial Supremacy*). But that supremacy may also be cyclical and contingent on the political relationship between the courts and the dominant partisan regime. See James M. Balkin, *The Cycles of Constitutional Time* (Oxford: Oxford University Press, 2020).

80. Louis Fisher, *Supreme Court Expansion of Presidential Power: Unconstitutional Leanings* (Lawrence: University Press of Kansas, 2017); Martin Sheffer, *Judicial Development of Presidential War Powers* (Westport, CT: Praeger, 1999); Gordon Silverstein, "Judicial Enhancement of Executive Power," in *The President, the Congress, and the Making of Foreign Policy*, ed. Paul E. Peterson (Norman: University of Oklahoma Press, 1994), 23–48; Gordon Silverstein, *Imbalance of Powers* (New York: Oxford University Press, 1997).

81. Stephen M. Griffin, *Long Wars and the Constitution* (Cambridge, MA: Harvard University Press, 2013).

82. If the president takes unilateral military action, even without the legitimate authority to do so, he has an advantage because Congress then faces the choice of whether to respond. Congress, on the other hand, always faces a collective action problem. The president does not face any such collective action problems—hence his advantage. Terry Moe and William Howell, "Unilateral Action and Presidential Power: A Theory," *Presidential Studies Quarterly* 29, no. 4 (December 1999): 850–873. Although Richard Neustadt famously described "three cases of command" in which one might expect that the president could issue a "self-executing order" but in which the president had to, in fact, persuade military generals and cabinet secretaries to do what he wanted them to do. See Richard E. Neustadt, *Presidential Power and the Modern Presidents: The Politics of Leadership from Roosevelt to Reagan* (New York: Free Press, 1990).

83. David P. Currie, "Prolegomena for a Sampler: Extrajudicial Interpretation of the Constitution," in Devins and Whittington, *Congress and the Constitution*, 18–38.

84. Donald G. Morgan, *Congress and the Constitution* (Cambridge, MA: Belknap Press 1966), 25; Susan R. Burgess, *Contest for Constitutional Authority: The Abortion and War Powers Debates* (Lawrence: University Press of Kansas 1992).

85. Zeisberg argues that the branches should engage in reasoning over foreign policy that is sensitive to the security realities they encounter and link their arguments about constitutional authority to their substantive agendas. She rejects the idea that there can be a single authoritative agreement about how to divide war powers authority between the branches of government, and argues instead for processual standards for constitutional interpretation in war powers in which each branch is able to develop an independent judgement that must be politically defended to the other branches. See Zeisberg, *War Powers*.

86. Keith Whittington, *Constitutional Construction: Divided Powers and Constitutional Meaning* (Cambridge, MA: Harvard University Press, 1999.) Whittington actually describes a more nuanced range of types of deliberation, but for simplicity's sake, I simply distinguish between interpretation and construction here.

CHAPTER 2: CONSTRUCTING THE AUTHORITY TO
INITIATE THE USE OF FORCE BEFORE 1898

1. That line between defense and offense is often traced to the Madison-Gerry amendment proposed at the constitutional convention, in which Madison suggested changing Congress's power from "make" war to "declare" war, so as to give the president the authority to "repel sudden attacks." In the brief debate over the "make war" clause, nearly all speakers expressed faith in the appropriateness of Congress's power to initiate wars. Charles Pinkney began by arguing that the power "to make war" should be vested in the Senate rather than in Congress as a whole. Pierce Butler replied that the Senate was also too big and made the one and only argument that the power "to make war" should be lodged in the president. James Madison and Elbridge Gerry then moved to "insert 'declare,' striking out 'make' war; leaving to the Executive the power to repel sudden attacks." Roger Sherman objected to the wording change. His concern was that the change in Congress's power from "make war" to "declare war" might empower the president to "commence" wars. While prescient over the long term, his worry did not seem to be shared by the other delegates. Gerry replied that he agreed with Sherman in principle but not about the implications of the amendment. He said, "I never expected to hear in a republic a motion to empower the Executive alone to declare war." Mr. Ellsworth of Connecticut argued it should be easy to get out of war and hard to get into it, implying initiation was a (time-consuming) legislative decision. George Mason then supported the "declare war" amendment because, he said, "I am against giving the power of war to the Executive, because not safely to be trusted with it . . . I am for clogging rather than facilitating war." The convention then voted 7 yes, 2 no. Mr. King then noted that "make war might be understood to 'conduct' it which was an Executive function," prompting Connecticut to change its vote to aye. That brief conversation has been at the heart of debates between politicians and scholars over the proper and intended distribution of war powers. See Max Farrand, ed., *The Records of the Federal Convention* (New Haven: Yale University Press 1911), 319.

2. Michael D. Ramsey, *The Constitution's Text in Foreign Affairs* (Cambridge, MA: Harvard University Press, 2007), 242.

3. Louis Fisher, *Presidential War Power*, 3rd ed. (Lawrence: University Press of Kansas, 2013), 17.

4. Stephen Griffin describes congressional power to initiate war as a defining characteristic of the original synthesis (*Long Wars and the Constitution* [Cambridge, MA: Harvard University Press 2013], 18). See also William Conrad Gibbons, "The Origins of the War Power of the Constitution," in *Congress and United States Foreign Policy: Controlling the Use of Force in the Nuclear Age*, ed. Michael Barnhart (Albany: State University of New York Press, 1987) 9–38; Ann Van Wynen Thomas and A. J. Thomas Jr., *The War Making Powers of the President* (Dallas: Southern Methodist University Press, 1982); Francis D. Wormuth and Edwin B. Firmage, *To Chain the Dog of War* (Dallas: Southern Methodist University Press, 1986).

5. Alexander De Conde, *The Quasi-War: The Politics and Diplomacy of the Undeclared War with France 1797–1801* (New York: Charles Scribner's Sons, 1966), 9.

6. De Conde, *Quasi-War*, 31.

7. 5th Cong., 8 Annals of Cong. 1455–1456.

8. He said that the Congress "could say whether the vessels should be employed offensively or defensively, but to say at what precise place they were to be stationed, was interfering with the duty of the commander-in-chief" (May 15, 1797, 5th Cong., 1st Sess., 7 Annals of Cong. 289–290).

9. 5th Cong., 8 Annals of Cong. 1459–1460.

10. May 15, 1797, 5th Cong., 1st Sess., 7 Annals of Cong. 361–362. Later, he went on to expound how Congress should not interfere with various directions the president might give to the military, using the specific example of what he considered to be the president's implied power to move troops from the interior to the coast: "That the Commander-in-Chief possessed the Constitutional power of employing these armed vessels as convoys in time of peace, he himself had no doubt, for he did not see any distinction in principle between employing a naval force to protect our merchantmen in the prosecution of a fair and lawful trade, or in enforcing the observance of the law of nations and employing the military in enforcing the execution of the municipal law." Note: in the *Annals of Congress*, the earliest congressional journal, members' remarks are reported in the third person. I have changed those to the first person for clarification about who is speaking and being spoken about.

11. May 15, 1797, 5th Cong., 1st Sess., 7 Annals of Cong. 363–364.

12. 5th Cong., 8 Annals of Cong. 1461–1462.

13. "*Be it enacted by the Senate and House of Representatives of the United States of America in Congress assembled*, That the President of the United States shall be, and he is hereby authorized to instruct the commanders of the public armed vessels which are, or which shall be employed in the service of the United States, to subdue, seize and take any armed French vessel, which shall be found within the jurisdictional limits of the United States, or elsewhere, on the high seas" ("An Act Further to Protect the Commerce of the United States," United States Statutes at Large, 1 Stat. 578, accessed September 7, 2023, http://avalon .law.yale.edu/18th_century/qw04.asp).

14. Confronted with questions about maritime prizes, the Supreme Court ruled that Congress had authorized, through a series of actions, an imperfect war. Bas v. Tingy 4 U.S. 4 Dall. 37 37 (1800).

15. Other aspects of these debates—such as the debate over Jackson's right to execute prisoners and Congress's right to oversee the implementation of military discipline—have been discussed in other chapters.

16. John Missall and Mary Lou Missal, *The Seminole Wars: America's Longest Indian Conflict* (Gainesville: University Press of Florida 2004), 38.

17. Missall and Missall, *Seminole Wars*, 40–41.

18. "I presume it will not be pretended, that either General Jackson or the President of the United States has the Constitutional right to wage war, for the purpose of making territorial addition to our Republic. The President of the United States has furnished the most conclusive evidence of the opinion which he entertains on the subject of his powers to place the United States in a belligerent attitude with foreign nations. We find, in all the orders from the War Department, the most cautious circumspection; the most apparent

reluctance to authorize the march of the American forces into Florida; the most positive injunctions to respect the Spanish authorities. This use of the military forces of the United States, for the purpose of conquest-of making important territorial additions to our Republic-must be viewed as an act of war against Spain, and, in that view, must be considered as an usurpation of the powers of the Congress of the United States-as a violation of the Constitution of the United States" (November 16, 1818, 15th Cong., 2nd Sess., 33 Annals of Cong. 621–622).

19. "The assertion of such a power to the commander-in-chief was contrary to the practice of the Government. By an act of Congress which passed in 1799, 'vesting the power of retaliation, in certain cases, in the President of the United States'—an act which passed during the quasi war with France, the President is authorized to retaliate upon any citizens of the French Republic, the enormities which may be practiced [*sic*], in certain cases, upon our citizens. Under what Administration was this act passed? It was under that which has been justly charged with stretching the Constitution to enlarge the Executive powers. Even during the mad career of Mr. Adams, when every means was resorted to for the purpose of infusing vigor into the Executive arm, no one thought of claiming for him the inherent right of retaliation" (November 16, 1818, 15th Cong., 2nd Sess., 33 Annals of Cong. 643–644).

20. As a personal critic of Jackson, and a future rival for the presidency, Clay obviously had a range of reasons to make these arguments.

21. Mr. Johnson, November 16, 1818, 15th Cong., 2nd Sess., 33 Annals of Cong. 665–666.

22. November 16, 1818, 15th Cong., 2nd Sess., 33 Annals of Cong. 1091–1092.

23. November 16, 1818, 15th Cong., 2nd Sess., 33 Annals of Cong. 679–680.

24. May 14, 1846, 29th Cong., 1st Sess., Cong. Globe 805.

25. 29th Cong., 2nd Sess., Cong. Globe 203 (1847), appendix.

26. Citing Story in his speech, the congressional record says that from "chapter 37, section 1486, page 34, he read the following: 'The power of the President, too, might well be deemed safe since tie could not of himself declare war, raise armies, or call forth the militia, or appropriate money for this purpose; for these powers all belong to Congress. In Great Britain, the King is not only commander-in-chief of the Army and navy, and militia, but he can declare war; and in time of war can raise armies and navies, and call forth the militia of his own will'" (January 20, 1848, 30th Cong., 1st Sess., Cong. Globe 192).

27. 29th Cong., 1st Sess., Cong. Globe 1049 (1846), appendix.

28. George Badger (Whig-NC), February 17, 1847, 29th Cong., 2nd Sess., Cong. Globe 430.

29. March 1, 1847, 29th Cong., 2nd Sess., Cong. Globe 519.

30. Meredith Gentry (Whig-TN) argued that "the President, as commander-in-chief of the army-and navy, has no right to wage war for objects and purposes not contemplated and sanctioned by Congress" and asked, "Where does the President find a sanction of the national will for his vast conquests and annexations?" 29th Cong., 2nd Sess., Cong. Globe 60 (1847), appendix.

31. 29th Cong., 1st Sess., Cong. Globe 902 (1846), appendix.

32. May 14, 1846, 29th Cong., 1st Sess., Cong. Globe 808.

33. March 30, 1848, 30th Cong., 1st Sess., Cong. Globe 555.

34. Of the 120 speeches that I coded as dealing with "initiation of hostilities," 84 were made before the year 1900. Only nineteen of these made what could be categorized as "broad" arguments about presidential power, and almost all argued that presidential discretion derives from some form of prior congressional authorization, or else from another nation beginning hostilities first. The only comment as broad as Yancey's prior to 1900 is a singular comment made by Representative Mills at the outset of the Spanish American War, arguing that if Hawaii is essential to the safety of the West Coast of the United States, the commander in chief would have a right to take it. He said, "We are told by the Navy Department, we are told by the naval experts, and for once in the history of the United States the line and the staff of the Navy have agreed, that the Hawaiian Islands are absolutely necessary for the protection of our Pacific coast. ... So greatly convinced of this are our military and naval boards of strategy, the President, who is Commander in Chief of the Army and Navy, and the General in charge of the Army, that they are reported to have agreed that in case this legislation is not enacted, it will be absolutely necessary to take military charge of the Hawaiian Islands in order to protect our Pacific coast." The few other members of Congress who speak on this topic argue that Hawaiian annexation would have to follow congressional action. See 31 Cong. Rec. 582 (1898), appendix.

35. 29th Cong., 1st Sess., Cong. Globe 951 (1846), appendix.

36. Robert C. Lieberman, "Ideas, Institutions, and Political Order: Explaining Political Change," *American Political Science Review* 96, no. 4 (December 2002): 697–712.

37. April 27, 1858, 35th Cong., 1st Sess., Cong. Globe 1777.

38. March 13, 1858, 35th Cong., 1st Sess., Cong. Globe 1073.

39. January 30, 1861, 36th Cong., 2nd Sess., Cong. Globe 621.

40. Rep. Conkling, February 1, 1861, 36th Cong., 2nd Sess., Cong. Globe 650.

41. January 18, 1861, 36th Cong., 2nd Sess., Cong. Globe 419.

42. April 19, 1862, 37th Cong., 2nd Sess., Cong. Globe 1719.

43. January 28, 1863, 37th Cong., 3rd Sess., Cong. Globe 531–534.

44. Jean Edward Smith, *Grant* (New York: Simon & Schuster 2001), 503.

45. Henry Bartholomew Cox, *War, Foreign Affairs, and Constitutional Power: 1829–1901* (Cambridge, MA: Ballinger 1984), 315.

46. "Be if further resolved, that if there be any naval force of the United States stationed in the waters of the Dominican Republic such naval force shall be withdrawn; and if there be any protectorate exercised over the Dominican Republic, or any aid given to the present government of that republic in resisting domestic or foreign enemies, such protectorate or aid shall be immediately discontinued" (41st Cong., 1st Sess., 43 Cong. Globe 217, 278 [1871]). A similar conversation did happen about a naval deployment to the Hawaiian islands. In 1895 Republican senator Henry Cabot Lodge proposed a resolution "instructing the Secretary of War" (later modified to ask the president, if not incompatible with the public interest") why Democratic president Grover Cleveland had moved US Navy ships away from the Hawaiian islands, and why he wasn't stationing at least one ship in Honolulu (53rd Cong., 3rd Sess., 27 Cong. Rec. 712). Democrats tended to say that the inquiry of their own Democratic president was inappropriate. John Palmer responded that "neither the Senate nor Congress, which consists of the two Houses, has the right to make a demand upon the

President, except under circumstances where the President would be guilty of an uncon-stitutional act" (53rd Cong., 3rd Sess., 27 Cong. Rec. 713). Despite the narrow Republican majority in the Senate, the resolution died without recorded vote.

47. 41st Cong., 1st Sess., 43 Cong. Globe 262.

48. 41st Cong., 1st Sess., 43 Cong. Globe 262.

49. March 28, 1871, 42nd Cong., 1st Sess., Cong. Globe 316.

50. Grant may have wanted to annex Santo Domingo as a destination for freed Black Americans, as did some members of Congress. The races of the people there figured prom-inently in congressional discussions about whether a treaty or annexation was good policy. Paul Frymer, *Building an American Empire: The Era of Territorial and Political Expansion* (Princeton: Princeton University Press, 2017), 212–218.

51. Grover Cleveland, "Proclamation 387—Continuing Neutrality of Citizens of the United States in the Civil Disturbance in Cuba," July 27, 1896, available at the American Presidency Project, http://www.presidency.ucsb.edu/ws/?pid=70793.

52. 54th Cong., 1st Sess., 28 Cong. Rec. 2109.

53. On the role of the "protecting Americans abroad" constitutional script during this time period, see Victoria Farrar-Myers, *Scripted for Change: The Institutionalization of the American Presidency* (College Station: Texas A&M University Press, 2007).

54. For a thorough account, read Wormuth and Firmage, *To Chain the Dog of War*, 37–40.

55. *Durand v. Hollins*. See discussion in chapter 6.

56. David Currie, *The Constitution in Congress: Descent into the Maelstrom* (Chicago: University of Chicago Press, 2014), 124.

57. James Buchanan, "Message to the Senate on the Arrest of William Walker in Nicara-gua," January 7, 1858, available at the American Presidency Project, http://www.presidency.ucsb.edu/ws/?pid=68291.

58. "Democrats in Congress:" And those who "conceived of Latin America as a fertile ground for the expansion of slavery." See Cox, *War, Foreign Affairs, and Constitutional Power*, 238. "supported their partisan ally Buchanan . . . ": January 22, 1858, 35th Cong., 1st Sess., Cong. Globe 362.

59. January 22, 1858, 35th Cong., 1st Sess., Cong. Globe 362–380.

60. January 22, 1858, 35th Cong., 1st Sess., Cong. Globe 358.

61. January 22, 1858, 35th Cong., 1st Sess., Cong. Globe 362–380. A senate report con-cluded that the arrest conformed to the Neutrality Act of 1818 and that given that the Nica-raguan government approved of the arrest, further action was unnecessary. Cox, *War, Foreign Affairs, and Constitutional Power*, 241.

62. Vivien A. Schmidt, "Discursive Institutionalism: The Explanatory Power of Ideas and Discourse," *Annual Review of Political Science* 11 (2008): 303; idem., "Reconciling Ideas and Institutions through Discursive Institutionalism," in *Ideas in Politics and Social Science Research*, ed. Daniel Beland and Robert Henry Cox (Oxford: Oxford University Press, 2011), 47–64; Rogers Smith, "Which Comes First, the Ideas or the Institutions?" in *Rethinking Po-litical Institutions: The Art of the State*, ed. Ian Shapiro, Stephen Skowronek, and Daniel Galvin (New York: New York University Press, 2006), 91–114; idem., "Ideas and the Spiral

of Politics: The Place of American Political Thought in American Political Development," *American Political Thought* 3, no. 1 (Spring 2014): 126–136; Lieberman, "Ideas, Institutions, and Political Order"; Mark Blyth, "Ideas, Uncertainty, and Evolution," in *Ideas in Politics and Social Science Research*, ed. Daniel Beland and Robert Henry Cox (Oxford: Oxford University Press, 2011), 83–105; George Thomas, "Political Thought and Development," *American Political Thought: A Journal of Ideas, Institutions, and Culture* 3, no. 1 (Spring 2014): 114–125.

CHAPTER 3: AUTHORITATIVE SOURCES AND CONSTITUTIONAL SCRIPTS

1. Bruce Peabody, "Congressional Attitudes toward Constitutional Interpretation," in *Congress and the Constitution*, ed. Neal Devins and Keith E. Whittington (Durham, NC: Duke University Press, 2005), 39–64; Donald. G. Morgan, *Congress and the Constitution: A Study of Responsibility* (Cambridge, MA: Belknap Press, 1966).

2. J. Mitchell Pickerill, *Deliberation in Congress: The Impact of Judicial Review in a Separated System* (Durham, NC: Duke University Press, 2004).

3. Andrew D. Martin, "Congressional Decision Making and the Separation of Powers," *American Political Science Review* 95, no. 2 (2001): 361–378.

4. Or to use Pierson's language, what were the mechanisms by which that institution reproduced itself? Paul Pierson, *Politics in Time: History, Institutions, and Social Analysis* (Princeton: Princeton University Press, 2004).

5. Victoria Farrar-Myers, *Scripted for Change: The Institutionalization of the American Presidency* (College Station: Texas A&M University Press, 2007).

6. Legal scholars, especially, focus on what war powers meant at the Founding because theories grounded in constitutional originalism makes such questions important to even modern decision making. See, prominently, David J. Barron and Martin S. Lederman, "The Commander in Chief at the Lowest Ebb: Framing the Problem, Doctrine, and Original Understanding," *Harvard Law Review* 121, no. 3 (2008): 689–804, and idem., "The Commander in Chief at the Lowest Ebb: A Constitutional History," *Harvard Law Review* 121, no. 4 (2008): 941–1112; Charles A. Lofgren, "War-Making under the Constitution: The Original Understanding," *Yale Law Journal* 81, no. 4 (1972): 672–702; John C. Yoo, "The Continuation of Politics by Other Means: The Original Understanding of War Powers," *California L Review* 84 (1996): 167; idem., "War and the Constitutional Text," *University of Chicago Law Review* 69, no. 4 (2002): 1639–1684; Michael D. Ramsey, *The Constitution's Text in Foreign Affairs* (Cambridge, MA: Harvard University Press, 2007). But political scientists and historians have of course considered the founding moment as well, although usually in broader context. See Sarah Burns, *The Politics of War Powers: The Theory and History of Presidential Unilateralism* (Lawrence: University Press of Kansas, 2019); Richard J. Ellis, *Founding the American Presidency* (Lanham, MD: Rowman & Littlefield, 1999); Louis Fisher, *Presidential War Power*, 3rd edition (Lawrence: University Press of Kansas: 2013); Francis D. Wormuth and Edwin B. Firmage, *To Chain the Dog of War* (Dallas: Southern Methodist University Press, 1986).

7. 26th Cong., 1st Sess., Cong. Globe 273 (1840), appendix.

8. 33 Annals of Cong. 665–666 (1818–1819), Proceedings and Debates of the House of Representatives of the United States, at the Second Session of the Fifteenth Congress, Begun at the City of Washington, Monday, November 16, 1818; 41 Cong. Rec. 1207 (1907); 30 Cong. Rec. 1094 (1897); 9 Cong. Rec. 242 (1879); 41 Cong. Rec. 1252 (1907); 40th Cong., Special Session, Cong. Globe 63–65 (1867), appendix; 43 Cong. Rec. 2451 (1909); 37th Cong., 2nd Sess., Cong. Globe 2966 (1862); June 28, 1862, 37th Cong., 2nd Sess., Cong. Globe 2969; June 28, 1862, 7 Cong. Rec. 329; 9 Cong. Rec. 49 (1879); 9 Cong. Rec. 242 (1879); 41 Cong. Rec. 1252 (1907); 37th Cong., 2nd Sess., Cong. Globe 2972 (1862).

9. Henry Cabot Lodge and Joseph Foraker, 1907.

10. The Founding was spectacularly unhelpful in defining the commander in chief clause. Unfortunately for us, there was no discussion at all at the Constitutional Convention of the decision to grant the president the title of "commander in chief." The phrase's inclusion in hastily drafted state constitutions does not significantly clarify the issue. When they declared independence from England, eleven of the colonies wrote state constitutions. These documents referred to the state militias in a variety of ways, but they do not definitively tell us what was meant by the phrase "commander in chief." Many of the state constitutions had explicit provisions requiring that the military power would be subordinate to the civil power, and many designated a civilian state official, usually the governor, as the head of the state military. Seven of those constitutions explicitly designated the governor as "commander in chief" of the state militias. But they don't define that authority any more than the Constitution of 1787 does. For a more extended discussion of the founding moment, see Barron and Lederman, "Commander in Chief at the Lowest Ebb: Framing the Problem, Doctrine, and Original Understanding."

11. Wormuth and Firmage, *To Chain the Dog of War.*

12. Though I do not find that members of Congress directly connected Montesquieu's theories to the specific authority of the commander in chief, generally their understanding of the Constitution and the balance of powers comports with the argument Sarah Burns makes about the separation of powers in *Politics of War Powers.*

13. Even when, as with the case of British generals freeing slaves on the battlefield, they were actually relevant precedents for the argument the member of Congress was making about military emancipation.

14. "as a foil": April 3, 1862, 37th Cong., 2nd Sess., Cong. Globe 1502; January 27, 1865, 38th Cong., 2nd Sess., Cong. Globe 439; 4 Part II Cong. Deb. 2685–2686 (1828), case of Marigny D'Auterive; April 19, 1834, 23rd Cong., 1st Sess., Cong. Globe 317; February 26, 1867, 39th Cong., 2nd Sess., I Cong. Globe 1854; March 28, 1879, 9 Cong. Rec. 106; 32 Cong. Rec. 2440 (1899); March 24, 1886, 17 Cong. Rec. 2695; January 17, 1907, 41 Cong. Rec. 1252; January 17, 1868, 40 Cong. Globe 591. "in reference to the British origin . . .": 37th Cong., 2nd Sess., Cong. Globe 113 (1862), appendix; January 8, 1863, 37th Cong., 3rd Sess., Cong. Globe 219; January 28, 1863, 37th Cong., 3rd Sess., Cong. Globe 531–534; April 3, 1862, 37th Cong., 2nd Sess., Cong. Globe 1502; 9 Cong. Rec. 239 (1879); February 18, 1886, 17 Cong. Rec. 1586.

15. For example, even during times of unified partisan government, most presidential

initiatives do not become law. See George C. Edwards III and Andrew Barrett, "Presidential Agenda Setting in Congress," in *Polarized Politics*, ed. Jon R. Bond and Richard Fleisher (Washington, DC: CQ Press 2000), 109–133.

16. In the rare exceptions where the court overrules the actions taken by the political branches in a timely way, their decisions have not always been honored. See, for example, the habeas corpus cases during the Civil War (which had little influence over Lincoln at the time).

17. Douglas L. Kriner, *After the Rubicon* (Chicago: University of Chicago Press, 2010).

18. *Washington:* June 28, 1862, 37th Cong., 2nd Sess., Cong. Globe 2966; May 3, 1864, 38th Cong., 1st Sess., Cong. Globe 2039; February 10, 1843, 27th Cong., 3rd Sess., Cong. Globe 254; December 21, 1852, 32nd Cong., 2nd Sess., Cong. Globe 106 (1853); December 27, 1853, 33rd Cong., 1st Sess., Cong. Globe 84 (1854); January 14, 1901, 34 Cong. Rec. 973; January 7, 1907, 41 Cong. Rec. 685; May 25, 1878, 7 Cong. Rec. 3803; May 27, 1878, 7 Cong. Rec. 3851; January 31, 1885, 16 Cong. Rec. 1136; 16 Cong. Rec. 3 (1885), appendix; 16 Cong. Rec. 150 (1885), appendix; March 9, 1886, 17 Cong. Rec. 2217; January 31, 1901, 34 Cong. Rec. 1721; April 18, 1898, 31 Cong. Rec. 4033. *Adams:* June 28, 1862, 37th Cong., 2nd Sess., Cong. Globe 2966; 33 Annals of Cong. 643–644 (1818–1819), Proceedings and Debates of the House of Representatives of the United States, at the Second Session of the Fifteenth Congress, Begun at the City of Washington, Monday, November 16, 1818; December 27, 1853, 33rd Cong., 1st Sess., Cong. Globe 84 (1854); November 14, 1877, 6 Cong. Rec. 392; May 25, 1878, 7 Cong. Rec. 3803; January 31, 1885, 16 Cong. Rec. 1136. *Jefferson:* March 28, 1871, 42nd Cong., 1st Sess., Cong. Globe 316; May 31, 1872, 42nd Cong., 2nd Sess., Cong. Globe 4117; March 14, 1884, 15 Cong. Rec. 1917; January 26, 1899, 32 Cong. Rec. 1107; 48 Cong. Rec. 860 (1912); February 7, 1898, 31 Cong. Rec. 1520. *Madison:* 9 Cong. Rec. 49 (1879), appendix; 33 Cong. Rec. 568 (1900), appendix; 29th Cong., 2nd Sess., Cong. Globe 99 (1847), appendix; June 28, 1862, 37th Cong., 2nd Sess., Cong. Globe 2969; 33 Annals of Cong. 679–680 (1818–1819), Proceedings and Debates. *Jackson:* 27th Cong., 1st Sess., Cong. Globe 475 (1841), appendix; 9 Cong. Rec. 35 (1879), appendix; May 9, 1879, 9 Cong. Rec. 1185; March 9, 1886, 17 Cong. Rec. 2217. *Polk:* March 14, 1900, 33 Cong. Rec. 2909; 33 Cong. Rec. 34 (1900), appendix; 33 Cong. Rec. 568 (1900), appendix; 30 Cong. Rec. 1098 (1897); 51 Cong. Rec. 6965 (1914). *Buchanan:* 9 Cong. Rec. 35 (1879), appendix; January 31, 1885, 16 Cong. Rec. 1136. *Lincoln:* 33 Cong. Rec. 568 (1900), appendix; March 20, 1902, 35 Cong. Rec. 3059; 40 Cong. Globe 348 (1869); 40 Cong. Globe 1244 (1869); 41 Cong. Globe 5397 (1870); 45 Cong. Rec. 5636 (1910); 49 Cong. Rec. 45 (1913), appendix; 49 Cong. Rec. 45 (1913), appendix; 53 Cong. Rec. 5557 (1916); 53 Cong. Rec. 5979 (1916); May 5, 1866, 39th Cong., 1st Sess., Cong. Globe 2413; July 9, 1866, 39th Cong., 1st Sess., Cong. Globe 3674; June 4, 1902, 35 Cong. Rec. 6294; April 20, 1871, 42nd Cong., 1st Sess., Cong. Globe 836; April 18, 1872, 42nd Cong., 2nd Sess., I Cong. Globe 2551; 3 Cong. Rec. 84 (1875), appendix; November 14, 1877, 6 Cong. Rec. 392; March 8, 1880, 10 Cong. Rec. 1372; March 14, 1884, 15 Cong. Rec. 1920. *Grant:* November 14, 1877, 6 Cong. Rec. 392. *McKinley:* June 25, 1902, 35 Cong. Rec. 7408; March 3, 1905, 39 Cong. Record 3933; 42 Cong. Rec. 2546 (1908); 42 Cong. Rec. 5161 (1908); 53 Cong. Rec. 43 (1916), appendix. *Roosevelt:* 43 Cong. Rec. 3396 (1909); 44 Cong. Rec. 4469 (1909); 48 Cong. Rec 2508 (1912).

19. March 30, 1848, 30th Cong., 1st Sess., Cong. Globe 555; January 28, 1863, 37th Cong.,

3rd Sess., Cong. Globe 531–534; January 14, 1862, 37th Cong., 2nd Sess., Cong. Globe 296; January 16, 1862, 37th Cong., 2nd Sess., Cong. Globe 342; 33 Annals of Cong. 601–602 (1818–1819), Proceedings and Debates; 33 Annals of Cong. 1091–1092 (1818–1819), Proceedings and Debates; 2 Part II Cong. Deb. 2103–2104 (1826), amendment of the Constitution; 39th Cong., 1st Sess., Cong. Globe 233 (1866), appendix; July 26, 1856, 34th Cong., 1st Sess., Cong. Globe 1756; 42nd Cong., Special Session Cong. Globe 308 (1871), appendix; May 27, 1878, 7 Cong. Rec. 3851; April 24, 1879, 9 Cong. Rec. 803; 9 Cong. Rec. 49 (1879), appendix.

20. 31 Cong. Rec. 290 (1898), appendix; April 30, 1917, 55 Cong. Rec. 1570; 31 Cong. Rec. 286 (1898), appendix; May 13, 1862, 37th Cong., 2nd Sess., Cong. Globe 2072; June 11, 1862, 37th Cong., 2nd Sess., Cong. Globe 2611; July 2, 1862, 37th Cong., 2nd Sess., Cong. Globe 3043; February 2, 1862, 37th Cong., 3rd Sess., Cong. Globe 629; 38th Cong., Special Session, Cong. Globe 46 (1863), appendix; June 30, 1886, 17 Cong. Rec. 6359; April 12, 1898, 31 Cong. Rec. 3730.

21. In *Martin v. Mott*, the court ruled that given Congress's delegation of the decision to call up the militia in 1795, and the declaration of war against Britain, the president had broad discretion to order state militia men to invade Canada, even though the Constitution did not specifically state that militias could be used for that purpose. Members referred to this precedent in the context of talking about the appropriate federal uses of state militias. *Cross v. Harrison* dealt with the governance of conquered territory and concluded that the commander in chief had authority under the laws of nations to make law in conquered territory until Congress legislated for it. Because it had important implications for the evolution of war powers, the case will be discussed in the next section. Notably, it was a precedent that ratified the consensus reached by Congress and the president during the Mexican War, and so when members of Congress referred to it thereafter, they often referred jointly to the court precedent and the historical precedent. For further discussion, see chap. 6. Members referred to the *Prize* cases to support arguments on either side of questions about whether the president had constitutional authority to recognize the existence of a rebellion or state of war. As they debated the measure, they asked whether the commander in chief had the implied constitutional authority to recognize a civil war abroad, or whether, as they ultimately determined, Congress could do so. The debate is relevant to questions about the initiation of force because recognizing a foreign insurgency could be seen as an act of aggression against, in this case, Spain. Horace Chilton (D-TX) referred to the *Prize* cases to argue that when Lincoln recognized the insurrection in the Southern states, he had done so under congressional statutory authority and not inherent presidential authority. (Such an interpretation would legitimize Congress's recognition of the Cuban revolution.) John Daniel (D-VA) also supported the resolution by arguing that the commander in chief had no implied authority to recognize war. Like Chilton, he used an American historical example to justify his reasoning. He argued that Polk had recognized the war with Mexico by repelling an invasion under congressional statutory authority and argued that the president was simply the executor of Congress's decisions. As Congress considered a resolution on April 15, 1898, to recognize "the belligerency" and the independence of Cuba, John Spooner (R-WI) and a supporter of McKinley, objected and argued that only the president as commander in chief could recognize a war among other countries. He referred to the *Prize*

cases and other historical precedents to argue that the power to recognize a nation was an executive one. 31 Cong. Rec. 286 (1898); January 5, 1904, 38 Cong. Rec. 459; 28 Cong. Rec. 2164 (1896); 28 Cong. Rec. 3012 (1896); 54th Cong., 1st Sess., 28 Cong. Rec. 1094; 55th Cong., 2nd Sess., 31 Cong. Rec. 290 (1898), appendix. For *Ex Parte Milligan* see 40 Cong. Globe 769 (1868); 43 Cong. Rec. 2540 (1909); 43 Cong. Rec. 308 (1909); 41 Cong. Rec. 691 (1907); 41 Cong. Rec. 1085 (1907). For the Eliason case, see *United States v. Eliason* 41 U.S. 291 (1842); 17 Cong. Rec. 6359 (1886); 41 Cong. Rec. 1252 (1907).

22. In 1826 Rep. Silas Wood (NY), arguing about amending the Constitution to allow for the direct election of senators, acknowledges that the president is "the organ of intercourse with other nations" and as such should be entitled to deference but also the "counsel of some department as permanent as the Senate" (2 Part II Cong. Deb. 1675–1676 [1826], amendment of the Constitution). In 1867 Republican senator Timothy Howe argued in favor of the Tenure of Office Act, arguing that constant attention to patronage prevented the president from attending to his other responsibilities such as being "the organ of the American nation in communicating with other nations" (39th Cong., 2nd Sess., Cong. Globe 1039–1040 [1867]). In 1869 Republican senator Matthew Carpenter argued that the president's role as "organ for communicating foreign powers" was actually largely conferred on him by the "act of Congress creating the Department of Foreign Affairs" (December 15, 1869, 41 Cong. Globe 140 [1870]). In reporting the proceedings of the commission that determined the outcome of the 1876 presidential election, Rep. Walbridge Field (R) used the language "organ between you and all foreign states" as a part of a description of the importance of the office and why it is important that the American public not perceive the president to be a fraud (5 Cong. Rec. 248, 7 [1877], Remarks of Members of the Electoral Commission). Also in 1877, President Ulysses Grant referred to both his constitutional and statutory authority as the "constitutional organ of communication with foreign states" to veto to House resolutions directing vague messages to foreign states (Ulysses S. Grant, "Veto Message," available at the American Presidency Project, accessed September 8, 2023, https://www.presidency.ucsb.edu/node/203803). In using that language, Grant cites an unnamed eminent writer on constitutional law, possibly George Curtis, who also did so. But in using that language Curtis himself was not asserting a broad power, just describing the Constitutional Convention's reasoning in placing the president at the head of treaty negotiations. He said, "The power to declare war having been vested in the whole legislature, it was necessary to provide the mode in which a war was to be terminated. As the President was to be the organ of communication with other governments, and as he would be the general guardian of the national interests, the negotiation of a treaty of peace, and of all other treaties, was necessarily confided in him." He also acknowledged the "concurrent authority" of the Senate (George Ticknor Curtis, *History of the Origin, Formation, and Adoption of the Constitution of the United* States [New York: Harper and Bros., 1861], 415).

23. For example, see the already mentioned cases of Grant's sending the navy to Santo Domingo during treaty negotiations and McKinley's floating of an intervention short of war in Cuba. (Further discussion in chap. 6).

24. 38 Cong. Rec. 456–485 (1904). Lodge also cites the "sole organ" logic in a 1907 debate

over an issue unrelated to the assertion of presidential authority to initiate the use of military force (41 Cong. Rec. 685 [1907]).

25. For cases that had already been resolved by the political branches, see *Cross v. Harrison*, *Martin v. Mott*, the *Prize* cases. Some of the major exceptions are *Durand v. Hollins*, *Ex Parte Merryman*, and *United States v. Curtiss-Wright Export Corporation*.

26. January 20, 1848, 30th Cong., 1st Sess., Cong. Globe 192; March 30, 1848, 30th Cong., 1st Sess., Cong. Globe 55; March 2, 1863, 37th Cong., 3d Sess., Cong. Globe 1382; March 2, 1863, 37th Cong., 3rd Sess., Cong. Globe 1383; March 14, 1864, 38th Cong. 1st Sess., Cong. Globe 1067; 40th Cong., Special Session, Cong. Globe 63–65 (1867), appendix; 5 Cong. Rec. 2162 (1877); 9 Cong. Rec. 1181 (1879).

27. "The power, to declare war may be exercised by congress, not only by authorizing general hostilities, in which case the general laws of war apply to our situation; or by partial hostilities, in which case the laws of war, so far as they actually apply to our situation, are to be observed . . . The latter course was pursued in the qualified war of 1798 with France, which was regulated by divers acts of congress, and of course was confined to the limits prescribed by those acts" (Joseph Story, *Commentaries on the Constitution of the United States; With a Preliminary Review of the Constitutional History of the Colonies and States, before the Adoption of the Constitution* [Boston: Hilliard, Gray, 1833], vol. 3, chap. 21, 1169).

28. Both Story and Kent use the same phrase (Story quotes Kent) to summarize the rationale for giving a single president the authority to enforce the laws and use defensive force. They both say that "the command and application of the public force, to execute the laws, to maintain peace, and to resist foreign invasion, are powers so obviously of an executive nature, and require the exercise of qualities so peculiarly adapted to this department, that a well-organized government can scarcely exist, when they are taken away from it" (Story, *Commentaries*, vol. 3, chap. 37, 1485; James Kent, *Commentaries on American Law* (New York: O. Halstead,

1826), lecture 13, 264.

29. Observations of this backward-looking tendency in congressional policymaking in the national security realm today has led to its being called legislative myopia; it may be partially grounded in interest groups' preference for stability. See Harold Hongju Koh, *The National Security Constitution: Sharing Power after the Iran Contra Affair* (New Haven: Yale University Press, 1990).

30. Curtis A. Bradley and Trevor W. Morrison, "Historical Gloss and the Separation of Powers," *Harvard Law Review* 126, no. 2 (2012): 428.

31. See, for example, Brian L. Beirne, "George vs. George vs. George: Commander-in-Chief Power," *Yale Law and Policy Review* 26, no. 1 (2007): 265–308; Cecilia Elizabeth O'Leary, *To Die For: The Paradox of American Patriotism* (Princeton: Princeton University Press, 1999).

32. Beirne, "George vs. George vs. George."

33. O'Leary, *To Die For*, 17.

34. In Congress, May 2, 1780: Instructions to the captains and commanders of private armed vessels which shall have commissions or letters of marque and reprisal. Passy, France: Benjamin Franklin, 1781.

35. On December 22, 1776, the Continental Congress empowered Washington "'to use every Endeavour, by giving Bounties and otherwise, to prevail upon the Troops, whose Time of Enlistment shall expire at the End of the Month, to stay with the Army so long after that Period as its Situation shall render their Stay necessary.' GW also is authorized to appoint a commissary of prisoners and a clothier general and establish their salaries, and Congress requests him 'to fix upon that System of Promotion in the Continental Army which in his Opinion, and that of the general Officers with him, will produce most general Satisfaction' and suggests to him 'whether a Promotion of Field Officers in the Colonial Line, and of Captains and Subalterns in the regimental Line would not be the most proper'" and "Resolved, That General Washington shall be, and he is hereby, vested with full, ample, and complete powers to raise and collect together, in the most speedy and effectual manner, from any or all of these United States, 16 batallions [sic] of infantry, in addition to those already voted by Congress; to appoint officers for the said batallions [sic]; to raise, officer, and equip three thousand light horse; three regiments of artillery, and a corps of engineers, and to establish their pay; to apply to any of the states for such aid of the militia as he shall judge necessary; to form such magazines of provisions, and in such places, as he shall think proper; to displace and appoint all officers under the rank of brigadier general, and to fill up all vacancies in every other department in the American armies; to take, wherever he may be, whatever he may want for the use of the army, if the inhabitants will not sell it, allowing a reasonable price for the same; to arrest and confine persons who refuse to take the continental currency, or are otherwise disaffected to the American cause; and return to the states of which they are citizens, their names, and the nature of their offences, together with the witnesses to prove them: That the foregoing powers be vested in General Washington, for and during the term of six months from the date hereof, unless sooner determined by Congress" ("To George Washington from John Hancock, 27 December 1776," *Founders Online*, National Archives, https://founders.archives.gov/documents/Washington/03-07-02-0356 [Original source: *The Papers of George Washington*, Revolutionary War Series, vol. 7, *21 October 1776–5 January 1777*, ed. Philander D. Chase (Charlottesville: University Press of Virginia, 1997), 461–463.]).

36. Wormuth and Firmage, *To Chain the Dog of War*, 106–107; *Journals of the Continental Congress*, 1774–1789, December 27, 1776, 1043–1046. For further discussion, see Barron and Lederman, "Commander in Chief at the Lowest Ebb: Framing the Problem, Doctrine, and Original Understanding."

37. Congress had the power to make treaties, and those treaties were to take precedence over any tariffs, taxes, or laws of any state or agreements that might be negotiated between a state and a foreign power. Congress had the power to determine the size of the army and navy. Congress also had the powers to "appropriate money," "agree upon the number of vessels of war, to be built or purchased, or the number of land or sea forces to be raised," and to "appoint a commander in chief of the army or navy." Only Congress could declare war or grant letters of marque and reprisal. Congress was given the powers to receive ambassadors although the states could do so if they had Congress's express permission. States were allowed to defend themselves for a short time when actually invaded or in immediate danger of invasion. States were prohibited from having an army or navy without Congress's

permission and were required to maintain a functioning militia. Specifically, the Articles declared that:

"The United States in Congress assembled, shall have the sole and exclusive right and power of determining on peace and war . . . entering into treaties and alliances, provided that no treaty of commerce shall be made . . . prohibiting the exportation or importation of any species of goods or commodities whatsoever[;] of establishing rules for deciding in all cases, what captures on land or water shall be legal, and in what manner prizes taken by land or naval forces in the service of the United States shall be divided or appropriated—of granting letters of marque and reprisal in times of peace—appointing courts for the trial of piracies and felonies committed on the high seas and establishing courts for receiving and determining finally appeals in all cases of captures."

38. Very early on in this project, at the point at which my undergraduate students and I were collecting speeches from the online congressional record, we noticed that there were a lot of references to George Washington, commander in chief of the Continental Army. We did not collect those, since we were focused on the post-1787 presidency. Since I was interested in how members of Congress thought about the *constitutional* commander in chief, these *preconstitutional* references seemed irrelevant and distracting. There were enough of these Washington shout-outs that it became a specific decision rule in our data collection process to exclude them from our collection process. I now wish I'd kept them, because, as already made clear, later analysis has told us that the precedents that Washington set as commander in chief of the Continental Army loomed large in the minds of nineteenth century members of Congress when they thought about the war powers of the Congress and the president. I leave it to others to go back through the fifty-eight thousand references to "commanders" and "chiefs" in the congressional record that my students and I dug through to find references to the US president. Members of Congress did refer repeatedly to precedents set during George Washington's presidency, notably about his actions to suppress the Whiskey Rebellion, that mostly related to his deference to the Militia Act when calling out the militia. Even excluding those specific references to Washington that we did not collect, and looking only at those speeches that referred only to the post-1787 commander in chief clause, it is clear that members of Congress frequently drew on the logic of Washington's relationship with the Continental Congress during the Revolutionary War.

39. As noted by Wilbur Zelinsky, representations of George Washington were common as early as the early nineteenth century. See Wilbur Zelinsky, *Nation into State: The Shifting Symbolic Foundations of American Nationalism* (Chapel Hill: University of North Carolina Press, 1988).

40. 29th Cong., 2nd Sess., Cong. Globe 308 (1847), appendix.

41. 29th Cong., 2nd Sess., Cong. Globe 308 (1847), appendix.

42. March 1, 1847, 29th Cong., 2nd Sess., Cong. Globe 519.

43. 29th Cong., 2nd Sess., Cong. Globe 166 (1847), appendix.

44. 29th Cong., 2nd Sess., Cong. Globe 166 (1847), appendix.

45. 29th Cong., 2nd Sess., Cong. Globe 166 (1847), appendix.

46. Paul Pierson and Theda Skocpol, "Historical Institutionalism in Contemporary

Political Science," in *Political Science: The State of the Discipline*, ed. Ira Katznelson and Helen V. Milner (New York: W. W. Norton, 2002), 693–721.

47. For discussions of the differences between historical institutionalist scholarship that focuses on institutional arrangements and ideational scholarship that emphasizes ideas, see Rogers M. Smith, "Which Comes First, the Ideas or the Institutions?" in *Rethinking Political Institutions: The Art of the State*, ed. Ian Shapiro, Stephen Skowronek and Daniel Galvin (New York: New York University Press, 2006), 91–114, and Brian J. Glenn, "The Two Schools of American Political Development," *Political Studies Review* 2, no. 2 (April 2004): 153–165.

48. For example, Gordon Silverstein argues that legal precedents shape politics by enshrining a set of ideas into law that then become the basis for policy regimes. See his *Law's Allure: How Law Shapes, Constrains, Saves, and Kills Politics* (Cambridge, UK: Cambridge University Press, 2009).

49. Elvin Lim, "Political Thought, Political Development, and America's Two Foundings," *American Political Thought* 3, no. 1 (Spring 2014): 146–156. See also Tulis and Mellow's analysis of how the *Federalist* rhetoric also facilitated an opposing logic by incorporating the politics it was trying to displace, and how that opposition rhetoric also affected development. Jeffrey K. Tulis and Nicole Mellow, *Legacies of Losing in American Politics* (Chicago: University of Chicago Press, 2018).

50. On the logic of constitutional scripts as dialogues, see Farrar-Myers, *Scripted for Change*. For general discussions of how attending to ideas and discourse can help us improve social science theories of change, see Mark Blyth, "Ideas, Uncertainty, and Evolution," in *Ideas in Politics and Social Science Research*, ed. Daniel Beland and Robert Henry Cox (Oxford: Oxford University Press, 2011), 83–105, and James W. Ceaser, "Foundational Concepts in American Political Development," in *Nature and History in American Political Development* (Cambridge, MA: Harvard University Press, 2006), 1–90.

51. Rogers Smith, "Ideas and the Spiral of Politics: The Place of American Political Thought in American Political Development," *American Political Thought* 3, no. 1 (Spring 2014): 126–136.

CHAPTER 4: HAIL TO THE CHIEF: A NEW SCRIPT FOR
A NEW CENTURY

1. Jeremy D. Bailey, *The Idea of Presidential Representation: An Intellectual and Political History* (Lawrence: University Press of Kansas: 2019).

2. William G. Howell and Terry M. Moe, *Relic: How Our Constitution Undermines Effective Government and Why We Need a More Powerful Presidency* (New York: Basic Books, 2016); B. Dan Wood, *The Myth of Presidential Representation* (Cambridge, UK: Cambridge University Press, 2009).

3. Or a conjuncture, perhaps, in Pierson's language. See Paul Pierson, *Politics in Time: History, Institutions, and Social Analysis* (Princeton: Princeton University Press, 2004), chap. 5.

4. John E. Mueller, *War, Presidents, and Public Opinion* (New York: Wiley, 1973).

5. Richard Brody, *Assessing the President* (Palo Alto: Stanford University Press, 1991);

Tim Groeling and Matthew A. Baum, "Crossing the Water's Edge: Elite Rhetoric, Media Coverage, and the Rally-Round-the-Flag Phenomenon," *Journal of Politics* 70, no. 4 (October 2008): 1065–1085; William D. Baker and John R. O'Neal, "Patriotism or Opinion Leadership?: The Nature and Origins of the 'Rally 'Round the Flag' Effect," *Journal of Conflict Resolution* 45, no. 5 (October 2001): 661–687.

6. William G. Howell, Saul P. Jackman, and Jon C. Rogowski, *The Wartime President: Executive Influence and the Nationalizing Politics of Threat* (Chicago: University of Chicago Press, 2013).

7. William Michael Treanor, "Fame, the Founding, and the Power to Declare War," *Cornell Law Review* 82 (1997): 695–772.

8. There are many similarities between nineteenth- and twentieth-century presidencies. Presidents from the earliest days of the republic faced political incentives to seek political power and to use it. See, for example, Daniel Galvin and Colleen Shogan, "Presidential Politicization and Centralization across the Modern-Traditional Divide," *Polity* 36, no. 3 (2004): 477–504; and Stephen Skowronek, *The Politics Presidents Make: Leadership from John Adams to Bill Clinton* (Cambridge, MA: Harvard University Press, 1997). Like today's presidents, those in the early republic also claimed national electoral mandates and occasionally asserted extensive military authority. Bailey, for example, shows that presidential claims to special democratic authority as "nationally elected representative" appeared repeatedly throughout the nineteenth and twentieth centuries (Bailey, *Idea of Presidential Representation*). Presidents' State of the Union rhetoric has also been consistent across the modern-traditional divide. See Ryan Lee Teten, "'We the People': The 'Modern' Rhetorical Popular Address of the Presidents during the Founding Period," *Political Research Quarterly* 60, no. 4 (December 2007): 669–682. Acknowledging these continuities, presidential scholars today rarely argue that there was a sudden change from a limited, "traditional" nineteenth-century presidency to a "modern" presidency, though such arguments are still made, as in Lewis L. Gould, *The Modern American Presidency* (Lawrence: University Press of Kansas, 2003). Arguments such as these were more popular not so long ago. For example, note the framework for texts like James Pfiffner's *The Modern Presidency*, 5th ed. (Belmont, CA: Thomson Wadsworth, 2008) and the midcentury classic Clinton Rossiter, *The American Presidency* (New York: New American Library, 1956).

9. Jeffrey Tulis, *The Rhetorical Presidency* (Princeton: Princeton University Press, 1987); Robert P. Saldin, "William McKinley and the Rhetorical Presidency," *Presidential Studies Quarterly* 41, no. 1 (March 2011): 119–134; Justin Rex, "The President's War Agenda: A Rhetorical View," *Presidential Studies Quarterly* 41, no. 1 (March 2011): 93–118; Ryan L. Teten, "Evolution of the Modern Rhetorical Presidency: Presidential Presentation and Development of the State of the Union Address," *Presidential Studies Quarterly* 33, no. 2 (June 2003): 333–346.

10. Samuel Kernell, *Going Public* (Washington, DC: CQ Press, 1997); Tulis, *Rhetorical Presidency*.

11. Tulis, *Rhetorical Presidency*, 128.

12. As noted by Forrest McDonald, "trivial doings became marketable products, for presidents and candidates were among the few people whose names newspaper readers

everywhere could recognize. Beginning around 1885 Americans were fed information (or misinformation or disinformation) about their president on a daily basis." McDonald, *The American Presidency: An Intellectual History* (Lawrence: University Press of Kansas, 1994), 434–435. Matthew Oyos also finds that Roosevelt enlisted the press specifically to help him establish broader authority over military affairs. See Oyos, "Theodore Roosevelt, Congress, and the Military: U.S. Civil-Military Relations in the Early Twentieth Century," *Presidential Studies Quarterly* 30, no. 2 (June 2000): 312–330.

13. Gil Troy, *See How They Ran: The Changing Role of the Presidential Candidate* (New York: Macmillan, 1991); Richard J. Ellis, *The Development of the American Presidency* (New York: Routledge, 2012), 46.

14. As Theodore Roosevelt put it, the president "is a steward of the people bound actively and affirmatively to do all he can for the people. . . . It is not only his right but his duty to do anything that the needs of the nation demanded unless such action was forbidden by the Constitution or by the laws. . . . Under this interpretation of executive power I did and caused to be done many things not previously done by the President and the heads of the departments. I did not usurp power, but I did greatly broaden the use of executive power." "Theodore Roosevelt's (1913) and William Howard Taft's Theories of Presidential Power (1916)," in *The Evolving Presidency: Addresses, Cases, Essays, Letters, Reports, Resolutions, Transcripts, and Other Landmark Documents 1787–1998*, ed. Michael Nelson (Washington, DC: Congressional Quarterly, 1999), 93–99.

15. John A. Dearborn, *Power Shifts: Congress and Presidential Representation* (Chicago: University of Chicago Press, 2021).

16. Stephen Skowronek, *Building a New American State: The Expansion of National Administrative Capacities 1877–1920* (New York: Cambridge University Press, 1982); Peri Arnold, *Remaking the Presidency: Roosevelt, Taft and Wilson, 1901–1916* (Lawrence: University Press of Kansas, 2009).

17. Skowronek, *Building a New American State*.

18. Arnold, *Remaking the Presidency*.

19. For example, 31 Cong. Rec. 4734 (1898) and 42 Cong. Rec. 5165 (1908).

20. Though of course American nationalism was constructed at many different points in time. David Waldstreicher, for example, notes its nascent beginnings at the time of the revolution. See Waldstreicher, "Rites of Rebellion, Rites of Assent: Celebrations, Print Culture, and the Origins of American Nationalism," *Journal of American History* 82, no. 1 (June 1995): 37–61. Benedict Anderson tells us that national identity is an idea that is at least partly cultivated by states, and that it is facilitated by the rise of a mass media and railroads and other mass transportation technologies. Anderson, *Imagined Communities: Reflection on the Origin and Spread of Nationalism* (New York: Verso Press, 1993).

21. Cecilia Elizabeth O'Leary, *To Die For: The Paradox of American Patriotism* (Princeton, New Jersey: Princeton University Press, 1999); Michael Kammen, *Mystic Chords of Memory: The Transformation of Tradition in American Culture* (New York: Vintage Books 1993).

22. Peter Mickelson, "Nationalism in Minnesota during the Spanish-American War," *Minnesota History* 41, no. 1 (Spring 1968): 1–12.

23. Cecilia O'Leary and Tony Platt, "Pledging Allegiance: The Revival of Prescriptive Patriotism," *Social Justice* 28, no. 3 (85) (Fall 2001): 43.

24. Susan-Mary Grant, "Americans Forging a New Nation, 1860–1916," in *Nationalism in the New World*, ed. Doyle Don H. and Pamplona Marco Antonio (Athens: University of Georgia Press, 2006), 80–98; Kammen, *Mystic Chords of Memory*; John Pettegrew, "'The Soldier's Faith': Turn-of-the-Century Memory of the Civil War and the Emergence of Modern American Nationalism," *Journal of Contemporary History* 31, no. 1 (January 1996): 49–73.

25. John Norton Pomeroy, *An Introduction to the Constitutional Law of the United States Especially Designed for Students, General and Professional* (Boston: Houghton, Mifflin, 1883). For example, on page 455, he says, "The 'captures' here spoken of, are the things taken by the armed forces of the government, and not the very act itself of taking. The word is used in both senses. We speak of the capture of a town, district of territory, ship, fort, army; and thereby imply the fact of their seizure. The clause cannot admit of this construction; otherwise a very large part of the disposition and management of the land and naval forces would be in the hands of Congress; and the 'Commander-in-Chief' would be an empty title, with little or no power except to enforce the mandates of the legislature. The policy of the Constitution is very different. It was felt that active hostilities, under the control of a large deliberative body, would be feebly carried on, with uniform disastrous results. All history teaches this truth, and shows that the army and navy must be wielded by a single will, must be instruments in one hand. The Constitution has therefore clothed the legislature with power to originate a war; to furnish the requisite supplies of money and materials; to authorize the raising of men; and to dispose of the results. All this is a complete check upon the Executive; for Congress may, by refusing to grant supplies or *raise* forces, drive the President to conclude a peace, or inaugurate a different policy in the conduct of actual hostilities. But all direct management of warlike operations, all planning and organizing of campaigns, all establishing of blockades, all direction of marches, sieges, battles, and the like, are as much beyond the jurisdiction of the legislature, as they are beyond that of any assemblage of private citizens. The only possible authority for Congress to pass measures in respect to the actual conduct of hostilities, is found in the last paragraph of Section VIII. Article I., which gives them power 'to make all laws which shall be necessary and proper for carrying into execution. . . . all powers vested by this Constitution in the government of the United States, or in any department or officer thereof.' But these measures must be supplementary to, and in aid of, the separate and independent functions of the President as commander-in chief; they cannot interfere with, much less limit, his discretion in the exercise of those functions." Pomeroy was cited by Henry Cabot Lodge in 1909 (43 Cong. Rec. 310 [1909]) and by Sen. John C. Spooner in 1907, both arguing for broad discretionary commander in chief powers (41 Cong. Rec. 1131 [1907]). Recall that my research project here was to examine congressional speeches, not all legal and historical textbooks. An examination of the changing treatment of presidential war powers in these texts does seem like a promising project for future research.

26. Mahan was both close to presidents and influential members of Congress like Henry Cabot Lodge. His ideas were part of the "intellectual formulation" of the new empire in the late nineteenth century. Walter LaFeber, *The New American Empire: An Interpretation of*

American Expansion 1860–1898 (Ithaca, NY: Cornell University Press, 1998, 85–95). At least one member of Congress referred to his work in connection with ideas about the commander in chief clause (45 Cong. Rec. 4167 [1910]).

27. LaFeber, *New American Empire*; see also Christina Duffy Burnett and Burke Marshall, "Between the Foreign and the Domestic: The Doctrine of Territorial Incorporation, Invented and Reinvented," in *Foreign in a Domestic Sense: Puerto Rico, American Expansion, and the Constitution*, ed. Christina Duffy Burnett and Burke Marshall (Durham, NC: Duke University Press, 2001), 1–36; also Gary Gerstle, *American Crucible: Race and Nation in the Twentieth Century* (Princeton: Princeton University Press, 2001), 26. Also Thomas Schoonover, *Uncle Sam's War of 1898 and the Origins of Globalization* (Lexington: University Press of Kentucky, 2003).

28. LaFeber, *New American Empire*, 1998 repr., 63–71.

29. LaFeber, *New American Empire*, 1998 repr., 95–100. Also Mark S. Weiner, "Teutonic Constitutionalism: The Role of Ethno-Juridical Discourse in the Spanish American War," in Burnett and Marshall, *Foreign in a Domestic Sense*, 48–81.

30. Victoria Farrar-Myers, *Scripted for Change: The Institutionalization of the American Presidency* (College Station: Texas A&M University Press, 2007); Stephen Kinzer, *Overthrow: America's Century of Regime Change from Hawaii to Iraq* (New York: Times Books 2006).

31. Scholars of American political development might call this a moment of "intercurrence" of "multiple orders." Karen Orren and Stephen Skowronek, "The Study of American Political Development," in *Political Science: The State of the Discipline*, ed. Ira Katznelson and Helen V. Milner (New York: W. W. Norton, 2002), 722–754.

32. 31 Cong. Rec. 6574 (1898)

33. "This fund being inadequate to the requirements of equipment and for the conduct of the war, the patriotism of the Congress provided the means in the war-revenue act of June 13 by authorizing a 3 per cent popular loan not to exceed $400,000,000 and by levying additional imposts and taxes." William McKinley, "Second Annual Message," the American Presidency Project, accessed September 8, 2023, https://www.presidency.ucsb.edu/node/205329.

34. January 29, 1862, 37th Cong., 2nd Sess., Cong. Globe 517.

35. In the interests of space and narrative clarity, I will not further describe those discussions about spending requests and state secrets here.

36. O'Leary, *To Die For*, 8.

37. James K. Polk, "Second Annual Message," December 8, 1846, available at the American Presidency Project, http://www.presidency.ucsb.edu/ws/?pid=29487.

38. May 22, 1846, 29th Cong., 1st Sess., 15 Cong. Globe 837.

39. 29th Cong., 2nd Sess., Cong. Globe 410 (1847), appendix.

40. Representative Thompson, July 25, 1848, 30th Cong., 1st Sess., Cong. Globe 977.

41. 29th Cong., 2nd Sess., Cong. Globe 213 (1847), appendix.

42. The only speaker to demand broad congressional obedience to the commander in chief was Senator Cowan, who said, "In the conduct of the war, by the terms of our submission the President is the Commander-in-Chief, and we are bound in the same way to obey him in all the measures he proposes to achieve the purpose of the war. That we would

not have adopted those measures makes no difference" (March 3, 1863, 37th Cong. 3rd Sess., Cong. Globe 1468).

43. January 9, 1863, 37th Cong., 3rd Sess., Cong. Globe 236.

44. February 6, 1865, 38th Cong., 2nd Sess., Cong. Globe 577.

45. February 23, 1866, 39th Cong., 1st Sess., Cong. Globe 987.

46. The pattern is the same whether or not you use raw counts or an annual average.

47. For example, 9 Annals of Cong. 3041–3042 (1798–1799); 37th Cong., 2nd Sess., Cong. Globe 284 (1862); 30th Cong., 1st Sess., Cong. Globe 342 (1848).

48. Representative Eliot (R), 37th Cong., 2nd Sess., Cong. Globe 80 (1862).

49. Representative Dalzell, 32 Cong. Rec. 1326 (1899).

50. Representative McLeary (R), 42 Cong. Rec. 5165 (1908).

51. 40 Cong. Globe 578 (1868); 10 Cong. Rec. 2296 (1880); 6 Cong. Rec. 421 (1877); 32nd Cong., 1st Sess., Cong. Globe 840 (1852); 33 Annals of Cong. 1091–1092 (1818–1819), Proceedings and Debates of the House of Representatives of the United States, at the Second Session of the Fifteenth Congress, Begun at the City of Washington, Monday, November 16, 1818; 37th Cong., 2nd Sess., Cong. Globe 192 (1862); 38th Cong., 1st Sess., Cong. Globe 1067 (1864); 39th Cong., 2nd Sess., Cong. Globe 623 (1867); 29th Cong., 2nd Sess., Cong. Globe 277 (1847); 40 Cong. Globe 547 (1868); 27 Cong., Rec. 1137 (1895).

52. "soldiers' duty": 4 Part II Cong. Deb. 1515–1516 (1828); 32nd Cong., 1st Sess., Cong. Globe 817 (1852); 37th Cong., 1st Sess., Cong. Globe 241 (1861); 38th Cong., 2nd Sess., Cong. Globe 136 (1865). "*Congress's duty*": 33 Annals of Cong. 665–666 (1818–1819), Proceedings and Debates; 37th Cong., 2nd Sess., Cong. Globe 80 (1862); 32nd Cong., 1st Sess., Cong. Globe 848 (1852), etc.

53. Senator Piles (R), 42 Cong. Rec. 5164 (1908).

54. 51 Cong. Rec. 6972 (1914).

55. "Why, sir, the destruction of the Spanish fleet was of itself enough to shed glory upon the Commander in Chief of the armies of these United States." Mr. Linney, January 31, 1900, 33 Cong. Rec. 1363 (1900).

56. Americans, of course, favored the war for many reasons, including market expansion, white racial supremacy, naval politics, and humanitarianism and the American "mission" in the world. See Paul T. McCartney, *Power and Progress: American National Identity, the War of 1898, and the Rise of American Imperialism* (Baton Rouge: Louisiana State University Press, 2006). That they felt good about it did not in fact make the war or their aims for it just. See Matthew Frye Jacobson, *Barbarian Virtues: The United States Encounters Foreign Peoples at Home and Abroad, 1876–1917* (New York: Hill and Wang, 2000).

57. When the 1896 Republican party platform was adopted, it included a strong statement supporting veterans, saying that "the veterans of the Union Armies deserve and should receive fair treatment and generous recognition. Whenever practicable they should be given the preference in, the matter of employment. And they are entitled to the enactment of such laws as are best calculated to secure the fulfillment of the pledges made to them in the dark days of the country's peril." This was much more robust than the 1892 platform, and there had been no pro-veteran rhetoric in the platform in 1888. Democrats

had no pro-veteran language in any of the three platforms for the same years. See Republican Party Platform of 1896, available at the American Presidency Project, https://www .presidency.ucsb.edu/node/273316.

58. June 23, 1902, 57th Cong., 1st Sess., 35 Cong. Rec. 7223.

59. 55th Cong., 2nd Sess., 31 Cong. Rec. 286 (1898), appendix.

60. March 25, 1898, 55th Cong., 2nd Sess., 31 Cong. Rec. 3222.

61. January 31, 1900, 56th Cong., 1st Sess., 33 Cong. Rec. 1363.

62. January 31, 1900, 56th Cong., 1st Sess., 33 Cong. Rec. 1363.

63. April 15, 1898, 55th Cong., 2nd Sess., 31 Cong. Rec. 3903, 3905.

64. April 15, 1898, 55th Cong., 2nd Sess., 31 Cong. Rec. 3903, 3905.

65. April 16, 1898, 55th Cong., 2nd Sess., 31 Cong. Rec. 3990.

66. January 19, 1900, 56th Cong., 1st Sess., 33 Cong. Rec. 1006.

67. April 27, 1898, 55th Cong., 2nd Sess., 31 Cong. Rec. 4312.

68. 56th Cong., 2nd Sess., 34 Cong. Rec. 11 (1901), appendix.

69. Christopher J. Deering, "Congress, the President, and Military Policy," *Annals of the American Academy of Political and Social Science* 499 (September 1988), 136–147.

70. Rep. Michael Griffin (R), January 30, 1899, 55th Cong., 3rd Sess., 32 Cong. Rec. 1255.

71. Rep. John Dalzell (R), January 31, 1899, 55th Cong., 3rd Sess., 32 Cong. Rec. 1326.

72. Rep. John Lacey (R), February 25, 1899, 55th Cong., 3rd Sess., 32 Cong. Rec. 2406.

73. Sen. Francis Warren (R), February 21, 1899, 55th Cong., 3rd Sess., 32 Cong. Rec. 2142.

74. January 25, 1899, 55th Cong., 3rd Sess., 32 Cong. Rec. 1047.

75. Sen. Francis Cockrell (D), February 16, 1899, 55th Cong., 3rd Sess., 32 Cong. Rec. 1921.

76. Mr. Gorman, February 25, 1899, 55th Cong., 3rd Sess., 32 Cong. Rec. 2377.

77. As noted by Mariah Zeisberg, Morgan had an interest in a Nicaraguan canal route and so had multiple reasons to oppose the treaty. See Zeisberg, *War Powers: The Politics of Constitutional Authority* (Princeton: Princeton University Press, 2013), 117.

78. January 4, 1904, 60th Cong., 1st Sess., 38 Cong. Rec. 435.

79. "Except as herein provided or specifically otherwise provided by statute the money herein appropriated for the pay and supplies of the Army shall be used only for the pay and supplies of the Army on duty in the United States and in the territory subject to the laws and jurisdiction of the United States; and no part of the money herein appropriated shall be used for the pay or supplies of any part of the Army of the United States employed, stationed, or on duty in any country or territory beyond the jurisdiction of the laws of the United States or in going to or returning from points within the same: Provided, that this prohibition shall not apply to cases of emergency within the discretion of the President arising at a time when the Congress of the United States is not in session. In every case when, while Congress is not in session, as aforesaid, any part of the Army shall be ordered for duty into any country or territory beyond the jurisdiction of the laws of the United States, it shall be the duty of the Secretary of War to report to the Congress at the beginning of the next ensuing session, the authority for such order, the number and designation of the troops ordered on duty in said foreign country, and the operation of said troops under said order; and no part of the money herein appropriated shall be used for the pay

and supplies of said part of the Army remaining in said foreign country beyond the term of 10 days after the beginning of the next ensuing Congress unless expressly authorized thereto by an act of Congress." 62nd Cong., 2nd Sess., 48 Cong. Rec. 10929.

80. 62nd Cong., 2nd Sess., 48 Cong. Rec. 10929 (1912).

81. 62nd Cong., 2nd Sess., 48 Cong. Rec. 10929 (1912).

82. 62nd Cong., 2nd Sess., 48 Cong. Rec. 10862, 10955 (1912).

83. As quoted in the 63rd Cong., 2nd Sess., 51 Cong. Rec. 6949.

84. 63rd Cong., 2nd Sess., 51 Cong. Rec. 6949.

85. 63rd Cong., 2nd Sess., 51 Cong. Rec. 6988.

86. January 16, 1907, 59th Cong., 2nd Sess., 41 Cong. Rec. 1208.

87. 63rd Cong., 2nd Sess., 51 Cong. Rec. 6944.

88. 63rd Cong., 2nd Sess., 51 Cong. Rec. 6999.

89. 63rd Cong., 2nd Sess., 51 Cong. Rec. 6965.

90. 63rd Cong., 2nd Sess., 51 Cong. Rec. 6951.

91. 63rd Cong., 2nd Sess., 51 Cong. Rec. 6972.

92. 63rd Cong., 2nd Sess., 51 Cong. Rec. 7104.

93. 63rd Cong., 2nd Sess., 51 Cong. Rec. 6945.

94. 63rd Cong., 2nd Sess., 51 Cong. Rec. 6951.

95. Louis Fisher, *Presidential War Power* (Lawrence: University Press of Kansas, 1995), 51.

96. John S. D. Eisenhower, *Intervention: The United States and the Mexican Revolution 1913–1917* (New York: W. W. Norton, 1993), 231–232.

97. He publicly declared the goal was to capture Villa, while simultaneously issuing slightly different orders to the War Department, limiting the forces to "the pursuit and dispersion of the band or bands that attacked Columbus, N. M." See James A. Sandos, "Pancho Villa and American Security: Woodrow Wilson's Mexican Diplomacy Reconsidered," *Journal of Latin American Studies* 13, no. 2 (November 1981): 293–311.

98. Concurrent Resolution 17, passed March 17, 2016, 53 Cong. Rec. 4395 (1916).

99. 64th Cong., 1st Sess., 53 Cong. Rec. 6348.

100. 64th Cong., 1st Sess., 53 Cong. Rec. 9875.

101. 64th Cong., 1st Sess., 53 Cong. Rec. 12611.

102. 64th Cong., 1st Sess., 53 Cong. Rec. 10818.

103. 64th Cong., 1st Sess., 53 Cong. Rec. 9887.

104. 64th Cong., 1st Sess., 53 Cong. Rec. 14065.

105. 64th Cong., 1st Sess., 53 Cong. Rec. 7452.

CHAPTER 5: SCRIPTS AND PRECEDENTS

1. The "laws of nations" metaphor might be thought of as similar to a ship's captain on the high seas, who was "often regarded as a sailor-diplomat" and was assumed to know and operate under both general orders and international law. Henry Bartholomew Cox, *War, Foreign Affairs, and Constitutional Power: 1829–1901* (Cambridge, MA: Ballinger, 1984), 51n.

2. For a thorough understanding of those "laws," see John Fabian Witt, *Lincoln's Code: The Laws of War in American History* (New York: Free Press, 2012).

3. For example, members referred to Vattel in 1818, 1862, and 1899. May 23, 1862, 37th Cong., 2nd Sess., Cong. Globe 2292 (1862); 33 Annals of Cong. 621–622 (1818–1819), Proceedings and Debates of the House of Representatives of the United States, at the Second Session of the Fifteenth Congress, Begun at the City of Washington, Monday, November 16, 1818; 32 Cong. Rec. 994 (1899). No references to Grotius are in the same paragraph as the references to the commander in chief, but in the longer speeches from which those excerpts are drawn, he is frequently mentioned. For example, 8 Annals of Cong. 2307–2308 (1798–1799); April 7, 1866, 39th Cong., 1st Sess., Cong. Globe 1830; 40 Cong. Globe 620–645 (1868); 33 Cong. Rec 34 (1900), appendix. Two citations of Kent's text are in close proximity to references to the commander in chief; dozens more appear in the extended speeches from which those excerpts are drawn. For example, see March 2, 1863, 37th Cong., 3rd Sess., Cong. Globe 1383 (1863); and June 14, 1864, 38th Cong., 1st Sess., Cong. Globe 2899.

4. For a discussion of the status of the laws of nations in constitutional foreign affairs power at the time of the Founding, see Michael D. Ramsey, *The Constitution's Text in Foreign Affairs* (Cambridge, MA: Harvard University Press, 2007). For an argument that incorporating international law principles into constitutional interpretation can reduce presidential unilateralism, see Michael J. Glennon, *Constitutional Diplomacy* (Princeton: Princeton University Press, 1990). Scholars today also debate whether customary international law should be given the status of federal law in US courts and whether it can override state laws. For background, see Louis Henkin, "International Law as Law in the United States," *Michigan Law Review* 82, nos. 5–6 (April–May 1984): 1555–1569. For an overview of modern debates, see Ernest A. Young, "Sorting Out the Debate over Customary International Law," *Virginia Journal of International Law* 42, no. 2 (Winter 2002): 365–512. On the argument that customary international law should not have privileged status, see Curtis A. Bradley and Jack L. Goldsmith, "Customary International Law as Federal Common Law: A Critique of the Modern Position," *Harvard Law Review* 110, no. 4 (February 1997): 815–876. On the argument that it should have such status, see Harold Hongju Koh, "Is International Law Really State Law," *Harvard Law Review* 111, no. 7 (May 1998): 1824–1862. These debates reflect core disagreements among nineteenth-century members of Congress as well.

5. Witt, *Lincoln's Code*.

6. Other scholars who have gone through the congressional record have noted the appearance of arguments about the laws of nations and its applicability to particular debates about war powers. See, for example, David J. Barron and Martin S. Lederman, "The Commander in Chief at the Lowest Ebb: A Constitutional History," *Harvard Law Review* 121, no. 4 (2008): 941–1112 and Cox, *War, Foreign Affairs, and Constitutional Power.*

7. In his long career, Trumbull was alternately a Democrat and a Republican.

8. January 29, 1862, 37th Cong., 2nd Sess., Cong. Globe 516.

9. January 29, 1862, 37th Cong., 2nd Sess., Cong. Globe 516.

10. Of course, he neglected to mention that the Constitution literally empowers not the president but the Congress to "define offenses against the law of nations" (January 29, 1862, 37th Cong., 2nd Sess., Cong. Globe 516).

11. January 29, 1862, 37th Cong., 2nd Sess., Cong. Globe 516.

12. January 29, 1862, 37th Cong., 2nd Sess., Cong. Globe 517.

13. January 29, 1862, 37th Cong., 2nd Sess., Cong. Globe 517.

14. January 29, 1862, 37th Cong., 2nd Sess., Cong. Globe 517.

15. 37th Cong., 2nd Sess., Cong. Globe 175 (1862), appendix; see also December 23, 1862, 37th Cong., 3rd Sess., Cong. Globe 147–151.

16. Senate Bill 169 passed the Senate 23–12, with all parties divided. The yays were 18 Republicans, 3 Democrats, 2 Unionists, and the nays were 5 Republicans, 4 Democrats, 2 Unionists, and 1 Opposition. The was signed into law on January 31, 1862. January 29, 1862, 37th Cong., 2nd Sess., Cong. Globe 520.

17. Jack Bauer, *The Mexican War 1846–1848* (Lincoln: University of Nebraska Press, 1984).

18. General Stephen Kearny, Las Vegas, New Mexico territory, August 15, 1846, available at http://newmexicohistory.org/people/general-kearnys-first-address.

19. "Resolved, That the President communicate to this House any and all orders or instructions to General Taylor, General Wool, General Kearny, Captain Sloat, Captain Stockton, or any other officer of the Government, in relation to the establishment or organization of civil government in any portion of the territory of Mexico which has or might be taken possession of by the army or navy of the United States; also, what forms of government such officers, or either of them, may have established and organized, and whether the President has approved and recognised [*sic*] said governments" (December 10, 1846, 29th Cong., 2nd Sess., 16 Cong. Globe 13).

20. The president could "discharge no function in relation to the war but such as resided in him as commander-in-chief of the army and navy of the country. As President he could legitimately take no part in a war of conquest—none whatever—none, none." Rep. Garrett Davis, December 10, 1846, 29th Cong., 2nd Sess., Cong. Globe 13.

21. December 26, 1846, 29th Cong., 2nd Sess., Cong. Globe 66.

22. December 30, 1846, 29th Cong., 2nd Sess., Cong. Globe 85.

23. 29th Cong., 2nd Sess., Cong. Globe 337 (1847), appendix.

24. 29th Cong., 2nd Sess., Cong. Globe 237 (1847), appendix.

25. December 10, 1846, 29th Cong., 2nd Sess., Cong. Globe 55.

26. 29th Cong., 2nd Sess., Cong. Globe 99 (1847), appendix. He also cites as governing authority the Supreme Court case *Talbot v. Seeman*.

27. "Congress might legislate upon the subject, but the obligation of the law of nations was binding till actually superseded by special legislation. It was the duty of the President to execute those laws; he must do it; he was sworn to do it; and he would be liable to impeachment if he did not." Rep. Thomas Bayly, 29th Cong., 2nd Sess., Cong. Globe 99 (1847), appendix.

28. 29th Cong., 2nd Sess., Cong. Globe 55 (1847), appendix.

29. "Letter from James K. Polk to the United States House of Representatives," December 25, 1846, in *A Compilation of the Messages and Papers of the Presidents*, vol. 6, ed. James Daniel Richardson, United States, Congress, Joint Committee on Printing.

30. James K. Polk, "Special Message," December 22, 1846, available at the American Presidency Project, http://www.presidency.ucsb.edu/ws/?pid=67945.

31. March 20, 1848, 30th Cong., 1st Sess., Cong. Globe 487.

32. January 19, 1848, 30th Cong., 1st Sess., Cong. Globe 188.

33. Calhoun said, "I would ask where is the limit to his power in Mexico? Has he also the power of making appropriations of money collected in Mexico, without the sanction of Congress? This he has already done. Has he the power to apply the money to whatever purpose he may think proper, and among others to raise a military force in Mexico without the sanction of Congress? That, also, he has already done. But if there be no limitation, then his powers are absolute and despotic in Mexico, and he stands in the two-fold character of the constitutional President of the United States and the absolute and despotic ruler of Mexico. To what must this conclusion lead? What may he not do? He may lay taxes at his pleasure either as to kind or-amount; he may establish the rules and regulations for their collection; he may dispose of them, without passing the proceeds into the treasury, to any object or for any purpose he may think proper, and is not liable or responsible to Congress or any other authority, in any respect whatever, in doing all this. He may, of course, raise armies, and pay them out of the proceeds of the taxes; he may wage war against the neighboring countries to the south of him at his pleasure . . . Nay, further, he may turn his army against his own country, and make it the instrument of its subjugation. Against all this there is no remedy, and can be none, if he has the power which must necessarily result from the principles which would invest him with the power of laying taxes" (March 18, 1848, 30th Cong., 1st Sess., Cong. Globe 479).

34. January 5, 1849, 30th Cong., 2nd Sess., Cong. Globe 150.

35. The speeches discussed in this section came up while Congress was considering a bill to raise ten new army regiments. The bill did not pass.

36. 57 U.S. (16 How.) 164.

37. There were also a handful of references to *Fleming v Page*. See 33 Cong. Rec. 1359 (1900); 33 Cong. Rec. 47 (1900), appendix; and 43 Cong. Rec. 2540 (1909).

38. Clifton Rumery Hall, *Andrew Johnson: Military Governor of Tennessee* (Princeton: Princeton University Press, 1916).

39. May 3, 1864, 38th Cong., 1st Sess., Cong. Globe 2013.

40. January 18, 1867, 39th Cong., 2nd Sess., Cong. Globe 561.

41. 40th Cong., Special Sess., Cong. Globe 63–65 (1867), appendix.

42. January 18, 1866, 39th Cong., 1st Sess., Cong. Globe 289.

43. 39th Cong., 2nd Sess., Cong. Globe 84 (1867), appendix.

44. April 21, 1866, 39th Cong., 1st Sess., Cong. Globe 2091.

45. February 15, 1866, 39th Cong., 1st Sess., Cong. Globe 871.

46. February 18, 1867, 39th Cong., 2nd Sess., Cong. Globe 1319.

47. January 17, 1866, 39th Cong., 1st Sess., Cong. Globe 271–275.

48. February 24, 1866, 39th Cong., 1st Sess., Cong. Globe 1019.

49. For example, Sen. Lyman Trumbull argued that "there is not in the Constitution a line or a word giving him any power whatever as President to inaugurate governments anywhere. Whatever power he has in the rebel States greater than that possessed by him in other States was his military power as Commander in-Chief of the Army, and when he exercises that power he is subject to the rules and regulations established by Congress." January 23, 1868, 40 Cong. Globe 705 (1868).

50. February 27, 1865, 38th Cong., 2nd Sess., Cong. Globe 1093–1094.

51. February 17, 1866, 39th Cong., 1st Sess., Cong. Globe 900–901.

52. December 18, 1865, 39th Cong., 1st Sess., Cong. Globe 73.

53. Republican Fernando Beaman of Michigan said that the president is "the Commander-in-Chief of the Army and Navy. He can declare martial law and repress rebellion, but he has no power to institute civil government. He may impose conditions, grant pardons, and proclaim an amnesty, but he cannot admit new States" (March 24, 1864, 38th Cong., 1st Sess., Cong. Globe 1245). Sen. Benjamin Wade (R-OH) said that representatives of military governments could not be considered civil officers and that Congress should not recognize senators appointed under newly organized government, such as the "two men from Louisiana, representing nobody and nothing except the will of the Commander-in-Chief of the Army of the United States." Lyman Trumbull argued that the commander in chief could not draw upon any powers of the executive branch when exercising military functions (February 27, 1866, 39th Cong., 1st Sess., Cong. Globe 1048). Sen. Jacob Howard (R-MI) drew the line at establishing political rights for the states: "He, the President of the United States, assumes, of his own motion, without authority of Congress, without calling together Congress, or in any way consulting or proposing to consult them, to issue to each of these provisional governors this imperial commission, [and] I will say, that it is not competent for a military commander in the field, whether he be 'Commander-in-Chief or acting in any other capacity under the Constitution of the United States, to impart political or legislative rights to the conquered community" (May 11, 1866, 39th Cong., 1st Sess., Cong. Globe 2551).

54. For a thorough treatment, see Eric Foner, *Reconstruction: America's Unfinished Revolution, 1869–77* (New York: Harper and Row, 1988).

55. Before treaty ratification and violence broke out, the Senate considered a resolution disclaiming US intentions to exercise sovereignty, but it was defeated when the vice president cast a tie-breaking vote. Cox, *War, Foreign Affairs, and Constitutional Power*, 321.

56. As well as those who objected to acquiring territory populated by nonwhites.

57. February 24, 1899, 55th Cong., 3rd Sess., 32 Cong. Rec. 2309.

58. January 24, 1899, 55th Cong., 3rd Sess., 32 Cong. Rec. 994.

59. January 20, 1899, 55th Cong., 3rd Sess., 32 Cong. Rec. 832.

60. January 26, 1899, 55th Cong., 3rd Sess., 32 Cong. Rec. 1093.

61. January 26, 1899, 55th Cong., 3rd Sess., 32 Cong. Rec. 1115.

62. January 26, 1899, 55th Cong., 3rd Sess., 32 Cong. Rec. 1107.

63. Senate, February 8, 1901, 56th Cong., 2nd sess., Cong. Rec. 2117.

64. Indeed, as noted by Michael Glennon, reliance on custom and precedent rarely, if ever, relies on the commensurability of such comparisons. Michael J. Glennon, "The Executive's Misplaced Reliance on War Powers 'Custom,'" *American Journal of International Law* 109, no. 3 (2015): 551–556.

65. William Howell and Jon C. Pevehouse, *While Dangers Gather: Congressional Checks on Presidential War Powers* (Princeton: Princeton University Press, 2007).

66. On the general subject of the partisan controls available to congressional majorities, one could begin with Gary W. Cox and Mathew D. McCubbins, *Setting the Agenda: Responsible Party Government in the U.S. House of Representatives* (Cambridge, UK: Cambridge

University Press, 2004). The precise relationships between ideology, party, and partisan controls in Congress are analyzed in their own vast scholarly literature. But in dealing with the rare, narrow questions of constitutional authority, party itself (and the relationship between partisan congressional majorities and the partisan in the White House) is a simple enough frame for starting to understand outcomes and evolution. Ideology, in particular, is not especially relevant to constitutional questions, though preferences that do not align with party are occasionally important. Later in this chapter, I separate out racial ideology and partisan preferences specifically.

67. This perspective resonates with the argument made by Bradley and Morrison. See Curtis A. Bradley and Trevor W. Morrison, "Historical Gloss and the Separation of Powers," *Harvard Law Review* 126, no. 2 (2012): 411–485.

68. Henry P. Monaghan, "Presidential War-Making," *Boston University Law Review* 50, no. 5 (1970): 19–33.

69. In fact, some presidential actions may have created antiprecedents, or historical markers of actions presidents cannot take. See Deborah Pearlstein, "The Executive Branch Anticanon," *Fordham Law Review* 89 (2020): 597–649.

70. Bradley and Morrison, "Historical Gloss." Others have tried to theorize about which historical episodes might become constitutionally binding or relevant precedents. Spiro, for example, argues that actions matter more than words, that conduct must be known to both branches, and that the other branch must acquiesce in the action to create "incremental elements of custom." Peter J. Spiro, "War Powers and the Sirens of Formalism," *New York University Law Review* 68 (1993): 1338.

71. Mariah Zeisberg, *War Powers: The Politics of Constitutional Authority* (Princeton: Princeton University Press, 2013), 252.

CHAPTER 6: SCRIPTS, CONGRESSIONAL PREFERENCES, AND BATTLEFIELD EMANCIPATION

1. Burrus M. Carnahan, *Act of Justice: Lincoln's Emancipation Proclamation and the Law of War* (Lexington: University Press of Kentucky, 2007); Noah Feldman, *The Broken Constitution: Lincoln, Slavery, and the Refounding of America* (New York: Picador Farrar, Straus and Giroux, 2021); Eric Foner, *Reconstruction: America's Unfinished Revolution, 1869–77* (New York: Harper and Row, 1988); John Hope Franklin, *The Emancipation Proclamation* (New York: Doubleday, 1963); Allen C. Guelzo, *Lincoln's Emancipation Proclamation: The End of Slavery in America* (New York: Simon and Schuster, 2004); Mark E. Neely, *Lincoln and the Triumph of the Nation: Constitutional Conflict in the American Civil War* (Chapel Hill: University of North Carolina Press, 2011); James Oakes, *Freedom National: The Destruction of Slavery in the United States 1861–1865* (New York: W. W. Norton, 2012); George Clarke Sellery, "Lincoln's Suspension of Habeas Corpus as Viewed by Congress," *Bulletin of the University of Wisconsin* 1, no. 2 (1907): 213–286; Silvana R. Siddali, *From Property to Person: Slavery and the Confiscation Acts 1861–1862* (Baton Rouge: Louisiana State University Press, 2005); Elbert B. Smith, *The Death of Slavery in the United States 1837–1865* (Chicago:

University of Chicago Press, 1967); John Syrett, *The Civil War Confiscation Acts: Failing to Reconstruct the South* (New York: Fordham University Press, 2005).

2. Martha S. Jones et al., "Historians Forum: The Emancipation Proclamation," *Civil War History* 59, no. 1 (March 2013): 7–31.

3. Carnahan, *Act of Justice.*

4. See, for example, Martin Bisgaard and Rune Slothuus, "Partisan Elites as Culprits? How Party Cues Shape Partisan Perceptual Gaps," *American Journal of Political Science* 62, no. 2 (April 2018): 456–469.

5. Daryl J. Levinson and Richard H. Pildes, "Separation of Parties, Not Powers," *Harvard Law Review* 119, no. 8 (June 2006): 2311–2386. Terry Moe and William Howell also note this dynamic in their theoretical argument about the centralization of authority in the executive in "Unilateral Action and Presidential Power: A Theory," *Presidential Studies Quarterly* 29, no. 4 (December 1999): 850–873.

6. Nathan Kalmoe, *With Ballots and Bullets: Partisanship and Violence in the American Civil War* (New York: Cambridge University Press, 2020).

7. Neustadt argues that one of the president's central informal resources is his ability to convince other elites, including members of Congress, and that his reputation among elites facilitates use of this resource. See his *Presidential Power and the Modern Presidents: The Politics of Leadership from Roosevelt to Reagan* (New York: Free Press, 1990).

8. Partisan cleavages are likely to be rooted in strongly held positions, which modern research suggests may be strongly related to constituency concerns. Mark Souva and David Rohde, "Elite Opinion Differences and Partisanship in Congressional Foreign Policy, 1975–1996," *Political Research Quarterly* 60, no. 1 (March 2007): 113–123.

9. For example, Sundquist argues that Congress enabled Truman's unilateralism during the Korean War to avoid appearing to support communism. James L. Sundquist, *The Decline and Resurgence of Congress* (Washington, DC: Brookings Institution, 1981). John Hart Ely argues that Congress acquiesced to presidential leadership during the Vietnam War in part to avoid responsibility for what happened there. *War and Responsibility: Constitutional Lessons of Vietnam* (Princeton: Princeton University Press, 1993). Similarly, Victoria Farrar-Myers notes the role that expansionist foreign policy preferences played in shifting war powers authority during the period from 1880 to 1920. See her *Scripted for Change: The Institutionalization of the American Presidency* (College Station: Texas A&M University Press, 2007).

10. Moreover, of course, party leaders' control over floor procedure has varied over time with the development of congressional institutions and the internal distribution of lawmaking power in Congress. See Eric Schickler, *Disjointed Pluralism: Institutional Innovation and the Development of the U.S. Congress* (Princeton: Princeton University Press, 2001).

11. For discussion, see Oakes, *Freedom National* (chap. 1).

12. Neely, *Lincoln and the Triumph of the Nation*, 131. Although many reference Lincoln's visit to McClellan at Harrison's Landing or the victory at Antietam as instigating the initial September proclamation. See for example John Fabian Witt, *Lincoln's Code* (New York: Free Press 2012), 210; or James M. McPherson, "How President Lincoln Decided to Issue the Emancipation Proclamation," *Journal of Blacks in Higher Education* 37 (Autumn 2002): 108–109.

13. For discussion, see Carnahan, *Act of Justice*, 135.

14. Abraham Lincoln, "Letter to Albert G. Hodges," April 4, 1864, available at the American Presidency Project, http://www.presidency.ucsb.edu/ws/?pid=104107.

15. "within US territory": Rep. Thomas Fitzsimons (Pro-Administration), 3 *Annals of Cong.* 1105–1106 (1791–1793), appendix to the History of the Second Congress; Mr. Hickman, February 5, 1862, 37th Cong., 2nd Sess., 32 Cong. Globe 611. "in both American and enemy . . .": Rep. Owen Lovejoy (R), February 5, 1862, 37th Cong., 2nd Sess., 32 Cong. Globe 32 613; Sen. James Grimes (R), June 21, 1862, 37th Cong., 2nd Sess., 32 Cong. Globe 2831; Representative Pomeroy (R), February 25, 1863, 37th Cong., 3rd Sess., 32 Cong. Globe 1242; Rep. Henry Dawes (R), February 2, 1863, 37th Cong., 3rd Sess., 33 Cong. Globe 653; Mr. Dawes, February 2, 1863, 37th Cong., 3rd Sess., 32 Cong. Globe 653; Rep. Michael Griffin (R), January 30, 1899, 32 Cong. Rec. 1255; Sen. William Borah (R), February 17, 1909, 43 Cong. Rec. 2540.

16. "direct campaigns:" Rep. William Davis (R), January 28, 1863, 37th Cong., 3rd Sess., Cong. Globe 531–534; Rep. James Johnson (D), January 27, 1868, 40th Cong., 2nd Sess., 39 Cong. Globe 769. "recommend": Rep. John Lovett (Federalist), 26 Annals of Cong., 1180–1181; 1183–1184 (1813–1814), Proceedings and Debates of the House of Representatives of the United States, at the Second Sess. of the Thirteenth Congress, begun at the City of Washington, Monday, December 6, 1813.

17. 29th Cong., 2nd Sess., Cong. Globe 308 (1847), appendix.

18. "undertake expeditions": Sen. Jacob Howard (R), June 28, 1862, 37th Cong., 2nd Sess., Cong. Globe 2966. "active and speedy measures": Rep. Andrew Johnson (D), 30th Cong., 1st Sess., Cong. Globe 379 (1848), appendix.

19. "draw the sword": Sen. James Doolittle (R), February 24, 1868, 40 Cong. Globe 1374. "open fire": Sen. Jacob Gallinger (R), January 10, 1899, 32 Cong. Rec. 532. "strike a blow": Rep. Robert Hitt (R), June 11, 1898, 31 Cong. Rec. 5772; Sen. George Wellington (R), February 18, 1902, 35 Cong. Rec. 1851; Sen. Charles Fairbanks (R), February 24, 1902, 35 Cong. Rec. 2122. "to attack the enemy . . . :" Rep. David Henderson (R), January 27, 1899, 32 Cong. Rec. 1163 (1899).

20. Rep. Henry Smith (R), March 29, 1902, 35 Cong. Rec. 3416.

21. Carnahan notes that applying the law of war to the South, rather than treating the Civil War as a domestic insurrection, was an iterative process that took place over time (*Act of Justice*).

22. Oakes, *Freedom National*.

23. Syrett, *Civil War Confiscation Acts*.

24. Franklin, *Emancipation Proclamation*, 16.

25. Franklin, *Emancipation Proclamation*, 51.

26. Feldman, *Broken Constitution*, 265.

27. Siddali, *From Property to Person*, 148.

28. U.S., *Statutes at Large, Treaties, and Proclamations of the United States of America*, vol. 12 (Boston, 1863), 589–592.

29. Feldman highlights those arguments that the Second Confiscation Act was unconstitutional to emphasize the revolutionary nature of emancipation in its rejection of the original federal compact (*Broken Constitution*, 275).

30. These debates have been analyzed many times over. See, for example, Oakes, *Freedom National*, and David J. Barron and Martin S. Lederman, "The Commander in Chief at the Lowest Ebb: A Constitutional History," *Harvard Law Review* 121, no. 4 (February 2008): 1009–1016. But even thorough examinations do not locate members' arguments in their rhetorical history.

31. John Quincy Adams spoke about such a wartime authority to emancipate slaves while discussing potential war with England on the floor of the House in 1842. His remarks were republished and circulated by the abolitionist William Lloyd Garrison in 1861 under the title *The Abolition of Slavery the Right of the Government from the War Power* (Boston: R. F. Walcutt, 1861). Carnahan describes Adams's development of this argument in *Act of Justice*, 14–20.

32. Witt, *Lincoln's Code*.

33. For further discussion of the development of the idea of battlefield emancipation in American law, see Carnahan, *Act of Justice*.

34. Witt, *Lincoln's Code*, 204–205.

35. William Whiting, *The War Powers of the President and the Legislative Powers of Congress in Relation to Rebellion, Treason, and Slavery* (Boston: John L. Shorey, 1862).

36. The battlefield emancipation position would not immediately destroy the federal consensus that slavery was a legitimate state legal institution (Oakes, *Freedom National*).

37. See, for example, further discussion of congressional debates in Oakes, *Freedom National*, and Carnahan, *Act of Justice*.

38. Powell was an enslaver, according to the *Washington Post*'s congressional slaveholding database (https://www.washingtonpost.com/history/interactive/2022/congress-slave owners-names-list/). Powell opposed the war and was subject to votes for his removal from the Senate. See *Biographical Sketch of the Hon. Lazarus W. Powell, (of Henderson, Ky.): Governor of the State of Kentucky from 1851–1855 and a Senator in Congress from 1859–1865 / Published by Direction of the General Assembly of Kentucky* (Frankfort, KY: Kentucky Yeoman Office, 1868).

39. 37th Cong., 2nd Sess., Cong. Globe 107 (1862), appendix.

40. Also an enslaver. *Washington Post*, database of slaveholders in Congress. See also 37th Cong., 2nd Sess., Cong. Globe 261–262 (1862), appendix.

41. *Washington Post*, database of slaveholders in Congress.

42. April 23, 1862, 37th Cong., 2nd Sess., Cong. Globe 1760.

43. Bogue identifies Senators King, Wilmot, Wilkinson, Chandler, Wade, Morrill, and Sumner as the most radical Republican senators on racial and slavery votes during the war, though he notes that there is scholarly disagreement about exactly how to define that faction. Allan G. Bogue, *The Earnest Men: Republicans of the Civil War Senate* (Ithaca, NY: Cornell University Press, 1981), 92.

44. Howard helped define the first antislavery platform of the Republican party. See Budd R. Ross, *The Early Bench and Bar of Detroit from 1805 to the End of 1850* (Detroit: Richard P. Joy and Clarence M. Burton, 1907), 90. He also "served as a Radical Republican, drafted the 13th Amendment, opposed presidential Reconstruction, and favored extreme punishment of the South through the Fourteenth Amendment and the Military Reconstruction Acts"

(William L. Richter, *Historical Dictionary of the Civil War and Reconstruction* [Lanham, MD: Rowman & Littlefield, 2004], 305). See April 19, 1862, 37th Cong., 2nd Sess., Cong. Globe 1719.

45. April 19, 1862, 37th Cong., 2nd Sess., Cong. Globe 1719.

46. June 28, 1862, 37th Cong., 2nd Sess., Cong. Globe 2966.

47. Wade was, according to Richter, not only antislavery since the 1840s but served as "the protector of less-rugged anti-slave senators who feared to physically fight it out with their duel prone Southern proslavery foes." He favored far more aggressive actions than Lincoln was willing to take, as he "introduced a more stringent plan of Reconstruction," the Wade-Davis Bill, "and tried to get Lincoln replaced by Secretary of the Treasury Salmon P. Chase in the election of 1864, only to be rebuffed by his own supporters back home." Richter, *Historical Dictionary of the Civil War and Reconstruction*, 637–638. May 3, 1862, 37th Cong., 2nd Sess., Cong. Globe 1917.

48. Richter argues that Sherman was not a radical himself but voted with Radical Republicans "because it was dangerous not to do so and expect to re-elected" (*Historical Dictionary of the Civil War and Reconstruction*, 555). Sherman would serve in Republican politics, including being secretary of state for William McKinley until the outset of the Spanish-American War. April 24, 1862, 37th Cong., 2nd Sess., Cong. Globe 1784.

49. Sumner spoke often and stridently against slavery, and openly advocated for emancipation. "Sumner, Charles," in *Encyclopedia Brittanica*, ed. Hugh Chisholm, vol. 26, 11th ed. (Cambridge, UK: Cambridge University Press, 1911), 81–82. See also Carnahan, *Act of Justice*, 5; June 28, 1862, 37th Cong., 2nd Sess., Cong. Globe 2964.

50. June 28, 1862, 37th Cong., 2nd Sess., Cong. Globe 2964.

51. May 20, 1862, 37th Cong., 2nd Sess., Cong. Globe 2193.

52. June 27, 1862, 37th Cong., 2nd Sess., Cong. Globe 2930.

53. 37th Cong., 2nd Sess., Cong. Globe 168 (1862), appendix.

54. Bingham had been a "conscience Whig" and a Republican by 1854. He would later help draft the Fourteenth Amendment. Richter, *Historical Dictionary*, 63.

55. Wilmot was the sponsor of the Wilmot proviso, a failed proposal to ban the slavery to western lands after the Mexican War, but was more of a free-soiler than a moral opponent of slavery as an institution. See Charles Buxton Going, *David Wilmot, Free-soiler* (United Kingdom: D. Appleton, 1924). May 1, 1862, 37th Cong., 2nd Sess., Cong. Globe 1877.

56. May 23, 1862, 37th Cong., 2nd Sess., Cong. Globe 2292.

57. May 26, 1862, 37th Cong., 2nd Sess., Cong. Globe 2325.

58. Fessenden turned against slavery while serving in Congress as a Whig and helped to organize the Republican Party. During Reconstruction he was considered a Radical Republican. Richter, *Historical Dictionary*, 232–234. Bogue considers him based on his voting record to not have been a part of the most radical antislavery Senate faction during the war. Bogue, *Earnest Men*, 93. January 22, 1862, 37th Cong., 2nd Sess., Cong. Globe 402. Guelzo calls Fessenden the "outstanding Republican moderate in the Senate" (*Lincoln's Emancipation Proclamation*, 72).

59. 37th Cong., 2nd Sess., Cong. Globe 235 (1862), appendix.

60. Among those who articulated these pro-Lincoln arguments were Senators Browning

and Cowan, who can be ranked among the most conservative Republican senators on issues related to race and slavery. Bogue, *Earnest Men*, 95.

61. May 1, 1862, 37th Cong., 2nd Sess., Cong. Globe 1858.

62. Guelzo, *Lincoln's Emancipation Proclamation*, 72.

63. July 12, 1862, 37th Cong., 2nd Sess., Cong. Globe 3234.

64. December 20, 1861, 37th Cong., 2nd Sess., Cong. Globe 130.

65. Wright, based on his voting record on issues related to race and slavery, was among the most centrist senators. Bogue, *Earnest Men*, 95. January 22, 1862, 37th Cong., 2nd Sess., Cong. Globe 407.

66. *Washington Post*, database of slaveholders in Congress.

67. 37th Cong., 2nd Sess., Cong. Globe 273 (1862), appendix.

68. January 29, 1862, 37th Cong., 2nd Sess., Cong. Globe 501.

69. Willey, based on his voting record on issues related to race and slavery, was among the most centrist senators. Bogue, *Earnest Men*, 95.

70. April 12, 1862, 37th Cong., 2nd Sess., Cong. Globe 1623.

71. Syrett, *Civil War Confiscation Acts*, 57.

72. "That on the first day of January in the year of our Lord, one thousand eight hundred and sixty-three, all persons held as slaves within any State, or designated part of a State, the people whereof shall then be in rebellion against the United States shall be then, thenceforward, and forever free; and the executive government of the United States, including the military and naval authority thereof, will recognize and maintain the freedom of such persons, and will do no act or acts to repress such persons, or any of them, in any efforts they may make for their actual freedom." Abraham Lincoln, *Preliminary Emancipation Proclamation*, September 22, 1862.

73. December 23, 1862, 37th Cong., 3rd Sess., Cong. Globe 147–51 (1863).

74. Guelzo, *Lincoln's Emancipation Proclamation*, 142.

75. Elsewhere in society, there were strong legal objections from newspapers and in a pamphlet by former Supreme Court justice Benjamin Curtis, as described by Feldman, which relied on "general in chief" arguments to oppose the act and battlefield emancipation (Feldman, *Broken Constitution*, 298).

76. February 10, 1863, 37th Cong., 3rd Sess., Cong. Globe 804.

77. 38th Cong., Special Sess., Cong. Globe 85 (1863), appendix.

78. February 2, 1863, 37th Cong., 3rd Sess., Cong. Globe 629.

79. April 1, 1864, 38th Cong., 1st Sess., Cong. Globe 1357.

80. February 11, 1864, 38th Cong., 1st Sess., Cong. Globe 567.

81. February 17, 1864, 38th Cong., 1st Sess., Cong. Globe 677.

82. February 3, 1864, 38th Cong., 1st Sess., Cong. Globe 439.

83. For a broader discussion of Congress's attempts to end slavery in law, and members' conclusion that an amendment was the only option, see James Oakes, "The Only Effectual Way: The Congressional Origins of the Thirteenth Amendment," *Georgetown Journal of Law and Public Policy* 15, no. 1 (Winter 2017): 115–136.

84. Benjamin A. Kleinerman, *The Discretionary President: The Promise and Peril of Executive Power* (Lawrence: University Press of Kansas, 2009), 197.

85. Neely, *Lincoln and the Triumph of the Nation*, 140.

86. March 17, 1864, 38th Cong., 1st Sess., Cong. Globe 1150.

87. March 17, 1864, 38th Cong., 1st Sess., Cong. Globe 1152.

88. Rep. Edwin Niblack (D-IN), February 19, 1867, 39th Cong., 2nd Sess., Cong. Globe 1354; Rep. Edwin Wright (D-NJ), February 19, 1867, 39th Cong., 2nd Sess., Cong. Globe 1355; Rep. Elijah Hise (D-KY), February 23, 1867, 39th Cong., 2nd Sess., Cong. Globe 1532; Senator Hendricks, July 13, 1867, 40th Cong., 1st Sess., Cong. Globe 626; Rep. Andrew Jackson Rogers (D-NJ), 39th Cong., 2nd Sess., Cong. Globe 87 (1867), appendix.

89. February 26, 1867, 39th Cong., 2nd Sess., Cong. Globe 1853.

90. February 19, 1867, 39th Cong., 2nd Sess., Cong. Globe 1355.

91. February 23, 1867, 39th Cong., 2nd Sess., Cong. Globe 1532.

92. July 13, 1867, 40th Cong., 1st Sess., Cong. Globe 626.

93. 39th Cong., 2nd Sess., Cong. Globe 1854 (1867).

94. February 6, 1867, 39th Cong., 2nd Sess., Cong. Globe 1039–1040.

95. February 6, 1867, 39th Cong., 2nd Sess., Cong. Globe 1039–1040.

96. January 17, 1868, 40 Cong. Globe 587–603 (1868).

97. In 1871 Democratic senator Francis Blair of Missouri recalled that "the command of the troops who were to put the acts into execution was taken away from the constitutional Commander in-Chief" (41st Cong., 3rd Sess., Cong. Globe 116 [1871], appendix). In 1879 Rep. Richard Townshend of Illinois was one of several Democrats arguing in favor of a bill to cut military appropriations for the army to explicitly refer to the controversial bill from a decade earlier (April 2, 1879, 46th Cong., 1st Sess., 9 Cong. Rec. 169). In 1908 Rep. Frank Clark (D-FL) raised the issue while arguing about racial segregation and a bill to fund street cars. In a wide ranging diatribe about the Reconstruction "laws—if such acts of a mutilated Congress, so palpably and avowedly in conflict with the Constitution can be called laws," he noted that "the President of the United States, who is the constitutional Commander in Chief of the Army, was deprived of all control over the Army" (February 22, 1908, 42 Cong. Rec. 43 [1908], appendix).

98. For example, when Polk made broad arguments in favor of his own authority, many Democrats echoed his language closely.

99. For example, Richard Nixon, referred to Lincoln's letter to Hodges when he defended the Huston Plan in his interview with David Frost. For a discussion of how the proclamation fits among past and future unilateral executive actions, see Graham G. Dodds, *Take Up Your Pen: Unilateral Presidential Directives in American Politics* (Philadelphia: University of Pennsylvania Press, 2013).

100. Mariah Zeisberg, *War Powers: The Politics of Constitutional Authority* (Princeton: Princeton University Press, 2013).

CONCLUSION

1. Louis Fisher, *Presidential War Power* (Lawrence: University Press of Kansas, 2005) and Stephen M. Griffin, *Long Wars and the Constitution* (Cambridge, MA: Harvard University

Press 2013), 18. See also William Conrad Gibbons, "The Origins of the War Power of the Constitution," in *Congress and United States Foreign Policy: Controlling the Use of Force in the Nuclear Age*, ed. Michael Barnhart (Albany: State University of New York Press, 1987); Ann Van Wynen Thomas and A. J. Thomas Jr., *The War Making Powers of the President* (Dallas: Southern Methodist University Press, 1982); and Francis D. Wormuth and Edwin B. Firmage, *To Chain the Dog of War* (Dallas, TX: Southern Methodist University Press, 1986).

2. John A. Dearborn, *Power Shifts: Congress and Presidential Representation* (Chicago: University of Chicago Press, 2021). Berman also suggests this is an important task when studying the relevance of ideas to political development. See Sheri Berman, "Ideas, Norms, and Culture in Political Analysis," *Comparative Politics* 33, no. 2 (January 2001): 231–250.

3. Douglas L. Kriner, *After the Rubicon* (Chicago: University of Chicago Press, 2010); William G. Howell and Jon C. Pevehouse, *While Dangers Gather: Congressional Checks on Presidential War Powers* (Princeton: Princeton University Press, 2007).

4. See chapter 5 for a more extended discussion. Curtis A. Bradley and Trevor W. Morrison, "Historical Gloss and the Separation of Powers," *Harvard Law Review* 126, no. 2 (December 2012): 411–485; Deborah Pearlstein, "The Executive Branch Anticanon," *Fordham Law Review* 89 (2020): 597–649. Also Mariah Zeisberg, *War Powers: The Politics of Constitutional Authority* (Princeton: Princeton University Press, 2013).

5. Griffin, *Long Wars*; Bradley and Morrison, "Historical Gloss."

6. For example, Fisher, *Presidential War Power*; John Hart Ely, *War and Responsibility: Constitutional Lessons of Vietnam* (Princeton: Princeton University Press, 1993).

7. As suggested by Zeisberg and others such as Harold Hongju Koh, *The National Security Constitution: Sharing Power after the Iran Contra Affair* (New Haven: Yale University Press, 1990).

8. These interwoven and competing ideas about the scope of war powers authority might be labeled "intercurrence." Karen Orren and Stephen Skowronek, "Institutions and Intercurrence: Theory Building in the Fullness of Time," *Nomos* 38 (1996): 111–146.

9. I hesitate to apply the term too forcefully because it is defined as the interactions between multiple political orders, and I am not convinced that competing interpretations of the commander in chief clause constitute political orders.

10. As such, this analysis follows other work that situates ideas and language in political development, for example, Robert C. Lieberman, "Ideas, Institutions, and Political Order: Explaining Political Change," *American Political Science Review* 96, no. 4 (December 2002): 697–712; James W. Ceaser, "Foundational Concepts in American Political Development," in *Nature and History in American Political Development* (Cambridge, MA: Harvard University Press, 2006), 1–90; Vivien Schmidt, "Reconciling Ideas and Institutions through Discursive Institutionalism," in *Ideas in Politics and Social Science Research*, ed. Daniel Béland and Robert Henry Cox (Oxford: Oxford University Press, 2011), 47–64; and George Thomas, "Political Thought and Development," *American Political Thought: A Journal of Ideas, Institutions, and Culture* (Spring 2014): 114–125.

11. Like Ryan C. Hendrickson, *The Clinton Wars: The Constitution, Congress, and War Powers* (Nashville: Vanderbilt University Press, 2002). See also Howell and Pevehouse, *While Dangers Gather*.

12. J. Mitchell Pickerill, *Deliberation in Congress: The Impact of Judicial Review in a Separated System* (Durham, NC: Duke University Press, 2004).

13. Victoria Farrar-Myers, *Scripted for Change: The Institutionalization of the American Presidency* (College Station: Texas A&M University Press, 2007); Zeisberg, *War Powers.* Future research should absolutely explore the racial and power dynamics of the development of defensive presidential power.

14. George I. Lovell, "Justice Excused: The Deployment of Law in Everyday political encounters," *Law and Society Review* 40, no. 2 (June 2006): 283–324. See, for example, the public's deliberation on constitutional war powers issues in the deliberative polling conducted by Steven Kull, Evan Scot Fehsenfeld, and Evan Charles Lewitus, "Americans on War Powers, Authorization for Use of Military Force, and Arms Sales" (working paper, Program for Public Consultation, School of Public Policy, University of Maryland, March 18, 2022, https://cissm.umd.edu/research-impact/publications/americans-war-powers-authorization-use-military-force-and-arms-sales).

15. Bruce Peabody, "Congressional Attitudes toward Constitutional Interpretation," in *Congress and the Constitution*, ed. Neal Devins and Keith E. Whittington (Durham, NC: Duke University Press, 2005), 39–64. See also John Yoo, "Lawyers in Congress," in the same volume, 131–150.

16. Louis Fisher, "Constitutional Analysis by Congressional Staff Agencies," in Devins and Whittington, *Congress and the Constitution*, 64–86; Elizabeth Garrett and Adrian Vermeule, "Institutional Design of a Thayerian Congress," in the same volume at 242–268.

17. As Josh Chafetz notes, political power is endogenous to politics. Josh Chafetz, *Congress' Constitution: Legislative Authority and the Separation of Powers* (New Haven: Yale University Press, 2017), 17.

18. For a discussion of the politically and socially constructed nature of "wartime," and its relationship to similarly constructed ideas about offense and defense, see Mary L. Dudziak, *War Time: An Idea, Its History, Its Consequences* (New York: Oxford University Press, 2012). For a discussion of the racial origins of the inherent powers doctrine that became enshrined in the *Curtiss-Wright case*, see Sarah H. Cleveland, "Powers Inherent in Sovereignty: Indians, Aliens, Territories, and the Nineteenth Century Origins of Plenary Power over Foreign Affairs," *Texas Law Review* 81, no. 1 (November 2002): 1–284.

Bibliography

Ackerman, Bruce. *We the People: Foundations.* Cambridge, MA: Belknap Press, 1991.

Adler, William D. *Engineering Expansion: The US Army and Economic Development, 1787–1860.* Philadelphia: University of Pennsylvania Press, 2021.

Alexander, Larry, and Frederick Schauer. "On Extrajudicial Interpretation." *Harvard Law Review* 110, no. 7 (May 1997): 1359–1387.

American State Papers: Documents, Legislative and Executive, of the Congress of the United States, part 5, vol. 3 (Washington, DC: Gales and Seaton, 1860).

Anderson, Benedict. *Imagined Communities: Reflection on the Origin and Spread of Nationalism.* New York: Verso Press, 1983.

Arnold, Peri E. *Remaking the Presidency: Roosevelt, Taft and Wilson, 1901–1916.* Lawrence: University Press of Kansas, 2009.

Bailey, Jeremy D. *The Idea of Presidential Representation: An Intellectual and Political History.* Lawrence: University Press of Kansas, 2019.

Baker, William D., and John R. O'Neal. "Patriotism or Opinion Leadership?: The Nature and Origins of the 'Rally 'Round the Flag' Effect." *Journal of Conflict Resolution* 45, no. 5 (October 2001): 661–687.

Balkin, James M. *The Cycles of Constitutional Time.* Oxford: Oxford University Press, 2020.

Barron, David J., and Martin S. Lederman. "The Commander in Chief at the Lowest Ebb: A Constitutional History." *Harvard Law Review* 121, no. 4 (February 2008): 941–1112.

———. "The Commander in Chief at the Lowest Ebb: Framing the Problem, Doctrine, and Original Understanding." *Harvard Law Review* 121, no. 3 (2008): 689–804.

Bauer, K. Jack. *The Mexican War 1846–1848.* Lincoln: University of Nebraska Press, 1974.

Beirne, Brian Logan. "George vs. George vs. George: Commander-in-Chief Power." *Yale Law and Policy Review* 26, no. 1 (2007): 265–308.

Béland, Daniel, and Robert Henry Cox, eds. *Ideas in Politics and Social Science Research.* Oxford: Oxford University Press, 2011.

Berman, Sheri. "Ideas, Norms, and Culture in Political Analysis." *Comparative Politics* 33, no. 2 (January 2001): 231–250.

Biographical Sketch of the Hon. Lazarus W. Powell, (of Henderson, Ky.): Governor of the State of Kentucky from 1851–1855 and a Senator in Congress from 1859–1865 / Published by Direction of the General Assembly of Kentucky (Frankfort, KY: Kentucky Yeoman Office, 1868).

Bisgaard, Martin, and Rune Slothuus. "Partisan Elites as Culprits? How Party Cues Shape Partisan Perceptual Gaps." *American Journal of Political Science* 62, no. 2 (April 2018): 456–469.

Blyth, Mark. "Ideas, Uncertainty, and Evolution." In Béland and Cox, *Ideas in Politics and Social Science Research,* 83–105.

Bogue, Allan G. *The Earnest Men: Republicans of the Civil War Senate.* Ithaca, NY: Cornell University Press, 1981.

Bradley, Curtis A., and Jack L. Goldsmith. "Customary International Law as Federal Common Law: A Critique of the Modern Position," *Harvard Law Review* 110, no. 4 (February 1997): 815–876.

Bradley, Curtis A., and Martin S. Flaherty. "Executive Power Essentialism and Foreign Affairs." *Michigan Law Review* 102, no. 4 (February 2004): 545–688.

Bradley, Curtis A., and Trevor W. Morrison. "Historical Gloss and the Separation of Powers." *Harvard Law Review* 126, no. 2 (December 2012): 411–485.

Brody, Richard. *Assessing the President*. Palo Alto: Stanford University Press, 1991.

Burgess, Susan R. *Contest for Constitutional Authority: The Abortion and War Powers Debates*. Lawrence: University Press of Kansas, 1992.

Burnett, Christina Duffy, and Burke Marshall. "Between the Foreign and the Domestic: The Doctrine of Territorial Incorporation, Invented and Reinvented." In Burnett and Marshall, *Foreign in a Domestic Sense*, 1–36.

Burnett, Christina Duffy, and Burke Marshall, eds. *Foreign in a Domestic Sense: Puerto Rico, American Expansion, and the Constitution*. Durham, NC: Duke University Press, 2001.

Burns, Sarah. *The Politics of War Powers: The Theory and History of Presidential Unilateralism*. Lawrence: University Press of Kansas, 2019.

Carnahan, Burrus M. *Act of Justice: Lincoln's Emancipation Proclamation and the Law of War*. Lexington: University Press of Kentucky, 2007.

Carter, Ralph G. "Defense Budgeting, 1981–1988: The Impacts of Ideology, Party, and Constituency Benefit on the Decision to Support the President." *American Politics Quarterly* 17, no. 3 (1989): 332–347.

Ceaser, James W. "Foundational Concepts in American Political Development." In *Nature and History in American Political Development*, 1–90. Cambridge, MA: Harvard University Press, 2006.

Chadsey, Charles Ernest. *The Struggle between President Johnson and Congress over Reconstruction*. New York: Columbia University, 1896.

Chafetz, Josh. *Congress' Constitution: Legislative Authority and the Separation of Powers*. New Haven: Yale University Press, 2017.

Cleveland, Sarah H. "Powers Inherent in Sovereignty: Indians, Aliens, Territories, and the Nineteenth Century Origins of Plenary Power over Foreign Affairs." *Texas Law Review* 81, no. 1 (November 2002): 1–284.

Conde, Alexander de. *The Quasi-War: The Politics and Diplomacy of the Undeclared War with France 1797–1801*. New York: Charles Scribner's Sons, 1966.

Cooper, Jerry. *The Rise of the National Guard: The Evolution of the American Militia 1865–1920*. Lincoln: University of Nebraska Press, 1987.

Cox, Gary W., and Mathew D. McCubbins. *Setting the Agenda: Responsible Party Government in the U.S. House of Representatives*. Cambridge, UK: Cambridge University Press, 2004.

Cox, Henry Bartholomew. *War, Foreign Affairs, and Constitutional Power: 1829–1901*. Cambridge, MA: Ballinger, 1984.

Currie, David P. *The Constitution in Congress: Descent into the Maelstrom*. Chicago: University of Chicago Press, 2014.

———. "Prolegomena for a Sampler: Extrajudicial Interpretation of the Constitution." In Devins and Whittington, *Congress and the Constitution*, 18–38.

Curtis, George Ticknor. *History of the Origin, Formation, and Adoption of the Constitution of the United States*. New York: Harper and Bros., 1861.

Dearborn, John A. *Power Shifts: Congress and Presidential Representation*. Chicago: University of Chicago Press, 2021.

Deering, Christopher J. "Congress, the President, and Military Policy." *Annals of the American Academy of Political and Social Science* 499 (September 1988): 136–147.

Deudney, Daniel H. "The Philadelphian System: Sovereignty, Arms Control, and Balance of Power in the American States-Union, circa 1787–1861." *International Organization* 49, no. 2 (1995): 191–228.

Devins, Neal, and Keith E. Whittington. "Introduction." In Devins and Whittington, *Congress and the Constitution*, 1–17.

Devins, Neal, and Keith E. Whittington, eds. *Congress and the Constitution*. Durham, NC: Duke University Press, 2005.

Dodds, Graham G. *Take Up Your Pen: Unilateral Presidential Directives in American Politics*. Philadelphia: University of Pennsylvania Press, 2013.

Dudziak, Mary L. *War Time: An Idea, Its History, Its Consequences*. New York: Oxford University Press, 2012.

Edwards, George C., III, and Andrew Barrett. "Presidential Agenda Setting in Congress." In *Polarized Politics*, edited by Jon R. Bond and Richard Fleisher, 109–133. Washington, DC: CQ Press, 2000.

Eisenhower, John S. D. *Intervention: The United States and the Mexican Revolution 1913–1917*. New York: W. W. Norton, 1993.

Ellis, Richard J. *The Development of the American Presidency*. New York: Routledge, 2012.

———. *Founding the American Presidency*. Lanham, MD: Rowman & Littlefield, 1999.

Ely, John Hart. *War and Responsibility: Constitutional Lessons of Vietnam*. Princeton: Princeton University Press, 1993.

Farrand, Max, ed. *The Records of the Federal Convention*. New Haven: Yale University Press, 1911.

Farrar-Myers, Victoria. *Scripted for Change: The Institutionalization of the American Presidency*. College Station: Texas A&M University Press, 2007.

Feldman, Noah. *The Broken Constitution: Lincoln, Slavery, and the Refounding of America*. New York: Picador Farrar, Straus and Giroux, 2021.

Fisher, Louis. *Congressional Abdication on War and Spending*. College Station: Texas A&M University Press, 2000.

———. "Constitutional Analysis by Congressional Staff Agencies." In Devins and Whittington, *Congress and the Constitution*, 64–86.

———. *Constitutional Dialogues: Interpretation as Political Process*. Princeton: Princeton University Press, 1988.

————. "Constitutional Interpretation by Members of Congress." *North Carolina Law Review* 63 (1985): 707–747.

————. "The Korean War: On What Legal Basis Did Truman Act?" *American Journal of International Law* 89, no. 1 (January 1995): 21–39.

————. *Military Tribunals and Presidential Power: American Revolution to the War on Terrorism*. Lawrence: University Press of Kansas, 2005.

————. *Presidential War Power*. Lawrence: University Press of Kansas, 2005.

————. *Presidential War Power*. 3rd edition. Lawrence: University Press of Kansas, 2013.

————. *Supreme Court Expansion of Presidential Power: Unconstitutional Leanings*. Lawrence: University Press of Kansas, 2017.

Fisher, Louis, and David Gray Adler. "The War Powers Resolution: Time to Say Goodbye." *Political Science Quarterly* 13, no. 1 (Spring 2008): 1–20.

Foner, Eric. *Reconstruction: America's Unfinished Revolution, 1869–77*. New York: Harper and Row, 1988.

Franklin, John Hope. *The Emancipation Proclamation*. New York: Doubleday, 1963.

Frymer, Paul. *Building an American Empire: The Era of Territorial and Political Expansion*. Princeton: Princeton University Press, 2017.

Galvin, Daniel, and Colleen Shogan. "Presidential Politicization and Centralization across the Modern-Traditional Divide." *Polity* 36, no. 3 (2004): 477–504.

Garrett, Elizabeth, and Adrian Vermeule. "Institutional Design of a Thayerian Congress." In Devins and Whittington, *Congress and the Constitution*, 242–268.

Garrison, William Lloyd. *The Abolition of Slavery the Right of the Government from the War Power*. Boston: R. F. Walcutt, 1861.

Gerstle, Gary. *American Crucible: Race and Nation in the Twentieth Century*. Princeton: Princeton University Press, 2001.

Gibbons, William Conrad. "The Origins of the War Power of the Constitution." In *Congress and United States Foreign Policy: Controlling the Use of Force in the Nuclear Age*, edited by Michael Barnhart, 9–38. Albany: State University of New York Press, 1987.

Glenn, Brian J. "The Two Schools of American Political Development." *Political Studies Review* 2, no. 2 (April 2004): 153–165.

Glennon, Michael J. *Constitutional Diplomacy*. Princeton: Princeton University Press.

————. "The Executive's Misplaced Reliance on War Powers 'Custom.'" *American Journal of International Law* 109, no. 3 (2015): 551–556.

Going, Charles Buxton. *David Wilmot, Free-Soiler*. United Kingdom: D. Appleton, 1924.

Gould, Lewis L. *The Modern American Presidency*. Lawrence: University Press of Kansas, 2003.

Grant, Susan-Mary. "Americans Forging a New Nation, 1860–1916." In *Nationalism in the New World*, edited by Don H. Doyle and Marco Antonio Pamplona, 80–98. Athens: University of Georgia Press, 2006.

Griffin, Stephen M. *Long Wars and the Constitution*. Cambridge, MA: Harvard University Press, 2013.

Grimmett, Richard F. *Instances of Use of United States Armed Forces Abroad 1798–2008*. Washington, DC: Congressional Research Service, 2010.

Groeling, Tim, and Matthew A. Baum. "Crossing the Water's Edge: Elite Rhetoric, Media Coverage, and the Rally-Round-the-Flag Phenomenon." *Journal of Politics* 70, no. 4 (October 2008): 1065–1085.

Guelzo, Allen C. *Lincoln's Emancipation Proclamation: The End of Slavery in America*. New York: Simon and Schuster, 2004.

Hall, Clifton Rumery. *Andrew Johnson: Military Governor of Tennessee*. Princeton: Princeton University Press, 1916.

Hallett, Brien. *Declaring War: Congress, the President, and What the Constitution Does Not Say*. New York: Cambridge University Press, 2012.

Hamilton, Alexander. "Pacificus No. I, [29 June 1793]," Founders Online, National Archives, http://founders.archives.gov/documents/Hamilton/01-15-02-0038.

Hart, James. *The American Presidency in Action, 1789: A Study in Constitutional History*. New York: Macmillan, 1948.

Hendrickson, Ryan C. *The Clinton Wars: The Constitution, Congress, and War Powers*. Nashville: Vanderbilt University Press, 2002.

Henkin, Louis. 1972. *Foreign Affairs and the Constitution*. Mineola, NY: Foundation Press, 1972.

———. "International Law as Law in the United States." *Michigan Law Review* 82, nos. 5–6 (April–May 1984): 1555–1569.

Howell, William G., and Jon C. Pevehouse. *While Dangers Gather: Congressional Checks on Presidential War Powers*. Princeton: Princeton University Press, 2007.

Howell, William G., and Terry M. Moe. *Relic: How Our Constitution Undermines Effective Government and Why We Need a More Powerful Presidency*. New York: Basic Books, 2016.

Howell, William G., Saul P. Jackman, and Jon C. Rogowski. *The Wartime President: Executive Influence and the Nationalizing Politics of Threat*. Chicago: University of Chicago Press, 2013.

Hoxie, R. Gordon. "The Office of Commander in Chief: An Historical and Projective View." *Presidential Studies Quarterly* 6, no. 4 (1976): 10–36.

Ingber, Rebecca. "The Obama War Powers Legacy and the Internal Forces That Entrench Executive Power." *American Journal of International Law* 110, no. 4 (October 2016): 680–700.

Jacobson, Matthew Frye. *Barbarian Virtues: The United States Encounters Foreign Peoples at Home and Abroad, 1876–1917*. New York: Hill and Wang, 2000.

Johnson, Robert David. *Congress and the Cold War*. New York: Cambridge University Press, 2006.

Jones, Martha S., Kate Masur, Louis Masur, James Oakes, and Manisha Sinha. "Historians Forum: The Emancipation Proclamation," *Civil War History* 59, no. 1 (March 2013): 7–31.

Kalmoe, Nathan. *With Ballots and Bullets: Partisanship and Violence in the American Civil War*. New York: Cambridge University Press, 2020.

Kammen, Michael. *Mystic Chords of Memory: The Transformation of Tradition in American Culture*. New York: Vintage Books, 1993.

Katznelson, Ira, and Helen V. Milner, eds. *Political Science: The State of the Discipline*. New York: W. W. Norton, 2002.

Katznelson, Ira, and John S. Lapinski. "At the Crossroads: Congress and American Political Development." *Perspectives on Politics* 4, no. 2 (June 2006): 243–260.

Kent, James. *Commentaries on American Law*. New York: O. Halstead, 1826.

Kernell, Samuel. *Going Public*. Washington, DC: CQ Press, 1997.

King, Archibald. *The Command of the Army: A Legal and Historical Study of the Relations of the President, the Secretaries of War and the Army, the General of the Army, and the Chief of Staff, with One Another*. Charlottesville, VA: Judge Advocate General's School, 1960.

Kinzer, Stephen. *Overthrow: America's Century of Regime Change from Hawaii to Iraq*. New York: Times Books 2006.

Kleinerman, Benjamin A. *The Discretionary President: The Promise and Peril of Executive Power*. Lawrence: University Press of Kansas, 2009.

Knight, Jack, and Lee Epstein. "On the Struggle for Judicial Supremacy." *Law and Society Review* 30, no. 1 (1996): 87–120.

Koh, Harold Hongju. "Is International Law Really State Law." *Harvard Law Review* 111, no. 7 (May 1998): 1824–1862.

———. *The National Security Constitution: Sharing Power after the Iran Contra Affair*. New Haven: Yale University Press, 1990.

Kriner, Douglas L. *After the Rubicon*. Chicago: University of Chicago Press, 2010.

Kull, Steven, Evan Scot Fehsenfeld, and Evan Charles Lewitus. "Americans on War Powers, Authorization for Use of Military Force, and Arms Sales." Working paper, Program for Public Consultation, School of Public Policy, University of Maryland, March 18, 2022. https://cissm.umd.edu/research-impact/publications.

LaFeber, Walter. *The New American Empire: An Interpretation of American Expansion 1860–1898 Thirty-Fifth Anniversary Edition with a New Preface*. Ithaca, NY: Cornell University Press, 1998.

Laurance, Edward J. "The Changing Role of Congress in Defense Policy-Making." *Journal of Conflict Resolution* 20, no. 2 (June 1976): 213–253.

Levinson, Daryl J., and Richard H. Pildes. "Separation of Parties, Not Powers." *Harvard Law Review* 119, no. 8 (June 2006): 2311–2386.

Lieberman, Robert C. "Ideas, Institutions, and Political Order: Explaining Political Change." *American Political Science Review* 96, no. 4 (December 2002): 697–712.

Lim, Elvin. "Political Thought, Political Development, and America's Two Foundings." *American Political Thought* 3, 1 (Spring 2014), pp. 146–156.

Lincoln, Abraham. "Abraham Lincoln's Letter to Albert G. Hodges 1864." In *The Evolving Presidency: Addresses, Cases, Essays, Letters, Reports, Resolutions, Transcripts, and Other Landmark Documents 1787–1998*, ed. Michael Nelson, 70–74. Washington, DC: Congressional Quarterly, 1999.

Lindsay, James M. "Parochialism, Policy, and Constituency Constraints: Congressional Voting on Strategic Weapons Systems." *American Journal of Political Science* 34, no. 4 (November 1990): 936–960.

Lofgren, Charles A. "War-Making under the Constitution: The Original Understanding." *Yale Law Journal* 81, no. 4 (1972): 672–702.

Lovell, George I. 2006. "Justice Excused: The Deployment of Law in Everyday Political Encounters." *Law and Society Review* 40, no. 2 (June 2006): 283–324.

Madison, James. *Debates of the Constitutional Convention, Madison's Notes*. Available at the Avalon Project, Yale University. Accessed January 15, 2018. http://avalon.law.yale.edu/18th_century/debates_815.asp.

———. "'Helvidius' Number 1, [24 August] 1793." Founders Online. https://founders.archives.gov/documents/Madison/01-15-02-0056.

Martin, Andrew D. "Congressional Decision Making and the Separation of Powers." *American Political Science Review* 95, no. 2 (2001): 361–378.

McCartney, Paul T. *Power and Progress: American National Identity, the War of 1898, and the Rise of American Imperialism*. Baton Rouge: Louisiana State University Press, 2006.

McDonald, Forrest. *The American Presidency: An Intellectual History*. Lawrence: University Press of Kansas, 1994.

McPherson, James M. "How President Lincoln Decided to Issue the Emancipation Proclamation." *Journal of Blacks in Higher Education* 37 (Autumn 2002): 108–109.

Meernik, James. "Congress, the President, and the Commitment of the U.S. Military." *Legislative Studies Quarterly* 20, no. 3 (August 1995): 377–392.

Mickelson, Peter. "Nationalism in Minnesota during the Spanish-American War." *Minnesota History* 41, no. 1 (Spring 1968): 1–12.

Mikva, Abner. "How Well Does Congress Support and Defend the Constitution?" *North Carolina Law Review* 61 (1983): 587–611.

Milkis, Sidney M. "Ideas, Institutions, and the New Deal Constitutional Order." *American Political Thought* 3, no. 1 (2014): 167–176.

Missall, John, and Mary Lou Missall. *The Seminole Wars: America's Longest Indian Conflict*. Gainesville: University of Florida Press, 2004.

Moe, Terry, and William Howell. "Unilateral Action and Presidential Power: A Theory." *Presidential Studies Quarterly* 29, no. 4 (December 1999): 850–873.

Monaghan, Henry P. "Presidential War-Making." *Boston University Law Review* 50, no. 5 (1970): 19–33.

Morgan, Donald G. *Congress and the Constitution: A Study of Responsibility*. Cambridge, MA: Belknap Press, 1966.

Mueller, John E. *War, Presidents, and Public Opinion*. New York: Wiley, 1973.

Murphy, Walter F. "Who Shall Interpret? The Quest for the Ultimate Constitutional Interpreter." *Review of Politics* 48, no. 3 (Summer 1986): 401–423.

Neely, Mark E. *Lincoln and the Triumph of the Nation: Constitutional Conflict in the American Civil War*. Chapel Hill: University of North Carolina Press, 2011.

Nelson, Michael, ed. *The Evolving Presidency: Addresses, Cases, Essays, Letters, Reports, Resolutions, Transcripts, and Other Landmark Documents 1787–1998*. Washington, DC: Congressional Quarterly, 1999.

Neustadt, Richard E. *Presidential Power and the Modern Presidents: The Politics of Leadership from Roosevelt to Reagan*. New York: Free Press, 1990.

Oakes, James. *Freedom National: The Destruction of Slavery in the United States 1861–1865.* New York: W. W. Norton, 2012.

———. "The Only Effectual Way: The Congressional Origins of the Thirteenth Amendment." *Georgetown Journal of Law and Public Policy* 15, no. 1 (Winter 2017): 115–136.

O'Leary, Cecilia Elizabeth. *To Die For: The Paradox of American Patriotism.* Princeton: Princeton University Press, 1999.

O'Leary, Cecilia, and Tony Platt. "Pledging Allegiance: The Revival of Prescriptive Patriotism." *Social Justice* 28, no. 3 (85) (Fall 2001): 41–44.

Orren, Karen, and Stephen Skowronek. "Institutions and Intercurrence: Theory Building in the Fullness of Time." *Nomos* 38 (1996): 111–146.

———. *The Search for American Political Development.* West Nyack, NY: Cambridge University Press, 2004.

———. "The Study of American Political Development." In Katznelson and Milner, *Political Science,* 722–754.

Oyos, Matthew M. "Theodore Roosevelt, Congress, and the Military: U.S. Civil-Military Relations in the Early Twentieth Century." *Presidential Studies Quarterly* 30, no. 2 (June 2000): 312–330.

Park, Jong Hee. "Structural Change in U.S. Presidents' Use of Force." *American Journal of Political Science* 54, no. 3 (July 2010): 766–782.

Peabody, Bruce. "Congressional Attitudes toward Constitutional Interpretation." In Devins and Whittington, *Congress and the Constitution,* 39–64.

Pearlstein, Deborah. "The Executive Branch Anticanon." *Fordham Law Review* 89 (2020): 597–649.

Peterson, Paul, ed. *The President, the Congress, and the Making of Foreign Policy.* Norman: University of Oklahoma Press, 1994.

Pettegrew, John. "'The Soldier's Faith': Turn-of-the-Century Memory of the Civil War and the Emergence of Modern American Nationalism." *Journal of Contemporary History* 31, no. 1 (January 1996): 49–73.

Pfiffner, James. *The Modern Presidency.* 5th ed. Belmont, CA: Thomson Wadsworth, 2008.

Pickerill, J. Mitchell. *Deliberation in Congress: The Impact of Judicial Review in a Separated System.* Durham, NC: Duke University Press, 2004.

Pierson, Paul. *Politics in Time: History, Institutions, and Social Analysis.* Princeton: Princeton University Press, 2004.

Pierson, Paul, and Theda Skocpol. "Historical Institutionalism in Contemporary Political Science." In Katznelson and Milner, *Political Science,* 693–721.

Pomeroy, John Norton. *An Introduction to the Constitutional Law of the United States Especially Designed for Students, General and Professional.* Boston: Houghton, Mifflin, 1883.

Powell, H. Jefferson. *The President's Authority over Foreign Affairs.* Durham, NC: Carolina Academic Press, 2002.

Prakash, Saikrishna B., and Michael D. Ramsey. "The Executive Power over Foreign Affairs." *Yale Law Journal* 111 (2001): 231–356.

Ramsey, Michael D. *The Constitution's Text in Foreign Affairs.* Cambridge, MA: Harvard University Press, 2007.

Raven-Hansen, Peter. "Constitutional Constraints: The War Clause." In *The U.S. Constitution and the Power to Go to War: Historical and Current Perspectives*, edited by Gary M. Stern and Morton H. Halperin, 29–54. Westport, CT: Greenwood Press, 1994.

Rex, Justin. "The President's War Agenda: A Rhetorical View." *Presidential Studies Quarterly* 41, no. 1 (March 2001): 93–118.

Richter, William L. *Historical Dictionary of the Civil War and Reconstruction.* Lanham, MD: Rowman & Littlefield, 2004.

Rohde, David. "Presidential Support in the House of Representatives." In Peterson, *President, the Congress and the Making of Foreign Policy*, 101–128.

Ross, Budd R. *The Early Bench and Bar of Detroit from 1805 to the End of 1850.* Detroit: Richard P. Joy and Clarence M. Burton, 1907.

Rossiter, Clinton. *The American Presidency.* New York: New American Library, 1956.

———. *The Supreme Court and the Commander-in-Chief.* Ithaca: Cornell University Press, 1951.

Saldin, Robert P. "William McKinley and the Rhetorical Presidency." *Presidential Studies Quarterly* 41, no. 1 (March 2011): 119–134.

Sandos, James A. "Pancho Villa and American Security: Woodrow Wilson's Mexican Diplomacy Reconsidered." *Journal of Latin American Studies* 13, no. 2 (November 1981): 293–311.

Savage, Charlie. *Power Wars: Inside Obama's Post-9/11 Presidency.* New York: Little, Brown, 2015.

Schickler, Eric. *Disjointed Pluralism: Institutional Innovation and the Development of the U.S. Congress.* Princeton: Princeton University Press, 2001.

Schlesinger, Arthur M., Jr. *The Imperial Presidency.* Boston: Houghton Mifflin, 1973.

Schmidt, Vivien A. "Discursive Institutionalism: The Explanatory Power of Ideas and Discourse." *Annual Review of Political Science* 11 (2008): 303–326.

———. "Reconciling Ideas and Institutions through Discursive Institutionalism." In Béland and Cox, *Ideas in Politics and Social Science Research*, 47–64.

Schoonover, Thomas. *Uncle Sam's War of 1898 and the Origins of Globalization.* Lexington: University Press of Kentucky, 2003.

Segal, Jeffrey A. "Separation-of-Powers Games in the Positive Theory of Congress and Courts." *American Political Science Review* 91, no. 1 (March 1997): 28–44.

Sellery, George Clarke. "Lincoln's Suspension of Habeas Corpus as Viewed by Congress." *Bulletin of the University of Wisconsin* 1, no. 2 (1907): 213–286.

Sheffer, Martin. *Judicial Development of Presidential War Powers.* Westport, CT: Praeger, 1999.

Shepsle, Kenneth A. "Congress Is a 'They,' Not an 'It': Legislative Intent as Oxymoron." *International Review of Law and Economics* 12, no. 2 (June 1992): 239–256.

Siddali, Silvana R. *From Property to Person: Slavery and the Confiscation Acts 1861–1862.* Baton Rouge: Louisiana State University Press, 2005.

Silverstein, Gordon. *Imbalance of Powers.* New York: Oxford University Press, 1997.

———. "Judicial Enhancement of Executive Power." In Peterson, *President, the Congress, and the Making of Foreign Policy*, 23–48.

———. *Law's Allure: How Law Shapes, Constrains, Saves, and Kills Politics*. Cambridge, UK: Cambridge University Press, 2009.

Sinclair, Barbara. "Can Congress Be Trusted with the Constitution? The Effects of Incentives and Procedures." In Devins and Whittington, *Congress and the Constitution*, 293–312.

Skowronek, Stephen. *Building a New American State: The Expansion of National Administrative Capacities 1877–1920*. New York: Cambridge University Press, 1982.

———. *The Politics Presidents Make: Leadership from John Adams to Bill Clinton*. Cambridge, MA: Harvard University Press, 1997.

Smith, Elbert B. *The Death of Slavery in the United States 1837–1865*. Chicago: The University of Chicago Press, 1967.

Smith, Jean Edward. *Grant*. New York: Simon & Schuster, 2001.

Smith, Rogers M. "Ideas and the Spiral of Politics: The Place of American Political Thought in American Political Development." *American Political Thought* 3, no. 1 (Spring 2014): 126–136.

———. "Which Comes First, the Ideas or the Institutions?" In *Rethinking Political Institutions: The Art of the State*, edited by Ian Shapiro, Stephen Skowronek, and Daniel Galvin, 91–114. New York: New York University Press, 2006.

Sollenberger, Mitchel A. "Presidential and Congressional Relations: An Evolution of Military Appointments." In *Congress and Civil-Military Relations*, edited by Colton C. Campbell and David P. Auerswald, 17–35. Washington, DC: Georgetown University Press, 2015.

Souva, Mark, and David Rohde. "Elite Opinion Differences and Partisanship in Congressional Foreign Policy, 1975–1996." *Political Research Quarterly* 60, no. 1 (March 2007): 113–123.

Spiro, Peter J. "War Powers and the Sirens of Formalism." *New York University Law Review* 68 (1993): 1338–1366.

Spitzer, Robert. *The Presidential Veto: Touchstone of the American Presidency*. Albany: State University of New York Press, 1988.

Stern, Gary M., and Morton H. Halperin. *The U.S. Constitution and the Power to Go to War*. Westport, CT: Greenwood Press, 1994.

Story, Joseph. *Commentaries on the Constitution of the United States; With a Preliminary Review of the Constitutional History of the Colonies and States, before the Adoption of the Constitution*. Volume 3. Boston: Hilliard, Gray, 1833.

Stuart, Douglas T. *Creating the National Security State: A History of the Law That Transformed America*. Princeton: Princeton University Press, 2008.

Sundquist, James L. *The Decline and Resurgence of Congress*. Washington, DC: Brookings Institution, 1981.

Syrett, John. *The Civil War Confiscation Acts: Failing to Reconstruct the South*. New York: Fordham University Press, 2005.

Teten, Ryan L. "Evolution of the Modern Rhetorical Presidency: Presidential Presentation and Development of the State of the Union Address." *Presidential Studies Quarterly* 33, no. 2 (June 2003): 333–346.

————. "'We the People': The 'Modern' Rhetorical Popular Address of the Presidents during the Founding Period." *Political Research Quarterly* 60, no. 4 (December 2007): 669–682.

Thomas, Ann Van Wynen, and A. J. Thomas Jr. *The War Making Powers of the President.* Dallas: Southern Methodist University Press, 1982.

Thomas, George. "Political Thought and Development." *American Political Thought: A Journal of Ideas, Institutions, and Culture* 3, no. 1 (Spring 2014): 114–125.

Treanor, William Michael. "Fame, the Founding, and the Power to Declare War." *Cornell Law Review,* 82 (1997): 695–772.

Troy, Gil. *See How They Ran: The Changing Role of the Presidential Candidate.* New York: Macmillan, 1991.

Tulis, Jeffrey. *The Rhetorical Presidency.* Princeton: Princeton University Press, 1987.

Tulis, Jeffery K., and Nicole Mellow. *Legacies of Losing in American Politics.* Chicago: University of Chicago Press, 2018.

Tushnet, Mark. "Evaluating Congressional Constitutional Interpretation: Some Criteria and Two Informal Case Studies." In Devins and Whittington, *Congress and the Constitution,* 269–292.

————. *The New Constitutional Order.* Princeton: Princeton University Press, 2003.

————. *Taking the Constitution away from the Courts.* Princeton: Princeton University Press, 1999.

Waldstreicher, David. "Rites of Rebellion, Rites of Assent: Celebrations, Print Culture, and the Origins of American Nationalism." *Journal of American History* 82, no. 1 (June 1995): 37–61.

Weaver, John D. *The Brownsville Raid.* New York: W. W. Norton, 1970.

Weiner, Mark S. "Teutonic Constitutionalism: The Role of Ethno-Juridical Discourse in the Spanish American War." In Burnett and Marshall, *Foreign in a Domestic Sense,* 48–81.

Weissman, Stephen R. *A Culture of Deference: Congress' Failure of Leadership in Foreign Policy.* New York: Basic Books, 1995.

Whiting, William. *The War Powers of the President and the Legislative Powers of Congress in Relation to Rebellion, Treason, and Slavery.* Boston: John L. Shorey, 1862.

Whittington, Keith. *Constitutional Construction: Divided Powers and Constitutional Meaning.* Cambridge, MA: Harvard University Press, 1999.

————. *Political Foundations of Judicial Supremacy: The Presidency, the Supreme Court, and Constitutional Leadership in U.S. History.* Princeton: Princeton University Press, 2007.

Witko, Christopher, Jana Morgan, Nathan J. Kelly, and Peter K. Enns. *Hijacking the Agenda: Economic Power and Political Influence.* New York: Russell Sage Foundation, 2021.

Witt, John Fabian. *Lincoln's Code: The Laws of War in American History.* New York: Free Press, 2012.

Wood, B. Dan. *The Myth of Presidential Representation.* Cambridge, UK: Cambridge University Press, 2009.

Wormuth, Francis D., and Edwin B. Firmage. *To Chain the Dog of War*. Dallas: Southern Methodist University Press, 1986.

Young, Ernest A. "Sorting Out the Debate over Customary International Law." *Virginia Journal of International Law* 42, no. 2 (Winter 2002): 365–512.

Yoo, John C. "The Continuation of Politics by Other Means: The Original Understanding of War Powers." *California Law Review* 84, no. 2 (1996): 167–305.

———. "Lawyers in Congress." In Devins and Whittington, *Congress and the Constitution*, 131–150.

———. "War and the Constitutional Text." *University of Chicago Law Review* 69, no. 4 (2002): 1639–1684.

Zeisberg, Mariah. *War Powers: The Politics of Constitutional Authority*. Princeton: Princeton University Press, 2013.

Zelinsky, Wilbur. *Nation into State: The Shifting Symbolic Foundations of American Nationalism*. Chapel Hill: University of North Carolina Press, 1988.

Index